WHY THE CHURCH?

Cultural Memory in the *Present*

Hent de Vries, Editor

WHY THE CHURCH?

Self-Optimization or Community of Faith

Hans Joas

Translated by Alex Skinner

STANFORD UNIVERSITY PRESS
STANFORD, CALIFORNIA

Stanford University Press
Stanford, California

English translation © 2024 by the Board of Trustees of the Leland Stanford Junior University. All rights reserved.

Why the Church? was originally published in German in 2022 under the title *Warum Kirche? Selbstoptimierung oder Glaubensgemeinschaft* © Verlag Herder GmbH, Freiburg im Breisgau, 2022.

No part of this book may be reproduced or transmitted in any form or by any means, electronic or mechanical, including photocopying and recording, or in any information storage or retrieval system, without the prior written permission of Stanford University Press.

Printed in the United States of America on acid-free, archival-quality paper.

Library of Congress Cataloging-in-Publication Data
Names: Joas, Hans, author.
Title: Why the Church? : self-optimization or community of faith / Hans
    Joas ; translated by Alex Skinner.
Other titles: Warum Kirche? English | Cultural memory in the present.
Description: Stanford, California : Stanford University Press, 2024. |
    Series: Cultural memory in the present | "Originally published in German
    in 2022 under the title Warum Kirche? Selbstoptimierung oder
    Glaubensgemeinschaft." | Includes bibliographical references and index.
Identifiers: LCCN 2024007605 (print) | LCCN 2024007606 (ebook) |
    ISBN 9781503638037 (cloth) | ISBN 9781503640795 (paperback) |
    ISBN 9781503640801 (ebook)
Subjects: LCSH: Mission of the church. | Dignity—Religious
    aspects—Christianity. | Christian sociology.
Classification: LCC BV601.8 .J6313 2024 (print) | LCC BV601.8 (ebook) |
    DDC 260—dc23/eng/20240315
LC record available at https://lccn.loc.gov/2024007605
LC ebook record available at https://lccn.loc.gov/2024007606

Cover design: Daniel Benneworth-Gray
Typeset by Newgen in Adobe Garamond Pro 11/13.5

*For Susanna Schmidt
and Joachim Hake*

Contents

	Preface to the English-Language Edition of Why the Church?	ix
1	Introduction	1
2	Why the Church? Can Transcendence Be Organized?	13
3	Problematic Predictions: Religion in a Secular Age	30
4	Do We Need Religion? On Experiences of Self-Transcendence	43
5	Faith or Self-Optimization? On the Cultural Role of the Church	59
6	A Christian through War and Revolution: Alfred Döblin's Narrative Work *November 1918*	73
7	Christianity without the Church? The Intellectual Trajectory of Leszek Kołakowski	91
8	Human Dignity: The Religion of Modernity?	106
9	Is Human Dignity Still Our Supreme Value?	120
10	The Church as Moral Agency?	124
11	The Church's Global Responsibility and Particular Obligations	135
	Notes	147
	Bibliography	165
	Name Index	177
	Subject Index	181

Preface to the English-Language Edition of Why the Church?

It was only after the original German-language edition of this book had been published that I discovered, with a degree of horror, that a book with the same title had appeared in French half a century earlier. *Pourquoi l'Église?* asked no less a figure than eminent theologian Jean Daniélou in 1972, a Jesuit whom Pope Paul VI had admitted to the College of Cardinals three years earlier. This is not the place—and it is perhaps not my job in any case—to compare these two books in depth. Yet such a comparison might well be instructive, at least with regard to the changed circumstances in which the question is being posed. Jean Daniélou was still writing under the influence of the great collective process of self-reflection that the Second Vatican Council represented for the Catholic Church. One can still sense an air of epochal awakening in his book, but also a kind of defiant attempt at self-assertion in the face of a culture in which atheism seemed to be marching inexorably toward ultimate triumph. In opposition to an increasingly hostile environment, it was not only faith itself that had to be defended but also faith in community, in the church as an institution, with its traditions and its authoritative interpretations of the Gospel. With great vigor, the author rejected the notion that the church might have to shrink to a small spiritual community of those still loyal to the faith: "I must say that a Christianity which would no longer be open to the poor, a Christianity which would not be available to all, a Christianity which would be limited to a small spiritual elite shut up in their chapels within a totally atheistic world, literally horrifies me: because this would mean that we abandon all of mankind to atheism, that we renounce our obligation to bring Jesus Christ to them."[1]

For him, there were two aspects to the church's raison d'être. First, everything in the church must be geared toward the idea of *caritas*, and second, there must be a profound privileging of "holiness."[2] In his aversion to the idea of a church reduced to a mere spiritual community, I feel close to Daniélou's views. But I find his perspective rather unclear and of little use under present circumstances because in the fifty years between the publication of his book and the present day, a profound disillusionment has set in with respect to the Catholic Church.

In the 1970s, many still hoped that the church's new post-conciliar self-understanding would lead to fundamental organizational reforms. Today, however, most have abandoned such hopes or even harbor fundamental doubts about the church's capacity for structural reform. At the same time, the pressure on the church has grown enormously due to the shortage of priests in most economically advanced countries, the widespread disappointment felt among women in view of the discrimination they still face within the Catholic Church and, in particular, the exposure of numerous cases of sexual and spiritual abuse—along with the routine cover-up of such incidents. In the United States, the uncovering of these terrible offenses and the debate on their causes and ways of preventing them began in 2002, much earlier than in Europe. For several years, a number of European commentators went so far as to claim that this problem was limited to the United States. Subsequently, however, Europe too has been gripped by this great convulsion, which has also swept through other religious groups and institutions beyond Catholicism. In Germany, the ensuing crisis of credibility has led to the great endeavor known as the "Synodal Way," which saw the participation of all the country's bishops and auxiliary bishops, an equal number of representatives of Catholic associations and the priesthood, as well as a few "independent figures," myself included. In early 2024, as I write this Preface, no final judgment is possible on where this process will lead at the national and global levels.

But that cannot be the focus at this point. I merely wished to explain the context in which this book emerged and how it differs from Daniélou's era. My goal in this book is not to present a concrete program of reform—although I certainly have strong opinions on the controversial issues identified above. If you are interested in my thoughts in this regard, I invite you to consult the volume in which renowned conservative Catholic philosopher Robert Spaemann and I discussed some of the key bones of contention.[3] My intention in the present book is to uncover a common benchmark beyond the various matters of controversy, one on which the disputing parties should be able to agree. My goal here is to help prevent further polarization in both church and society—and to do so in an idiom that breaks free of the discourses at large within the church, within Christianity and within Christian theology. Daniélou's *sainteté*, "holiness," has to mean something quite different today. Far greater attention must be paid than in Daniélou's book to the tension between the church's institutional claim to sacredness and the offenses against human dignity—that is, the "sacredness of the person"[4]—manifest in the abuse of children, young people and women.

There is no need to go into detail here about how I pursue that project in the present book (for that, see the Introduction). But I would like to comment briefly on two points in order to avoid likely misunderstandings. First, this is not a book exclusively about the Catholic Church. On the contrary, I advocate a *pluralist* understanding of Christianity. What I mean by this is that Christianity de facto exists in a multitude of forms, strands and organizations. To dispute this is to assert that only one's own brand of the faith is truly Christian. But I also wish to suggest that it would be a good thing if many Christians took this *pluralism* as an opportunity to learn from one another in terms of both theological self-understanding and forms of social organization. I would also like to emphasize that my line of argument in this book draws substantially on Protestant thinkers such as Ernst Troeltsch and H. Richard Niebuhr and that, as a Catholic and nontheologian, I was appointed to the honorary professorship named after Ernst Troeltsch by the wholly Protestant Faculty of Theology—an institution steeped in tradition and founded by Friedrich Schleiermacher—at Humboldt University of Berlin.

Second and finally, the ideas informing this book are derived from a much broader project dedicated to the history of moral universalism. The first two volumes of the associated trilogy have already been published in English translation. These are chiefly concerned with refuting the historical narratives propagated by Max Weber and Georg Wilhelm Friedrich Hegel.[5] The third volume puts forward a narrative that is intended as an alternative to both—though important aspects of this narrative can already be found in outline form in the final sections of the first two volumes. If, at its core, Christianity is a moral universalism, then—to quote my key contention in the present book—this must find expression in its organizational structures. I do not mean that this moral universalism must take the form of a centralized and hierarchical global organization on the

Catholic model. But efforts must be made to avert the ever-present threat of a relapse into merely particularist orientations such as nationalism. As it happens, this problem is not unique to Christianity, as it is not the only religion with universalist aspirations.

Looking at the present book and Jean Daniélou's volume together can help clarify that my assessment of the social causes of secularization and my view of atheism also differ in crucial ways from the ideas that guided the French theologian and so many others.[6] Of course, there is no need to take his work as representative of the 1960s, the era of the Council or the subsequent years; naturally, by the same token, I cannot simply claim that my trains of thought are representative of our time. Still, the coincidence of the same title and the differences between the books may perhaps inspire readers to come up with their own answers to the question of why the church exists at all—that perennial source of astonishment—and in what form it ought to do so.

Hans Joas
Berlin, January 2024

WHY THE CHURCH?

1

Introduction

The impetus for this book came from the journalist Volker Resing, for many years editor-in-chief of the monthly *Herder Korrespondenz*, a thought-leading journal among Catholic Christians in Germany. Resing was previously responsible for initiating the lengthy debate between eminent Catholic philosopher Robert Spaemann (d. 2018) and myself, which he moderated and excerpts of which he published in 2018 as a book titled *Beten bei Nebel: Hat der Glaube eine Zukunft?* (Praying in the dark: Does faith have a future?). Over many a shared lunch, but also in an extended circle with editors from the Herder publishing house, we discussed which question was inflaming passions in Christian circles in Germany today—much as the question of whether religion has any future at all did in the early days of the new century. At that time, a debate that had taken off a few decades earlier in the social sciences was attracting growing attention on a much broader basis.

The debate in question revolved around attempts to critique and overcome so-called secularization theory, in other words, the idea that economic and scientific-technological modernization ineluctably results in the weakening of all religion. More than ever before, this debate was gripping the wider public in the churches and beyond. In line with this, "Do we need religion?" was the topic of the first keynote lecture at the first Ecumenical Church Congress ever held in Germany in 2003, which I had the honor of giving. Drawing inspiration from that gathering, I also published a short book of my own essays under the same title in 2004.[1]

Now, the exponents of secularization theory, as defined above, have by no means fallen completely silent. The turn away from the churches, especially the Catholic Church, which was already under way in certain countries, has intensified following the exposure of countless cases of sexual and spiritual abuse by clerics and the habitual cover-up of these cases by church officials—or the inadequate acknowledgment of their own wrongdoing. This turning away is undeniable and is not difficult to understand. No wonder, then, that the proponents of a scholarly position that had been on the defensive are once again becoming more vocal, convinced that they can confirm the global decline of religion after all. Perhaps the most prominent author among them was the leading scholar of value change, Ronald Inglehart, who died in 2021. In 2004, he and coauthor Pippa Norris came up with an original way to reconcile the basic idea of advancing secularization due to modernization with the simultaneous but—on this premise—seemingly paradoxical finding of an increasingly religious world.[2] They did so by taking greater account of the demographic dimension, that is, the different birth rates and variable population growth of societies depending on their degree of secularization. While his proposed explanation was problematic in many respects,[3] it was still an important step forward. In more recent works, however, Inglehart again tended to fall back on conventional secularization theory.[4] His key evidence in this regard was the increase in the number of people who no longer belong to a religious community in the United States. I will come back to this later.

First, however, it should be noted that in the discussions mentioned above we were quick to agree about another issue: for many Christians today the pressing question is not whether religion or Christianity has any future at all but whether there is any need for a church in that future. Many contemporaries view the Christian ethos of love for one's neighbor as plausible, at least in essence, and also find Christian forms of spirituality attractive. As a result, they have a hard time imagining that this heritage will one day lose its vigor completely and vanish from the scene. In any case, many of them are determined to hold fast to it personally, even in the face of strong resistance to Christianity in a secularized world. But they increasingly ask themselves why one cannot be a Christian without belonging to a church. So the pressing question today is not "Do we need religion?" but "Do religious people—do Christians—need a church?" Might a free, in other words, institutionless Christianity better facilitate the spread of the

Christian message? Do clergy and church do more to obscure than to convey this message? What would be missing—many Catholic Christians are now asking themselves—if there were no more priests, bishops or popes?

Historically, these questions are by no means entirely new. In many a rebellious movement in church history and within Protestantism, especially in its more radical forms, and in reaction to ossification within the Reformed churches, they were posed long ago. Sectarian splinter groups and attempts to retreat into mysticism have featured in the history of the churches since time immemorial. In fact, in the theology of the Enlightenment era, the distinction between church and Christianity became central, both in the sense of individuals' claim to determine for themselves what the Christian ethos demanded of them and in terms of the unbiased perception of Christianity in all its historical and cultural diversity—but also in light of its congruence with other religious traditions. At present, however, these impulses do not seem to stem primarily from intellectual and political motives—in contrast to the past, when there were protests against the church's entanglement with feudal power structures, the lower classes harbored utopian hopes of overthrowing the prevailing order, and the middle classes aspired to autonomy at both the political and intellectual levels. The wellspring of these shifts is now more likely to lie in cultural tendencies toward individualization. Beyond the field of religious institutions, these are bringing to an end the era of permanent membership in organizations and lifelong loyalty to political parties, and certainly the selfless commitment of the "party soldier." Once again, we can identify precursors in the shape of the religious quest movements around 1900 with their distinction between the spiritual and the religious, and in the hopes expressed by thinkers such as pragmatist philosopher John Dewey in the 1930s, who believed that the "religious" sphere would have to emancipate itself from all institutional forms, from all traditional mythologies and dogmas and from any claim to exclusivity in order to finally develop without constraint.[5] Under these circumstances, many people find that they can extol their faith only in light of its invigorating, comforting, inspiring effect and thus as something that helps them personally, perhaps even something that enables them to achieve autonomy and take action to help others. But this makes it more difficult for them to ascribe a constitutive role in their personal development to the church as an institution, to describe the Catholic Church, for example, through the metaphor of the

"Mother Church";[6] they may also struggle to acknowledge possible restrictive effects of faith that arise from commitment to ideals and that entail a profound shift in people's lives—away from a focus on realizing their own potential and the optimization of the self.

So why the church? Quite deliberately, the title of this book asks "why?" and not "what for?" In the aforementioned speech, "Do We Need Religion?," I distinguished between two possible meanings of this question.[7] It may imply that we are looking for benefits of some kind that individuals, society or humanity might derive from religion, such as happiness, stable morality, mental health, social cohesion or peace. This way of posing the question features a disturbingly autosuggestive undertone. Ultimately, everyone knows that even the most convincing proof of the utility of faith does not lead to faith. So we have to discern another meaning in the word "needs," namely, whether something may in fact be dispensable under certain conditions. When it comes to religion, this pertains to the "extra-ordinary" human experiences that are articulated in faith. Hence, when it comes to the church, the goal cannot be to seek to legitimize it as an institution because it fulfills a purpose or proves "functional" for a certain "system." Instead, the imperative must be to reflect on the factors that once prompted believers in Jesus Christ to create and imbue with life an institution that differs from all other contemporary social forms such as family and kinship, but also those characteristic of the polity. After all, not all religions have brought forth such an institution. Reflection on these historical causes, however, if convincing, may itself engender reasons and motives to hold fast to the social form of the church in the present and to actively participate in it—despite all the disappointment, even despair, about its concrete form in place and time.

That is what the present book is about. Rather than a monograph, it is a collection of essays that, instead of dealing with the topic in systematic, step-by-step fashion, illuminate it from a number of different angles. Forming the consistent background to all of them, however, is my long-term project of providing a systematic, historically grounded alternative to so-called secularization theory, but also to the grand, influential historical narratives centered on a world-historical process of disenchantment (as in the work of Max Weber), world history as divine reason coming to know itself (as expounded by Hegel) or the emergence of secular reason (as in the writings of Jürgen Habermas). This alternative consists of a global history of moral universalism, that is, grasping the diversity of religious and philosophical sources of an ethos directed at all of humanity. For now, all I will say about this is that it places Christianity in a light that allows for a new perspective on the church.[8]

The first essay most directly addresses this connection between moral universalism and appropriate forms of social organization. This chapter asks whether the human relationship to transcendence is even amenable to organization. Only against this background, in other words, after clarifying the deeper meaning of the church as institution, can we meaningfully probe power, authority and the separation of powers in the church. While these issues arise in all human institutions and organizations, they do not appear in every setting in the way typical of truly political institutions. I therefore express reservations here about rallying cries for the democratization of the church.

This key text is followed by a chapter that concisely summarizes my view of the failure of "predictions" of secularization and disenchantment. I also take the opportunity to reflect on the limits of historical forecasting in general and predictions about religion in particular. My reflections in this chapter raise the question, which I am unable to pursue further in the present book, of when in the history of Christianity the idea that it might ever perish arose last in antiquity and first in "modernity." For more than a millennium—I surmise—it was inconceivable, despite the significance of apocalyptic statements in Christianity, that the world could continue to exist if Christianity disappeared.[9] Today, however, many commentators refer to our entry into a "post-Christian" age as if this were a foregone conclusion.

These two chapters are followed by my thoughts on experiences of self-transcendence and then by an essay that attempts—even more clearly than the previous one—to set the meaning of Christian faith apart from the influence of present-day notions of self-optimization and to derive from this some consequences for the cultural role of the churches today. I place particular emphasis on access to a sphere of experience in which individuals can go beyond the limits of the self, for example, in the liturgy and by entering into "sacred spaces." Religious education, even in its rational forms, depends on access to this sphere.

The next pair of chapters links two texts that are particularly close to my heart but which may well irritate some readers. The first presents an interpretation of Alfred Döblin's great "narrative work," written in exile, on the German Revolution of 1918–19. In the context of his own conversion to Catholic Christianity and in light of his experiences of emigration and exile, Döblin articulated a view of Germany's political history in the first half of the twentieth century that I believe to be of truly explosive import. Beyond all established forms of political Catholicism or of any sort of politics calling itself Christian, he asks how a person who took the message of the Gospel completely to heart while simultaneously seeking to be a root-and-branch realist with regard to human beings ought to have behaved within and toward this history. Döblin does this in prose brimming with vividness, next to which any kind of analytical speech necessarily falls short.

The second is dedicated to the intellectual development of perhaps the greatest Polish philosopher of the twentieth century, Leszek Kołakowski. Once a prominent Marxist, Marxist dissident and historian of Marxism, he is little remembered today. I have two reasons for dedicating a chapter to him here. First, his gradual journey from Stalinist critic of religion and church hater in the early days of communist Poland to a positive assessment of Christianity—and eventually even of the church itself—reads like an object lesson illuminating the path of a secular thinker who, displaying great scrupulousness and authenticity, eventually finds his way to Christianity or at least into its vicinity. In the sense of interest to us here, Kołakowski seems to me to have followed a more consistent path than Habermas, a figure who is vastly more discussed today. I suggest that the route taken by his thought, once distant from Christianity and later close to it, can help us find "a new language" for the Christian faith. Second, as Kołakowski proceeded along his intellectual path, in the 1960s he produced a fundamental historical work, still largely unknown in Germany and the English-speaking world, that examines the pursuit of a nondenominational or even noninstitutional Christianity in the period between the Reformation and the Enlightenment. This book sheds much useful light on the question "Why the church?," which makes it worthy of in-depth treatment in the present context.

The fourth pair of chapters focuses on the idea at the core of what philosophers call moral universalism. I am referring to the notion of universal human dignity, the equal dignity of all human beings, which they did not acquire through any sort of feat and which no misdeed can deprive them of. For many Christians and Jews, but also for many nonbelievers, this idea represents the ultimate moral and political ideal—one whose demise they cannot imagine and which they are determined to defend. But this raises the question of whether this universalist ideal and especially its impact on the field of sexual morality and the associated sensibilities can and should constitute the essence of a new religion—beyond all traditional religion—or whether it can and should exist only in connection with specific, and in this sense particular, religious or nonreligious formations. The first study is dedicated to this issue, while the second, much shorter one was composed in a state of shock at the gross violations of human dignity represented by the torture practiced by members of the US Armed Forces in Iraq. It asks whether the widespread implementation of the ideal of human dignity is still realistic today or whether it is merely a fair-weather phenomenon that soon proves illusory at times of crisis such as military conflict.

The volume concludes with a discussion that builds on ideas I put forth in my short 2016 book *Kirche als Moralagentur?* (Church as moral agency?). At the time, the two largest Christian churches in Germany were expressing unconditional support for a liberal immigration policy. In light of this, though I did not question their political role as such, as I was sometimes accused of doing, I did articulate reservations about the unambiguous way in which Christian arguments were being made in a single policy field. I highlighted the selective derivation of political consequences from the ethos of the Gospel with respect to migration policy without thinking through the implications, while the same did not apply, for example, to matters of peace and disarmament. In the first of the two texts combined here I recall my arguments on this topic in the above-mentioned book, while in the second I address the statements of some of the most prominent critics of and commentators on my position (from Annette Schavan to Peter Dabrock). I do so to clarify the core of my argument that moral universalism can be lived only while simultaneously taking account of incommensurable particular obligations. As important as the moral universalism of Christianity is to my understanding of the church, the church must not become a mere agent of morality, not even in the name of a universalist morality.

As this overview shows, the present book is neither a manifesto for church reform nor a guidebook on the Synodal Way in Germany or in the world. Of course, this does not mean that I have no opinions about controversial issues such as the ordination of women, compulsory priestly celibacy, sexual morality or the nontransparency of developmental processes within the church. I have already expressed these opinions or made them apparent in many of my publications.[10] But in the highly charged situation of crisis currently facing the church, I want to do much more than communicate these opinions and their rationales: my hope is that the ideas presented in this book might help ensure that the disputes between reformers and preservers go beyond a mere power struggle. After all, nothing is gained if one side wins in the short term but the institution suffers in the long term. The common goal must be to reflect on every institutional question in light of our guiding ideals and with a view to strengthening the church in its mission of propagating the ideal of universal human dignity. Only by redoubling its efforts in pursuit of this goal can the church gain new self-confidence and renewed vigor—and not solely by remedying its shortcomings, as important as this obviously is. Some merely defend existing institutional forms without showing that they have served and continue to serve this ideal. Others want to change them, but they cite only political democracy as a positive role model, while failing to develop their own bespoke vision, one centered on the meaning of the church. As I see it, both are failing to focus on the goal identified above. It is this that I wish to foreground here, and this seems imperative even if we have no future path clearly laid out in front of us.

In Germany in particular, debates about the church and church reform often take place in an atmosphere of impending doom. This contrasts markedly with the fact that the globalization of Christianity has made the present one of the greatest phases of expansion in its entire history.[11] Logically, of course, European decline and global expansion do not contradict each other; empirically, they may occur simultaneously. In conclusion, however, I want to briefly address whether it is not more convincing—as Inglehart claims—to speak of a global decline of religion in our time. I limit myself to remarks on the two great powers of the present, whose world-historical collision represents one of the great dangers of the twenty-first century: the United States and China. Is the United States now catching up with European secularization after a historic delay? Is China becoming a world power without religion?

The assumption that the United States is catching up with European secularization and is thus conforming to the classic path of modernization-plus-secularization is supported by the rapid increase in the proportion of US citizens who state in surveys that they do not belong to any religious community. This increase has become particularly evident since the early 1990s. While the proportion was 10 percent in 1997, for example, it rose to 15 percent ten years later, reached 20 percent in 2014[12] and, according to the Pew Research Center survey published in December 2021, is now as high as 29 percent. What once looked like a mere rounding error is thus said to be poised to account for a quarter of the American population.[13] Of course, researchers in the sociology of religion have long been aware that it is risky to base statements about religiosity mainly on data about membership in churches and religious communities. After all, one can be a member without in any serious sense orienting one's own conduct of life toward faith. By the same token, one can also be a believer without belonging to a religious organization at the time a survey is undertaken. Hence, there can be no question of interpreting the mere increase in nonmembers ("religiously unaffiliated," "nones") straightforwardly as an increase in irreligious let alone antireligious attitudes. To come to such a far-reaching conclusion, we would have to break down more precisely which attitudes and behaviors with regard to religion and religious communities the "nones" exhibit. Whether such a breakdown is possible, however, depends on the categorizations prespecified in a given survey. Here, attempts to at least distinguish between confirmed atheists, agnostics and people who describe themselves as "nothing in particular" with regard to religion have proved helpful.

If we make this kind of distinction, it becomes clear that the number of staunch atheists is only about one-fifth of all the religiously unaffiliated individuals in the United States. Any attempt by organized atheists to be recognized as spokespersons for all the religiously unaffiliated is therefore unwarranted, at least in the United States. Agnostics also make up a similarly large (or small) proportion of this group. More than half of the religiously unaffiliated are in fact people who, while they do not currently identify with any specific religious community, can by no means be described as areligious in their attitudes. While more than a quarter of Americans today do not belong to a religious community, only a much smaller proportion deny the existence of God (4 percent according to some studies or, if those who consider the question of God unanswerable, the "agnostics," are included, 10 percent). The group of the unaffiliated is in fact highly heterogeneous; it includes almost half of all US Americans of Asian descent, because their traditions typically evade the "denominationalization" of faith, and a growing proportion of low-income blacks. A particularly striking finding is that in the short span of four years (2010 to 2014), one in four of the unaffiliated joined a religious community, mostly a Christian one. This suggests that for a significant portion of the "nones" in the United States, nonaffiliation is only a temporary phase in their lives. This is quite different in other countries where nonreligious or antireligious beliefs are well established and have been passed down across generations.

But this is not to detract from the fact that the increase in "nones" does indeed seem to be historically significant. Various explanatory factors are brought into play in the literature, such as the decline in marriages and parenthood, since the unmarried and the childless are twice as likely as married people and those with children to belong to no religious community. However, political attitudes seem to be the most significant factor responsible for this change. Since the 1970s, Christian churches and religious communities—including so-called mainline Protestants, Evangelicals and even the Catholic Church—have increasingly been perceived as allies of the political right in the United States, which means that Democrats and left-wingers feel less and less represented by them. Repelled by this, often people decide to pursue their religious or spiritual path outside these organizations. This could be described (following Spanish American sociologist of religion José Casanova) as the punishment that looms when Christian churches and groups simply become part of the culture wars instead of being sites of their resolution.

This is not the place to go into these issues in depth.[14] It should be noted, however, that this political explanation for the declining importance of the churches is different from one that emphasizes modernization processes. While the former prompts us to seek the cause of the churches' loss of credibility, even among Christians, in their one-sided political positioning, the latter treats the weakening of the churches as an inevitable consequence (whether welcome or regrettable) of economic and scientific-technological progress.

Finally, anyone approaching China through the lens of modernization theory would expect a high level of religiosity there and a low one in the United States. Yet in the first instance the findings paint exactly the opposite picture. Obviously, when it comes to the situation in China, the decades-long repression of all religions by the communist state played a crucial role. Particularly during the Maoist "Cultural Revolution" this repression was so severe that some referred in triumphant tones to the overcoming of all religion on Chinese soil. Of course, the Marxist critique of religion and continuity with Stalinist policies in the Soviet Union played a major role in this repressive policy, but the oppression was in fact greater than in the Soviet Union and the European communist states. In order to understand this, we must recognize how much China's own religious traditions were perceived in the twentieth century even by noncommunist reformers as obstacles to economic modernization, as mere cults and superstitions that lacked the institution-building power of Christianity. Thus, for many Chinese, it was the institution of the church that underlay the strength of Christians and the West. Many communists were additionally motivated by the struggle against imperialism. If one's own religious traditions appeared as an impediment to modernization, while Christianity was viewed as a tool of Western imperialism and Buddhism, with its organizational structures, as an instrument of Japanese imperialism, then radical secularism seemed like the only route to China's rebirth.

After Mao's death, but especially from the early 1980s onward, an epoch-making process of religious revitalization began in China, which was paralleled by an equally significant process of economic and scientific-technological modernization.[15] The revitalization of religion applies to the country's own religious traditions as well as Christianity. I will not be going into the diverse forms of expression of this revival, its significance to ethnic conflicts (Uyghurs, Tibet) or the differences between the Catholic Church and Protestant free churches in China. Although state repression in the religious field has increased massively again under Xi Jinping, it would be wrong to interpret this as a sign of deeply rooted Chinese secularism. On the contrary, it seems more convincing to attribute this repression to the widespread perception that the option of faith is becoming ever more popular in China. Even prior to any form of institutionalization, many people see in it the potential for a search for existential meaning and reassurance that goes beyond history and politics, a phenomenon that can in itself be seen as a threat to existing power structures. At the institutional level, pretensions to total state control are colliding with supranational religious institutions' aspiration to resist such control. The question of how to assess these clashing aspirations and their prospects of success is one of the great historical challenges of the present. Confucianism's relative political passivity after the collapse of the empire in 1911–12 has been attributed in part to the fact that it lacked a church and thus became a "soul without a body" in the absence of the imperial state.[16] It makes sense to probe the meaning of the institution of the church in these contexts as well.

To conclude, I would like to mention that this book is dedicated to two individuals who have made the Catholic Academy in Berlin one of the liveliest sites of cultural and religious dialogue in the German capital and a meeting place for all those who are willing to listen to each other. They have also turned it into a home for me personally. With gratitude and in friendship, I dedicate this book to Susanna Schmidt, director from 1997 to 2006, and Joachim Hake, director since 2007.[17]

2

Why the Church?

Can Transcendence Be Organized?

"Church sociology"—this term took on ever more negative connotations in the social sciences, and especially in the sociology of religion, from the early 1960s onward. It was increasingly used to refer to a type of research that supposedly allowed itself to be turned into a mere instrument of church leaders, for example, through collecting and evaluating data that they required or by helping rationalize organizational structures in the churches. This form of commissioned church sociology served aspiring sociologists of religion as a mere foil against which they defined their own projects, such as studies on new forms of spirituality that could be identified outside church institutions. These researchers laid claim to a broader horizon and an intellectual independence that they denied to so-called church sociologists. The splitting of the field into two camps—church sociologists and those who (often under the influence of Thomas Luckmann) mainly studied micro-phenomena of contemporary religious life and were guided by the idea of the ever-advancing privatization of religion—had an ironic consequence: both sides neglected to subject the institution of the church to fundamental analysis from a sociological perspective. For one camp, "church" was simply the unquestioned prerequisite of their work; for the other, it was chiefly a relic of the past that would virtually disappear in the near future, by the year 2000 at the latest—as renowned Austrian American sociologist Peter Berger put it in the *New York Times* in 1968, a remark he lived to regret and later retracted.[1]

As I see it, a sociology of the church, unlike a church sociology with a purely practical orientation, must take as its starting point the astonishing and thought-provoking fact that there is such a thing as the church in the first place. We take it too much for granted that in our world, despite a multitude of social changes, there is an institution that, notwithstanding all the conflicts and divisions, can claim a near-continuous tradition of almost two thousand years. Even those for whom this claim sounds too Catholic and who emphasize the great rupture of the Reformation will not deny the great continuity of institutions since the Reformation. No one can dispute that this is a remarkable phenomenon; some may even be tempted to see it as a kind of miracle. Very few states in the world can claim this sort of uninterrupted continuity. Japan and, to a certain extent, China, come closest. But these are states, in other words, political entities based on power and a specific territory. While these states themselves have a religious dimension, they are not religious communities that aspire to extend beyond a limited territory and encompass the whole of humanity; that is, they do not possess a universalist orientation. There are religious traditions of enduring vitality in the world that are older than Christianity, such as Buddhism and Judaism, but, for all the importance of monasticism and monasteries in Buddhism and networks of synagogues in Judaism, they have not developed an institutional structure comparable to the "church" of the Christians. It is in fact fair to say that none of the so-called world or universal religions has produced a similar institutional form, while the same is self-evidently true of the tribal or national religions, given their socially limited reach. Confucianism has developed no independent institutional structures, which made organized resistance to the forced communist secularization under Mao practically impossible. Islam, for all its institution-building strength and despite rudimentary clerical structures among the Shia, knows no church. Some say that it has never undergone a reformation, while others assert that its greatest lack is something akin to the papacy—and thus an authority capable of decisively rejecting the arbitrary politicization of religion. Although it is quite common for reference to be made to a Daoist "church" in China's history, it would scarcely make sense to suggest that a universalist orientation is at work in Daoism that resembles that of Christianity. Often, we find a stronger fusion of religion and ethnicity in these religious traditions than in Christianity—Judaism and Hinduism being cases in point—or the merging of religion with empire or state, as traditionally in the Chinese case.

Despite the absence of a structure similar to that of the Christian Church in other world religions, however, the first step toward understanding them in the historical–social scientific sense must be to acknowledge the organizational challenges facing all those religions that aim beyond a specific people and a specific state to encompass all human beings. Though it is right "not to exclude the social dimension from the essence of religion," which means that we must necessarily ascribe a social form to all religion, we will fall short if we think that this alone allows us to capture the specific organizational problem of "universalist" religions such as Christianity.[2] Today, scholars tend to refer less often to world religions than to post-Axial religions. Drawing on the ideas and terminology of German philosopher Karl Jaspers,[3] this means that in the religious history of humanity there were breakthroughs toward an understanding of transcendence and moral universalism that removed these religions from simple identification with specific peoples, cultures, states or empires. All these breakthroughs entailed the emergence of ideals that were radically different from the heroic ethos of tribal societies and the martial spirit of archaic empires. But these new ideals, such as the renunciation of violence, could not be realized under the existing conditions; moreover, they are far from being realized today, and perhaps they are fundamentally unattainable through human action. Yet it is precisely because these ideals are difficult or impossible to realize that they could be preserved only if there were institutions dedicated to safeguarding them or if new ones emerged. In order to keep these ideals alive, pass them on to future generations and bring more people into contact with them, to protect the members of the community thus created, breathe fresh life into the ideals again and again through shared rituals and facilitate forms of coexistence that are in greater harmony with the ideals than the general conduct of life permits—for all these reasons, new institutions were needed. This is the sociological dynamic that led to the emergence of Buddhist monasticism and the formation of philosophical schools and "academies" around Greek and Chinese wisdom teachers.[4] At least in some respects, these institutions are functional equivalents of the church in Christianity. So while not all world religions have developed a church, they have produced forms of organization that reflect their sources of inspiration, and on a scale that mirrors the extent to which these inspirations drove them beyond existing social forms.

At this point, however, I will pursue these sociological interreligious comparisons no further, instead limiting myself to Christianity. Even within the latter, the church is not the only social form of organization of the faithful. My goal will be to give the social form of the church a clearer profile in comparison with these other forms of social organization among Christians, while also considering what the churches might learn from them.

The attempt to examine the church and other forms of institutional self-organization among Christians sociologically has—according to the general view in the social sciences—an unambiguous point of origin from a history-of-science perspective. I am referring to the conversations between two colleagues and friends who, at the beginning of the twentieth century, even lived under the same roof in Heidelberg, albeit in separate dwellings: Ernst Troeltsch, the famous Protestant theologian and historian of Christianity, and Max Weber, who, with a background in economics and jurisprudence, was to become the most important founder of the discipline of sociology. In their writings, Troeltsch and Weber both espoused an important and highly consequential distinction between two types of social organization among Christians: the "church" and the "sect."[5] Both seem to have claimed to have invented this conceptual distinction, but since we cannot reconstruct their conversations and daily interactions, we will probably never determine definitively who has the greater claim to originality in this regard. However, we now know that the ground had already been laid for this distinction in various writings by nineteenth-century Protestant church historians, which takes some of the drama out of the "Weber or Troeltsch?" question.[6] No similar development occurred among Catholic thinkers. A strong supranaturalism, in other words, the idea of the church's "supernatural" foundation, long hindered any attempt to subject it to any sort of sociological analysis. Jesus's assurance (Mt 16:18) that not even the "gates of hell" (or "the power of death") would overpower the church seemed sufficient to explain and guarantee institutional continuity. Even Romano Guardini, certainly one of the most open-minded Catholic thinkers of the twentieth century, still held in the 1960s that the church was a "mystery" that fundamentally eluded psychological, sociological and historical explanations.[7] On the Protestant side, in Germany and Scandinavia the churches were for a long time so integrated into state power structures that there too no need arose to truly subject the church's specific features to examination. However, as mentioned above, this gradually changed in the nineteenth century. In the English-speaking world, meanwhile, a representative thinker like John Locke, in his famous "Letter concerning Toleration" of 1685–86, could describe the church as a purely voluntary association of individuals, "a voluntary society of men, joining themselves together of their own accord in order to the public worshipping of God, in such manner as they judge acceptable to him, and effectual to the salvation of their souls."[8] The pursuit of spiritual salvation is seen here as a purely individual matter that *may* bring people together, but this aggregation can never be more than a mere association.

So, we have three fundamental intellectual approaches to the sociology of the church, and all of them must be overcome if this sociology is not to be doomed to failure, because they are incapable of reconstructing the church's self-understanding or fail to provide the latter with any kind of grounding. The three elements that must be jettisoned are the supernatural claim that the church—as divinely founded—should not be regarded as a human institution in the first place; the idea that it is merely part of the state or, as church-critical polemics sometimes put it, its "extended arm"; and the assertion that the church is nothing more than the voluntary aggregation of its members in the manner of a club or association. While on the Catholic side an authoritarian-hierarchical and inordinately centralized understanding of the church was reinforced in the nineteenth century under the protective shield of supranaturalism, in the German Protestant areas the gradual dissolution of the state church and growing religious heterogeneity diminished resistance to a sociologically informed understanding of the church. As mentioned above, Troeltsch and Weber were able to base their analyses on the efforts of theologians, most of whom are forgotten today. For Troeltsch, one of the main findings of his brilliant sociological study of the history of Christianity (*Die Soziallehren der christlichen Kirchen und Gruppen*, translated as *The Social Teaching of the Christian Churches*) of 1912 was that neither the Gospels nor the history of early Christianity provided truly unambiguous benchmarks or guidelines for the formation of Christian religious communities. He thus contended that both the church type and the sect type were inherent in Christianity from the outset. The church, he believed, has a greater capacity to accommodate and integrate many diverse members; it is better able to adapt to its environment and forge compromises between religious ideals and political-economic conditions. The reason for this greater ability to integrate and adapt, for Troeltsch, is that churches make a strong distinction between the subjective moral and spiritual qualities of their members and the objective treasury of grace and salvation available to the institution as a whole and its hierocratic elite. "Lord Jesus Christ, who said to your Apostles: Peace I leave you, my peace I give you, look not on our sins, but on the faith of your Church" are the words spoken during the "Rite of Peace" in every Catholic mass. Sects, on the other hand, Troeltsch stated, are voluntary associations made up of a smaller number of more attentive and stricter Christians who emphasize their distance from the world and the moral purity of their organization. They demand strict Christian conduct from their members and develop precise ideas and control mechanisms to that end; they often tend toward eschatological beliefs.

While working on his book on the history of Christianity, Troeltsch felt an increasing need to go beyond this simple binary scheme and to introduce a third type. He vacillated between terms such as "mysticism" and "spirituality." This third type, he concluded, had the least potential for the formation of communities because here the personal emotional life of individuals was central and only highly fluid forms of shared life could emerge from it. Historically, it was long possible to consider this a marginal phenomenon, such as the Pietists' conventicles, which did not lead them out of their respective churches; this third type is not even mentioned by Weber. Today, however, after another century of increased individualization, especially in the religious sphere, it seems that Troeltsch demonstrated greater foresight than Weber, who viewed contemporary mystical tendencies as mere manifestations of regression and irresponsibility.

It is often overlooked that Troeltsch did not declare the triadic scheme to be complete but referred to only three *main* types of the social organization of Christianity. In addition to these main types, then, he fully allowed for the possibility of others. One example of his perspective on this issue is the "Salvation Army." In a lengthy review essay on a 1915 sociological study of that organization,[9] he asked how Christians could come to take the army as a model for their organization—and, incidentally, not for the first time in history, as evident, for instance, in the early development of the Jesuit Order. Far more interesting, however, than an attempt to expand

and perhaps complete his typology, or to establish how empirically apt the types might be in a given case, is a different question: Why should such a typology be so important in the first place?

The reason for this is, I believe, quite profound. The sociology of Weber, Troeltsch and others blazed a trail that differs from idealist and materialist modes of thinking. Under the influence of idealist philosophies, it was bound to seem as if institutions emerged from ideals themselves. Church historians had increasingly found this unsatisfactory as they grappled with speculative constructions influenced by Hegel. For materialists, on the other hand, ideals have no inherent power at all; they are never more than projections of material desires and needs, distorted expressions of real interests. Troeltsch and Weber, however, attributed agency neither to ideals nor to interests but only to people—with their ideals and interests. Consequently, the institutions of Christianity should not simply be seen as emanations of Christian ideals but must be understood as the result of believers' attempts to preserve their ideals vis-à-vis a world that makes realizing them difficult. These institutions in turn affect how the ideals are understood. Hence, one of the most original features of Troeltsch's history of Christianity was his consistent interpretation of dogmatic differences between churches and sects partly as a consequence of their different forms of organization and not simply as the cause of their separation.

Here we encounter a profoundly pluralist understanding of Christianity. Sects and spiritually oriented communities are not denounced in derogatory fashion as deviations from the only true church, but neither are churches condemned as necessarily corrupt, decadent or authoritarian, as typically implied in sectarian polemics. It must be recognized that the priestly-sacramental church with its adaptation to the world will always be perceived as unsatisfactory by individual Christians, and perhaps even by large groups or entire social movements. These individuals or groups will then resist what they perceive as the objectification and relativization of the Gospel and seek alternative forms of organization based on personal religiosity and ethical commitment. However, these organizations will in turn be experienced by some individuals as narrow-minded and oppressive, leading them either to attempt to liberalize sectarian life or to yearn to return to the freer atmosphere of the churches. Individuals can change membership over the course of their lives without losing their Christianity; in the United States this is a mass phenomenon. Religious communities, meanwhile, vary greatly in their ability to retain members—and their children—over the long term. Seen in this light, it is highly unlikely that any particular type of organization, be it church, sect or loose spiritual community, will ever hold sway exclusively in the future of Christianity. What ultimately matters is that every institution within Christianity must always be viewed in light of its history as a social movement oriented toward a universalist ideal.

As brilliant as Troeltsch's book was in methodological terms, it remained empirically incomplete. Orthodox Christianity was completely absent, as were the Anglican Church and the entirety of Christianity outside Europe. His account ended with the late eighteenth century and, as far as Catholicism was concerned, with the Reformation. Like many Protestants, Troeltsch considered post-Reformation Catholicism a mere remnant of pre-Reformation times. Troeltsch himself recognized the glaring lack of an adequate account of Saint Augustine and his doctrine of the City of God and remedied it with an important book published in 1915.[10] He also continually added annotations to his personal copy, amounting to three hundred additional printed pages in a new edition.[11]

In our context, the details of Troeltsch's additions and self-revisions can be left aside. However, I will discuss here two developments after Troeltsch that are of utmost importance to an adequate sociological understanding of the church today. One of these developments can be grasped only against the background of the religious situation in the United States—a situation characterized by the peaceful coexistence of a multitude of Christian religious communities. The other comes into focus if we pay greater attention to post-Reformation Catholicism.

In the United States, of course, one refers not so much to churches and sects as to "denominations." This term was introduced into the sociology of religion in 1929 by H. Richard Niebuhr, the younger brother of Reinhold Niebuhr, arguably the most-renowned American Protestant theologian of the twentieth century. In his book *The Social Sources of Denominationalism*,[12] the younger Niebuhr showed that the differences between Christian groups in the United States could scarcely be explained on the basis of theological distinctions. Instead, he emphasized the significance of ethnic origin, class affiliation and the "color line," in other words, racism and racial segregation. For a universalist religion like Christianity, he believed, such a state of affairs was scandalous. In this condition, the church was merely mirroring social divisions without offering any hope of overcoming them. Even at the Lord's table, he contended, rich and poor sat separately. For him, then, the denominations were a negative phenomenon, emblems of a process in which the church endorses the very thing the Gospel condemns.

Over time, however, the positive aspect of denominations increasingly came to the fore in studies on the United States, namely, the fact that, under conditions of religious freedom and religious pluralism, the various Christian currents are fundamentally willing to recognize each other. When this aspect is emphasized, furthermore, it soon becomes clear that denominations need not be, as Niebuhr thought, a late stage in the development of sects, a moderated form of their original rigidity. Neither Methodists nor Congregationalists were ever sects, as the Quakers once were. They are in fact something like a loyal opposition within the Christian realm, minorities with a strong willingness to respect others or a majority.[13] This American phenomenon, for which there are parallels in the countries of the British Commonwealth, has also become important outside this cultural sphere through increasing religious pluralization.

The other key correction to Troeltsch and Weber comes from sociologist Werner Stark. Of Bohemian Jewish stock, Stark immigrated to Britain and then the United States, converted to Catholicism and spent the last decade of his life (1975–85) in Salzburg.[14] He raised two main objections to Troeltsch's and Weber's sociology of the church. First, he criticized both these classical figures for having failed to distinguish sufficiently between a universal and a spatially limited church (such as the Protestant territorial churches [*Landeskirchen*]). Second, he emphasized the role of religious orders within the church and contrasted their revitalizing function for the latter with the conflict-ridden interaction between sect and church.[15]

For Stark, universality is the church's most crucial characteristic—universality in relation to both social inequality and cultural difference. Stark saw submission to existing structures of social inequality as the great temptation for the medieval church. Meanwhile, he considered the churches' kowtowing to nationalism their great temptation "in modern times." Of course, the hierarchy of the church was never simply one of descent, but meritocratic principles often took a back seat to those of aristocratic lineage and the estates-based order. The churches' opposition to nationalism, colonialism and imperialism, Stark contended, was often barely discernible.

Even in the absence of de jure identification with a state, he underlined, the churches were often de facto aligned with specific social orders.

However, countermovements against such identification have arisen time and again. These movements share motives with sects—but with a crucial difference: "The withdrawal of religious orders from the Universal Church is never as total as the withdrawal of religious sects from an established church, and, above all, it is not as final. After retreat comes re-entry, after a turning away from their community, a turning back towards it. It is a case of *reculer pour mieux sauter*. Whereas the sect gives up the establishment as hopeless and thenceforth goes its own way, the order merely gathers strength with the hope, nay with the expectation, that the day will come when it will conquer and remodel the whole Church."[16] Of course, this raises all sorts of empirical questions, since the orders themselves have their own organizational problems, and they too always risk succumbing to particularist regression. Interpretative questions also arise about how exactly Weber and Troeltsch envisioned things like the emergence of monasticism,[17] the great reform movements of Cluny, for example, or the Franciscan renewal, and how they perceived the Jesuits or the self-reform of the Catholic Church. I am going to leave these questions to one side here. Instead, in five brief points, I will systematize the significance of my reflections based on Ernst Troeltsch, H. Richard Niebuhr and Werner Stark to our present-day situation.

1. *Universality*. This seems to me more important than ever in our time, in which Christianity is undergoing a tremendous global expansion. As Karl Rahner put it, over the course of its history even the Catholic Church has for the most part been the universal church only *in potentia* rather than *in actu*.[18] During the First Vatican Council (1869–70), the faithful from the European colonies were still represented by bishops from the colonial powers. The Second Vatican Council (1962–65) marked an epochal turning point in this regard. Today's pope does not come from Europe, and the equation of Christianity with European or Western culture is becoming ever more untenable. The question for all Christian religious communities is how to consistently accommodate this growing globality within their organizational structures. It is crucial, however, not to equate universality with hierarchical centralism. The most important thinker to explore the potential of federal structures, and student of Troeltsch and

Weber, Paul Honigsheim, pointed to the Orthodox churches, in which the national branches enjoy considerable autonomy and "unity is symbolized in essentially mystical fashion through the gathering of their leaders rather than being perceived in juridical terms through a centrally governing head."[19] In Latin Christianity too, especially in the fifteenth century, the "conciliarist" movement attempted to subordinate the authority of the pope to that of an assembly of representatives of the entire Christian community and thus pave a way out of the divisions and conflicts within the church. The ecumenical movements have often been guided by the idea that theological differences need not prevent close cooperation to the point of communion.

2. *Denominationalism.* It is not easy for the Catholic Church to recognize other Christian communities as fundamentally equal, a point laid bare once again in the controversies surrounding the 2000 declaration of the Vatican Congregation for the Doctrine of the Faith titled *Dominus Iesus*. Mutual respect, however, does not mean relativizing one's own truth claims, as is sometimes asserted, but only a revised understanding of the relationship between the inevitable truth claim in dialogue and an understanding of institutional structures as the embodiment of the claimed truth. It does not seem justified to me to label such a distinction between dialogical truth claims and institutional claims to possession of the truth "ecclesiological relativism,"[20] just as it is unjustifiable to dismiss the insight into the never definitive possession of truth as a relativistic abandonment of truth claims. Often, the changed attitude of the Catholic Church's Magisterium toward religious freedom since the Second Vatican Council has not yet fully translated into its attitude to other Christian churches and groups such that its own self-understanding is genuinely transformed in the process. It is crucial not to confuse the desire for unity among all Christians with the claim to successfully represent this unity already. The Catholic Church can only provide orientation toward worldwide unity. It must never cease to encourage inner diversity, and it will inevitably endure the fate of new divisions.[21]

3. *Sects* are characterized by the principle of voluntary association. Such voluntary associations may also exist within the church. I am not well versed in canon law, but to my knowledge it states that "the Christian faithful are at liberty freely to found and direct associations for purposes

of charity or piety or for the promotion of the Christian vocation in the world and to hold meetings for the common pursuit of these purposes."[22] There is no mention of permission from or recognition by the ecclesiastical authorities. However, controversies have arisen time and again in this regard, in Germany most recently in relation to the pregnancy counseling organization Donum Vitae. It would be a tremendous step forward if such voluntary initiatives could flourish without being tied to the hierarchy's apron strings.

4. *Religious orders.* In the history of the church, the role of religious orders has often been crucial to spiritual renewal. It is important to distinguish here between communities of monks and nuns who seek to live an exemplary Christian life through intensive personal togetherness at a fixed location, and religious orders per se. The latter are supralocal organizations with their own goals and strategies and may (like the Jesuits) dispense entirely with a fixed monastic community in a particular place. For a long time, sociology contributed very little to the study of religious orders;[23] it is only in the era of globalization that interest has begun to grow, especially in the Jesuits as the first global network in history.[24] As apparent in the Liturgical Movement after the First World War, however, lay people can also play a decisive role in such a revitalization of the church. At a time when the number of new entrants into religious orders is low, at least in the Western world, networks of active lay people such as Sant'Egidio can be expected to become increasingly important. From the point of view of spiritual renewal, this surely represents a particularly interesting recent development.

5. *Mysticism.* If individuals are concerned only about themselves and their personhood, then the connection to transcendence and to the moral universalism of Christianity is severed; in such cases, faith becomes a self-made combination of beliefs and practices informed by the criteria of feeling good and self-help. "Spiritual" thus becomes the antithesis of institutionally bound religiosity. But if this connection is preserved, the mystical dimension may constitute a particularly important element for Christianity under conditions of radical individualization.

Troeltsch had no wish to dissolve churches and sects in favor of loosely structured mystical communities, as is sometimes imputed to him. Instead, he envisioned a synthesis of the three main forms of social organization among Christians as he had distinguished them in his history of

Christianity. This perspective of a synthesis of church, sect and mysticism needs to be refined today by factoring in the issues set out above relating to denominations, universality and religious orders (or other Christian communities). His plea for an "elasticized" people's church (*Volkskirche*) has become famous.[25] For him, elasticity meant that it was vital for the church to make space for "ruggedly and radically religious spirits" without making their way of life the norm for everyone.

The era in which Troeltsch developed these ideas was in many ways very different from our own. He wrote under the conditions of a state in which "an unbaptized lieutenant [was] as inconceivable as a confessionless railway conductor,"[26] and he expected the foreseeable collapse of social democratic hopes for progress to lead to a sharp growth in sects among the German lower classes. Communism and fascism were, of course, beyond the scope of his imagination in his writings prior to the First World War. In this respect, everything he wrote must be rethought and qualified in many ways. But when it comes to the most crucial issue of all, he was absolutely not the cliché of the "cultural Protestant." "The greatness of religion consists of its contrast with culture, its difference from science and social-utilitarian morality, its mustering of supramundane and superhuman powers, its development of the imagination and its orientation toward that which lies beyond the senses."[27] Still, that cliché has weighed heavily on the reception of Troeltsch's ideas. Yet the notion of the Christian religion as at variance with culture ultimately means that all those who are seized by the ideals of moral universalism and who articulate these ideals religiously by reference to a supramundane—in other words, transcendent—divine source of all holiness, must in fact produce forms of social organization. And these forms must never cease to be measured against these ideals and the demands emanating from them. So can transcendence be organized? Yes—it cannot be preserved merely by individuals in the absence of organization. But no—it transcends any particular organization.

Those who refer to organization, however, cannot remain silent about power and domination. Inevitably, they must consider what the most appropriate degree and mode of participation for members might be. Two aspects must be taken into account here from the outset. First, paying attention to the dimension of power in the church-as-organization must not lead us to simply reject one extreme—forgetfulness of power—only to embrace the other extreme, an unbounded concept of power. In debates on church reform, under the influence of Nietzschean French philosopher and cultural historian Michel Foucault, some are currently inclined to understand pastoral action, every gesture or a habitus of humility, and even theological arguments primarily or exclusively in terms of a struggle for power. Of course, it may be productive to look at small-scale interactional phenomena from this point of view. But in doing so, we must not lose sight of the ideal that is constitutive of Christianity and of the church. In fact, this ideal opens our eyes to a counter-concept to power. Just as there are, and must be, structures in the university through which the undeniable differences in power are methodically suspended, so that what counts in academic debate is not power but exclusively the better argument, so the religious ideal of Christianity itself must remain the benchmark for all reflections on the best organizational structure for the church; it must not be obscured by a seemingly critical theory of power.[28]

Second, we have to remember that the question of power arises not just in relation to the internal distribution of power within organizations but also with respect to their ability to take action to achieve their organizational goals and to maintain their autonomy vis-à-vis their environment, and thus in relation to the external world. If, as in the Reformation, the power imbalance between the clergy and the so-called laity within the church is, for good reasons, diminished, this may result in greater reliance and dependence on the state as a nonecclesiastical power. We would have to wonder whether this is truly beneficial.

As I see it, from my reflections on the moral-universalist character of Christianity and on the two aforementioned insights into power and organization, it follows that the church should understand itself as a cooperative (*Genossenschaft*) of those moral universalists who see in the Gospel of Christ the most emphatic articulation of this ideal. Influenced by the great legal historian Otto von Gierke,[29] I prefer to speak of a "cooperative" rather than a "community" in order to avoid the opposition to "society" inherent in the concept of community and the possible romanticization of the social relations within it. The church, then, should be envisioned as a cooperative of believers that requires hierarchical structures in order to guarantee its ability to act in pursuit of its ideals despite the influence of external powers.

The hierarchical character of an organization, even a cooperative, is always in danger of degenerating. This happens when leadership is practiced in the form of domination. Then the church is imagined as a quasi state, and this tendency becomes particularly pronounced when it is fostered by the state, turning the church into a state institution. This has happened frequently and over long periods in the history of Christianity. If the church as quasi state also deviates in important normative respects—such as the transparency of organizational processes and their legal auditability by those affected—from the standards developed by the liberal-democratic constitutional state, then a gap opens up between ideal and reality, which is in this respect greater in today's Catholic Church than in the state. But as a cooperative of those oriented toward an ideal, the church cannot avoid being judged in light of its own constitutive ideal.

This may sound like a demand for the "democratization" of church structures. Yet when this demand is made, it is crucial to clarify precisely what it entails. Of course, in a democratic society, particular institutions may face certain demands arising from the spirit of a democratic culture. But it is by no means the case that every institution in a democracy, not even every publicly financed one, must itself be organized on the model of political democracy if it is to meet the standards of democratic culture. Each of these institutions must be able to focus mainly on pursuing its own institutional goal. Universities, for example, must be judged chiefly by whether their organizational structures enable excellent research and teaching. This restricts the potential for democratic codetermination in many ways and leads to differing opportunities for participation for different so-called status groups. In the detail, much will be, and will remain, controversial and contested here. As it happens, especially in societies with a long democratic tradition (such as the United States), the transformation of these institutions through what is called "democratization" is often met with incomprehension. The structure of public broadcasting in Germany, meanwhile, is the outcome of the struggle to organize media beyond the private sector while simultaneously avoiding purely state-led entities, in other words, domination by a given democratically elected government. On this premise, programming decisions can certainly not be made "democratically" by the employees of a TV or radio station; they must be made in complex ways—or be controlled—by the representatives of various social forces. The specific problems involved in organizing the military in a democracy are of course another case in point—and it is in this context that we can see most clearly that the democratic spirit cannot simply mean democratization of internal organizational structures.

When it comes to the Catholic Church, the democratization perspective requires us to recall additional organizational problems.[30] In a global organization, every decision-maker is responsible not only to those affected and involved locally but also to the organization as a whole and thus to those higher up the hierarchy, for whom quite different priorities may hold sway than those that seem to make sense at the local level. For example, critics of the idea that the royal road to church reform is for pastors or bishops to be bound by majority decisions by committees rightly point out that this will inevitably result in the collision of two logics within the person of the cleric: that of universal hierarchy and that of local participation. This problem can certainly be defused by clarifying decision-making responsibilities, but the potential for conflict and the "risk of secession" inherent in such an arrangement is unmistakable.

Another problem thrown up by any kind of democratization must also be faced. At German universities, the perceived legitimacy of decisions made by student bodies is often low because only a tiny fraction of the student "electorate" actually participates in elections. Much the same applies to the existing participatory structures in the church. If everything proceeds as usual, this may go unnoticed; silence is often interpreted as approval. But the picture shifts in cases of conflict. Then the entire arsenal of struggle over these decisions comes into play. These struggles may end in outcomes that are ultimately accepted by all. But they may also bring about even greater alienation from the organization than the sense of disappointment sometimes felt at the decisions of officeholders.

It therefore seems to me wise and appropriate to look for a term other than "democratization" when discussing church reform. The idea that it might be beneficial to consider "synodal structures" makes sense against this background. Understandably, some suspect that this merely involves periodically plastering a pleasing patina on clerical power structures in the absence of serious change.[31] Yet the synodal paradigm might just harbor the potential to develop an organizational structure that is truly appropriate for the church today. The key features of this structure would have to be, first, "checks and balances"; second, appropriate ways of representing all believers; and third, the right balance of centralism and decentralism. The great idea expounded by French Enlightenment thinker and theorist of the state Montesquieu and then by the founding fathers of the United States in the eighteenth century was, after all, that of clear leadership and clear control structures as complementary rather than fundamentally opposed. This is the only way to systematically reconcile the capacity for action with consensus building.[32] At all levels of the church, from parishes to dioceses to the universal church, structures could emerge that avoid both untrammeled clerical power and the paralysis often engendered by participatory decision-making. Furthermore, it seems inevitable that a world-spanning church whose center of gravity is moving ever further away from European cultural hegemony as the Christian population of Europe shrinks while it expands in other parts of the world must strike a new balance between unity and diversity and also openly acknowledge this fact. This relates to organizational structures but must extend into lived faith. There are issues in which culturally self-evident "truths" are blended into the Christian message that do not have the same claim to universal validity as the message of the Gospel itself. It may be a liberating step not to insist on cross-cultural consensus with respect to every culturally imbued dispute. Just as, at the organizational level, the final decision on decision-making structures can only be made centrally, when it comes to decisions about the obligations arising from faith, the center must also decide where decentralized room for maneuver should not only be tolerated but consciously opened up. This could accommodate demands for a different position for women or homosexuals and others without tearing the church apart and stymying its missionary efforts through endless internal wrangling.

3

Problematic Predictions
Religion in a Secular Age

Some time ago I was a guest on the popular German TV show *Scobel* on the 3sat channel. The topic of the evening was conveyed by a phrase more hackneyed than humorous, "the emptiness of the churches," which played on the fact that in German this sounds exactly like the more familiar expression for "the churches' teachings."[1] This trite beginning signaled the slant of the clips shown during the broadcast: our churches and other places of worship are mostly empty and thus largely dispensable; no one today is interested in the messages of the Christian faith, while esotericism and Asian forms of spirituality are flourishing in the West. A biologist, who also claimed to be a religious studies scholar, asserted that for two thousand years Christianity had been no more than an extension of the state—since before the crucifixion of Christ, strictly speaking! The broadcast began by showing the demolition of the so-called Immerath cathedral, a church that fell victim to open-cast mining in the northern Rhenish brown coal field—though this was not mentioned, with the church's destruction merely serving to illustrate the superfluousness of large-scale church buildings in the present age. We might characterize the historical picture implied by all this as follows. Although Christianity, given its proximity to the state, bears a significant degree of responsibility for every form of political oppression and social inequality in the parts of the world it has influenced, almost everyone in Germany adhered to it until well into the postwar period and the days of the so-called economic miracle. Subsequently, however, an unparalleled and continually self-reinforcing collapse occurred, which is now resulting in the complete marginalization of Christianity and casts doubt on—or renders absurd—any notion of Germany or Europe as a culture profoundly shaped by Christianity.

I am of course well aware of the signs of declining Christianity and advancing secularization in Germany and in a number of other countries. Since 2000, around 500 Catholic churches have been redesignated in Germany, and 140 of these have indeed been torn down. But if we really want to understand the precise nature and causes of this weakening of Christianity, we have to engage far more deeply with the subject. In spatial terms we must be willing to look beyond Germany and Central or Western Europe, while in temporal terms we must think beyond the present era. If we do so, it soon becomes apparent that—from a global perspective—the weakening of religion in these European countries is clearly the exception. It is true that this phenomenon pertains in some, though by no means all, ex-communist countries in Europe, most strikingly the Czech Republic, East Germany and Estonia. It is also to be found in an array of Western European countries (the United Kingdom, Sweden, France, the Netherlands), though it is always worth scrutinizing the relationship between the majority and the minority of seriously "practicing" Christians in each country. Particularly in the case of Sweden, the term "vicarious religion" has been put forward to convey the benign attitude of those who do not attend church on Sunday toward those who do so, as it were, on everyone's behalf.[2] This benevolence is for the most part not bestowed upon churchgoers in East Germany, so the term would be a quite inappropriate means of describing the situation there. Only in a very small number of non-European societies shaped by European settlers are there similarly strong trends toward secularization (New Zealand and Uruguay are the most frequently mentioned). Comprehensive communist repression of religion now exists chiefly in North Korea; China, by contrast, despite the antagonism of the state, which has intensified again recently, is undergoing a multifaceted revival of both indigenous religious traditions (such as Buddhism and Daoism) and (mostly Protestant) Christianity. Developments in South Korea have been dramatic. There, one of the most rapid economic and scientific-technological processes of modernization in the history of the world went hand in hand with a revitalization of older religious traditions and a vigorous process of Christianization. Christianity is growing rapidly in many African countries, even though some of the most astute observers, such as the great Protestant theologian Paul Tillich, once assumed that the end of colonial rule would cause Christianity in Africa, as a European implant, to wither. This growth is largely but not entirely due to demographic factors. According to reliable estimates, the number of Christians in Africa is currently growing by twenty-three thousand people a day.[3] In the shape of so-called Pentecostalism, today Christianity continues to spread in Latin America, Africa, East Asia and, in the face of immense resistance, even some parts of India.[4]

In light of these developments, the so-called secularization thesis has now lost its plausibility for most researchers in the field, though not all. Here I have to sound a warning about a common misunderstanding. This thesis has never simply stated that secularization *exists*. It is thus neither confirmed by indisputable cases of the weakening of religion nor refuted by the resurgence of religion. Instead, this thesis or theory claimed to *explain* the weakening of religion. It asserted a close causal connection between modernization and secularization: the more modern a society (in terms of economic and scientific-technological development), the weaker religion is within it or the more it is limited to the private sphere. But this very assumption has increasingly proved to be a false generalization of phenomena found in European history. It has always been clear that it does not apply to the United States—an indisputably modern society but also one that is religiously vigorous and even productive of religion. By "productive of religion" I mean a society that gives rise to new religious movements that are capable of surviving and even of spreading, as in the case of the United States, which saw the emergence of Mormonism in the nineteenth century and Pentecostalism in the twentieth century. The thesis of secularization also fails to explain the major differences within Europe, which can by no means be described as a uniformly secular continent, given that the regional differences are substantial and cannot simply be put down to differing levels of modernization. It is now becoming clear that almost nowhere outside Europe do the facts corroborate this thesis. Even its few remaining proponents concede that the stronger population growth in religiously vital societies is making the world increasingly religious.[5] According to them, the tendency is for the population of modern—and thus, as they assume, highly secularized—societies to die out due to the low number of births or to be radically changed through the impact of migrants and the religiosity they bring with them.

But the loss of credibility suffered by the secularization thesis has manifold consequences. I will discuss three of them here. First, if modernization as such is not the explanation for secularization, but instances of the weakening of religion are undeniably real, we clearly need a different explanation for this religious decline. By no means are most critics of the secularization thesis postmodern opponents of all grand historical narratives or comprehensive theoretical attempts at explanation. They consider just one specific theory and one particular grand narrative, the theory of secularization, to have failed. Second, if modernization and secularization are no indissoluble dyad, then the common interpretation of the prehistory of modern secularization also begins to look shaky: the narrative, going back to Max Weber, of a millennia-long process of disenchantment. We must, however, make a clear distinction between the critique of the conception of disenchantment and criticisms of the theory of secularization. Third, if we think through seriously the erroneous predictions arising from the thesis of secularization and the narrative of disenchantment, we find ourselves confronted by truly fundamental issues entailed in such assertions of historical trends in general. These often have a prophetic air. But there are genuine and false prophets. What we say about the future always forms part of contemporary struggles over this future. This state of affairs also demands consideration and explains the title of this chapter.

Secularization: Not a Necessary Corollary of Modernization

At the beginning of this chapter I indicated that I believe the notion of the taken-for-granted Christianness of Germany or Europe as a whole until the era of the postwar economic miracle to be wrong. By the early eighteenth century the first commentators had already begun to predict the disappearance of Christianity from Europe. To my knowledge, such views had not in fact been expressed for more than a millennium, since the era when Saint Augustine "considered a mass return to heathenism quite conceivable" after Alaric I's sack of Rome in 410.[6] Now, though, a growing number of people began to express such views. Prussian king Frederick the Great, for example, articulated such thoughts in his correspondence with Voltaire, while the French Revolution saw violent practical efforts to speed along this alleged process. We should keep in mind that Friedrich Schleiermacher, the greatest Protestant theologian of the nineteenth century, could address his brilliant speeches on religion of 1799 to "the educated among its despisers" only because these despisers existed in large numbers—both educated and uneducated. In the *Vormärz* (the period of German history prior to the Revolution of March 1848 in the states of the German Confederation) and in the Revolution of 1848 itself, the Protestant (state) church's loyalty to the Prussian dynasty, the king, government and army alienated much of the liberal bourgeoisie and the nascent labor movement in Prussia from Christianity—with lasting consequences. By the late nineteenth century, Berlin was already one of the most secularized cities in the world, in significant part because Protestant Christianity had become bourgeoisified and the lower classes felt repelled or excluded by this bourgeoisie and the pastors' nationalist views. The period after the First World War and the Nazi movement strengthened the cultish and anti-Semitic efforts to draw on a form of supposed Germanic religiosity predating Christianity, with its Jewish roots, or to strip Christianity of all Jewish elements. Jesus Christ, it was claimed, did not bring salvation; instead, we must be saved from Jesus Christ—this was the dominant view in the circle around Mathilde Ludendorff, the wife of the general of the emperor and key figure of *völkisch* religious circles. In order to achieve the "dejudaization" of Christianity, a theological Institute for the Study and Elimination of Jewish Influence on German Church Life was even founded in Eisenach in 1939. Had the Second World War ended differently, these incipient efforts to establish a new (Christian or anti-Christian) racist anti-universalism would probably have made a major impact; the Christian dimension, in the sense of a universalism of love, was also essentially absent from the organization of so-called German Christians.

These outline remarks are an attempt to demonstrate that we undoubtedly require an alternative to explanations of secularization focused on modernization. This alternative is readily available. I call it the "political sociology of religion" and regard British sociologist David Martin as its pioneer.[7] This approach foregrounds churches' and religious communities' stance on the major political questions of a given era: the "social question," for example, as it was called in the nineteenth century; the national question, which was so crucial to the loyalty of the Poles, Irish, Croats and Bavarians to their Catholic Church; the democratic question; the rights of the individual; the emancipation of women; and the issue of religious pluralism. The patchwork religious map of Europe, where highly religious regions sometimes border on highly secular ones, can be understood only from such a historically nuanced perspective. This also allows us to see how far from inevitable certain processes of secularization were and are. What matters is the character of the institutional relationship between state and church or state and religious communities. Excessive proximity to the state and a power-backed religious monopoly were always a danger to the churches if political and economic dissatisfaction spread among the general population. This is the rational core of the biologist's statement as cited at the start of this chapter. But how wrong it is to generalize from this is evident in her consummate ignorance of the history of tensions between church and state, as well as the tremendous significance of the dualism of state and church in European history. My favorite example from recent German history involves a Catholic school in the Eichsfeld region of Thuringia, where I once gave a talk. It was forced to close in the context of Bismarck's Cultural Struggle (Kulturkampf)—after which it was reopened. Later the Nazis closed it—and it was subsequently reopened. The next to close it were the communists—after which it was reopened once again. Three political regimes in Germany came and went, and this Christian school survived them all. The notion of the churches' and the whole of Christianity's steadfast closeness to the state must sound strange indeed in the Eichsfeld region, which—rather like Asterix's Gaulish village holding out against the might of the Roman Empire—has remained an island of the Catholic faith as the various political regimes have arisen and fallen away.

Tensions of this kind are not solely part of the past. They may also take new and unexpected forms. This applies, for example, to immigration policy in Germany, with the churches putting forward moral arguments in support of mass immigration and backing government policy, potentially alienating disadvantaged social milieus.[8] New challenges always arise in regard to questions of war and peace as well. The increased need for individualistic forms of spirituality also seems significant to me. While this need may very well be satisfied within the major religious communities and traditions, it may also be a threat to them. Again, this is the rational core of the claim that esotericism and new forms of spirituality are on the increase. But it is empirically incorrect to extrapolate from religious or quasi-religious quest-centered movements, which often lead merely to short-lived membership or practice and are mostly not passed on to the children of those involved, to the impending dissolution of all religious institutions.

I would like to make two additional comments on this complex to avoid misunderstandings. An emphasis on political questions does not mean that the political dimension is all that matters and that there is no religious sphere as such or that, as Marxism suggests, religious forms are merely the displaced expression of material interests. But the turn to and away from particular religions and even secular worldviews and value systems mostly occurs not on the basis of individual doctrinal statements but via holistic forms of identification. Hence, religious biographies are determined in part by key political inflection points. And finally, it may be some time before the consequences of such pivotal political forks in the road kick in. We know from the United Kingdom that for a long time men's distance from the church did not prompt them to leave it because their mothers, wives and lovers often acted as a countervailing force. But if women too lose their ties to the church, thus "feminizing" unbelief, the result may be an avalanche of departures. And if due to historical circumstance the parental generation fails to keep their children in the religious community, then galloping secularization, occurring after some delay, is likely. This sounds more gloomy than I mean it to be. One may also read the three-hundred-year history of the weakening of Christianity in Europe, as I have outlined it here, as the history of repeated instances of partially successful rejuvenation, as a reason not to underestimate the vitality of Christianity even in the secularized parts of Europe and to contemplate the undeniable relevance of its message, liturgical practice and welfare and social activities.

The Limits of the Narrative of Disenchantment

Only since the seventeenth and eighteenth centuries has Europe seen the emergence of an intellectually developed and aggressively espoused new alternative to the Christian faith in the shape of what the great Canadian philosopher Charles Taylor, in his monumental 2007 work *A Secular Age*, called the rise of the "secular option."[9] Prior to its appearance there was certainly religious indifference, hatred toward some or all clergy or the church, for example, in light of its role as exploitative landowner, but—apart from Judaism and the views of some intellectuals—no self-confident alternative to Christianity in Europe. How did this new worldview manage to emerge and spread? The key question here is whether the explanation for modern European secularization lies in the conditions of the eighteenth, nineteenth and twentieth centuries themselves or whether this epoch-making shift has a lengthy prehistory. Just as the theory of secularization claims to explain the development of the last two centuries, the narrative of disenchantment claims to explain the long-term historical background to this secularization. "Disenchantment" is not "secularization," though the two are constantly confused. For Max Weber, the main source of this narrative, "disenchantment" in fact meant a history extending across two and a half millennia, beginning with the Hebrew prophets (and certain parallel phenomena in other cultures such as Buddha). Weber drew a line that led from these prophets and the philosophy of the Greeks, after setbacks in the Middle Ages, to the new prophetic awakening in the Reformation and the early modern scientific revolution, from there to the establishment of a causal-mechanistic worldview and the Enlightenment, but subsequently also to the profound crisis of meaning in the European fin de siècle around 1900 and on the eve of the First World War. This narrative proved tremendously suggestive. Much as Nietzsche ascribed to Christianity a constitutive role in a historical process that inevitably led to the overcoming of Christianity—because the ethos of truthfulness also led to historical Bible criticism—Weber, however great his distance from Nietzsche in the detail, also constructed a narrative that leaves no room for an intellectually responsible and vital religiosity in our era.

To try to put forward a detailed critical discussion of this narrative would be to push the present text far beyond its limits. In my book *The Power of the Sacred* I tried to show, in hundreds of pages, what is wrong with this narrative and what an alternative to it might look like.[10] Above all, the narrative of disenchantment suffers from the ambiguity of its core concept, that of "disenchantment." This term refers to the prophets' struggle against magic ("demagification"), a loss of meaning with respect to everyday action and life ("desacralization") and the weakening of notions of radical transcendence as expressed in Jesus's statement to Pilate: "My kingdom is not of this world" ("immanentization" or "detranscendentalization"). Because Weber failed to distinguish between these three meanings, he turned these different processes into successive phases of one single world-historical process of disenchantment, which is then supposed to have facilitated both modernization *and* secularization.

To make my core criticism understandable, I use the distinction between three conceptual pairs, which constantly flow into one another in relevant debates.[11] I am referring to the pairings sacred/profane, transcendent/immanent (or mundane) and religious/secular. The terms "sacred," "transcendent" and "religious" are not synonyms. The concept of the "sacred" (or "holy") is an attempt to convey a universal anthropological phenomenon, one that arises from human experiences of self-transcendence. The concept of the "transcendent" refers to ideas of a division between the realm of the divine and the earthly, as well as the locating of the true and the good in the realm of the divine; these ideas by no means represent a universal anthropological phenomenon but instead emerged historically in identifiable places and at particular points in time. Finally, the concept of the religious makes sense only if it contrasts with something; this has fully been the case only since the rise of the "secular option" in the Europe of the seventeenth and eighteenth centuries.[12] If this distinction between three contrasting pairs, which I have mentioned here only very briefly,[13] makes sense, then it follows that there must be three different processes of shift from one side to the other: *this means there are processes of sacralization and profanization (or desacralization); there are processes of transcendentalization and immanentization (or detranscendentalization); and there are processes of religious revitalization and secularization.* It is in no way imperative to conceptualize these different processes as naturally succeeding one another. Things may proceed in either direction.

I would like to illustrate this with reference to a single example. In Max Weber's account, the Reformer Calvin plays a key role: Weber asserts that his thinking embodies the "completion" or apogee of religious disenchantment through radical hostility to magic. Weber certainly exaggerates when, without citing evidence,[14] he writes that "the strict Puritan had the corpses of his loved ones dug under without any formality in order to assure the complete elimination of superstition. That meant, in this context, cutting off all trust in magical manipulations"—for Calvin certainly approved of funerary rites.[15] Fundamentally, however, it is true that Calvin insisted on the "negation of any grounds for a *mundane* separation of sacred and profane—in other words of any basis for distinguishing certain places, times, numbers, objects, actions, and so on, as holy."[16] Yet in Calvin's thinking, of course, the point of this battle against all "idolatry of created things" (*Kreaturvergötterung*) is not total desacralization, let alone secularization, but rather the intensified, indeed exclusive sacralization of God, that is, his radical transcendentalization.[17] By citing this example, I aim to at least begin to lend plausibility to the argument that when it comes to ascetic Protestantism, we must understand demagification as transcendentalization. Much the same may be said about what Weber called the "prophetic age."[18] Again, we have to understand the prophetic struggle against magic not as the precursor of later secularization but merely as a step toward a demagified religion. After all, as Weber himself wrote,[19] in the first instance demagification opens up the potential for a form of religious faith that places greater emphasis on morality and conscience or one of a more mystical hue. Hence, we can at least tentatively tease apart what Weber folds into the single concept of disenchantment. This is bound to prompt us to ask whether *demagification, desacralization, detranscendentalization* and *secularization* are not in fact completely different processes. On this premise it is not obvious that we ought to declare that any one of these processes lays the ground or sets the pace for the others. Instead, this perspective points to a plethora of different challenges that religious traditions must cope with or that may be their ruin.

While in Weber's work itself the process of disenchantment stood center stage as a phenomenon in the history of *religion*, in the broader public debate it is the connection between the history of *science* and disenchantment that plays the greater role. This latter connection also crops up in Weber's work, where its relationship with the history of religion is quite unclear. The idea that it is the progress of science itself that robbed religion of its credibility cannot in fact be plausibly argued in light of our present-day state of knowledge. No one today, for instance, would seriously portray all the key figures in the early modern history of science as motivated by a desire for secularization; generally speaking, scholars have recognized that it was often religious motives that prompted the great natural scientists to study nature, for example, as the book of God.[20] For the same reason it cannot be satisfactory to put the emergence of a worldview of immanence down to the empirical advances of the sciences. To gain an appropriate view of such matters, we are faced with at least three key tasks, which I can mention only briefly here. First, in addition to the causal-mechanistic worldview, to which the sciences, supposedly, inevitably gave rise, we must take account of all those intellectual approaches that emerged in response to this worldview and that limit or overcome it without detaching themselves from the modern sciences. Kant's philosophy, with its focus on the conditions of possibility for human knowledge and moral freedom; the historicist and hermeneutic tradition of Herder, Humboldt and Schleiermacher, with its emphasis on human expression; and the complex attempts to synthesize these new philosophies in the work of Hegel do not tally with the notion of the triumphant march of the causal-mechanistic worldview. Second, we must ask how the ideas about transcendence found in religious traditions, such as Judaism or Christianity, change if the spatial metaphors for the localization of transcendence (in "heaven") are no longer available. The simplistic notion that the astronomy of the early modern era clearly did away with these ideas of transcendence because they were associated with these spatial metaphors is by no means an accurate summation of the history of religious discourse on cosmology. Third, when it comes to the newly emerging worldview of immanence, we have to distinguish between those versions that aim, in the spirit of the Enlightenment, to retain the moral universalism of the transcendence-focused religions, perhaps in a secularized form, and those for which science and the pathos of immanence are a means of eliminating this moral universalism, for example, through a supposedly scientific racial doctrine and a population policy based on it. The terms "disenchantment" and "enchantment" certainly do not equip us to perform these tasks. If one wishes to narrow the meaning of the term "disenchantment" so that it is limited to "demagification," then the empirical question must be how attempts to combat magic or superstition in the modern age actually played themselves out and what role religious or other motives played in this.[21] We might also examine the role played by references to science in the different processes of demagification, detranscendentalization, desacralization and secularization; in none of these cases should we work on the assumption of an automatic, one-sided effect. Articulations of religious faith are shaped in a range of ways by these debates within and with the sciences, but the outcome is always open rather than determined by the sciences. My brief survey of these issues here is chiefly intended to lend plausibility to the conceptual distinction I have proposed. The history of demagification since the Reformation is not the same as that of detranscendentalization, and neither can be equated with desacralization in the sense of the loss of a motivating relationship with the world. To uncover possible effects of one process on the others and to evaluate the role played by each of them in relation to secularization (in the sense of a weakening of all religion), we have to get past the concept of disenchantment.

Secularization as a Polemical Concept

So, while secularization theory and the narrative of disenchantment, however positive or melancholy they may be, present a specific view of the future as quite certain, if my thinking is correct, the future is in fact indeterminate and thus more open than many scholars are willing to countenance. That is, the future, including that of the churches and religion, depends in significant part on conscious human action. This does not mean that this future can be planned and molded at will. But just as Christians and their churches or communities are entangled in the past history of secularization and are to some extent responsible for it—secularization is not akin to a "tsunami" that descended upon Western cultures unpredictably and from "outside," destroying everything in its path, contrary to the views articulated in 2012 by one American cardinal (Donald Wuerl)—they are also enmeshed in its future history. But many commentators talk about the future in the idiom of false certainties and on the basis of problematic predictions. There are several reasons for this. For one thing, there is a general tendency to exaggerate the sciences' capacity for prediction. It is true that unexpected events have a sobering effect here. The prestige of economics, for example, suffered following the financial crisis of 2008 in much the same way as that of the social sciences after the unforeseen collapse of communism in Europe in 1989 and after. But the tendency to overestimate the ability of the sciences to make predictions often reappears before long. Secularization theory, which responded with surprise to the growth of Pentecostalism and the increased public presence of religion in many modern societies, and the narrative of disenchantment, with its implications for the future, are of course more than just failed or poor forecasts. In fact, they represent a concealed philosophy of history that fails to own up to its status as such. Many schools of thought of this kind exist. The implausibility of such a philosophy of history, though in this case an openly espoused one, suddenly became clear to me decades ago, when I was confronted in East Germany with the belief that socialism was unquestionably "a whole era ahead." Since its advocates thought they knew where history was headed, a socialist society simply had to be further ahead historically, even if its aged blocks of flats were crumbling, its urban infrastructure was in a state of decay and its industry could not compete within the global economy. But such seemingly secure knowledge about the future is taken for granted not only in Marxism. Statements presupposing a historical tendency toward political centralization or toward larger states can be found in contexts ranging from discussions of educational federalism in Germany to the debate on the prospects for an "ever-closer" European Union, with opponents of such developments being vilified as backward, nostalgic or dangerous.

No thinker has analyzed the militantly ideological character of such assertions of historical tendencies as astutely as the great German historian Reinhart Koselleck, who died in 2006. In his book *Critique and Crisis*,[22] he showed just how much the Enlightenment thinkers of the eighteenth century worked with assertions of historical inevitability. Far from value-free hypotheses about empirically observed tendencies, these were tools in the battle of ideas. Time and again, prominent thinkers, instead of openly fighting against the absolutist state on the political level, argued—within the frame of a particular philosophy of history—that it was outmoded. The assertion of its inevitable disappearance thus became a weapon, but one whose true nature those wielders did not acknowledge. Precisely the same may often be said of Enlightenment predictions—and later forecasts that built on them—of the disappearance of Christianity or of religion as a whole. Rather than reject religious faith, or as a means of supporting its rejection, many thinkers argued that it was outmoded or backward or no longer in keeping with the times. It is remarkable and almost odd that Koselleck's sensitivity to such rhetorical strategies seems to have let him down precisely in the case of the thesis of secularization, when he himself referred, for example, to a "post-Christian" or "post-theological age."[23] But this is irrelevant to our discussion. My only goal in this chapter has been to consider the facts of present-day secularization in this part of the world without illusion, while placing them within a historical and global framework and thus freeing us from the self-imposed browbeating inherent in prophecies of decline, whether openly stated or camouflaged.

4

Do We Need Religion?

On Experiences of Self-Transcendence

"Embarrassing Incident" is the title of a poem by Bertolt Brecht from the year 1943.[1] Written in his Californian exile, it gives an account of a major celebration among German émigrés on the occasion of the sixty-fifth birthday of Brecht's friend and admired colleague Alfred Döblin, whom he calls in this poem one of his "most revered gods." The birthday celebration took place in a small theater in Santa Monica close to Hollywood, and they had all come: Brecht and his wife, Helene Weigel; Heinrich and Thomas Mann; Lion Feuchtwanger; Hanns Eisler, who had composed a special piece for this occasion; and the great actors Fritz Kortner, Peter Lorre and Alexander Granach, all three of whom read from Döblin's books.[2] This tribute to the impoverished and isolated Döblin, who had been a leading novelist and leftist political writer in the Weimar Republic, was going just as well as its organizers had planned. But suddenly the unexpected happened. Döblin began his speech of thanks. He announced that he, the Jewish intellectual, had found his way to the Christian faith and been baptized as a Catholic. Brecht captured this occurrence as follows:

> Then the celebrated god himself stepped onto the platform reserved
>   for artists
> And declared in a loud voice
> Right in front of my sweat-drenched friends and students
> That he had just been afflicted with an illumination and now
> Had become religious and with unseemly haste

> He provocatively clapped a moth-eaten cleric's bonnet on his head
> Fell lewdly to his knees and shamelessly
> Struck up a saucy hymn, thus offending
> The irreligious sentiments of his listeners, some of them
> Mere youths.
> For the last three days
> I haven't dared show my face
> Among my friends and students
> I'm so
> Embarrassed.

This episode provides us with an initial answer to the question I am posing here. Religiosity—in one possible translation of Brecht's response—is a sign of weakness. Human beings are in need of religion only when they are too weak to live without it. Although the tone of the poem is more or less malicious, Brecht was certainly capable of treating his friend with greater empathy. In his journals, he articulated "the sympathetic horror felt when a fellow prisoner succumbs to torture and talks,"[3] and he adduced the many terrible blows of fate that had brought matters to such a pass and that must be considered extenuating circumstances: the loss of two sons, lack of success, illness and problems in his marriage. For Brecht, all this explains Döblin's conversion as a breakdown, but the basic idea clearly remains the same: to be religious means to be weak, and one should not yield to such weakness, at least not publicly. One's friends are embarrassed if one shows one's weakness in broad daylight.

Döblin is unlikely ever to have seen Brecht's poem, but the embarrassment and outrage felt by his friends, some of whom caused a stir by leaving the celebration early, and the cooling of his friendship with Brecht can surely not have escaped him. The views of Döblin's leftist kindred spirits were quite out of sync with his own self-esteem. In literary terms, Döblin was as prolific as ever; the power of his language and even the brash Berlin tone, which continued to feature in many of his commentaries, do not suggest a broken man. In a similar set of circumstances, he ironically fends off the insinuation that he became a believer because of illness, stating: "I am not sick, I was not sick, and I will never be sick."[4] And he wrote a powerful dialogue on religion because he wanted to translate Christianity "into his own language." Here, he distinguished between two types of weakness, as if to counter the interpretations of his friends: the first entails "declining strength," the second "waning resistance."⁵ Thus for him, it was the other way around: those who flee from their relationship with God and indulge in false certainties are the weak ones.

What do we feel when we look back on this "embarrassing incident" today, several decades later? Is it not Brecht's response itself that we find embarrassing, because it reveals the embarrassing certainty of Brecht's own beliefs? His faith was not, of course, a faith in God, but there is no doubt that Brecht felt he knew the answer to questions about the meaning of life, and this answer was political. He assumed that the laws of history had been discovered by the science of Marxism and that human history would progress until communism itself had been achieved. But does this "faith in history" not seem very aged today? Was not the term "scientific communism," used in communist countries to refer to an academic discipline and academic posts at universities and colleges, the butt of jokes long before the collapse of the regimes in Eastern Europe? One could not go on forever blaming the failure to realize utopian dreams on unfavorable conditions. When the colossus that was the Soviet Union collapsed, it had definitely become impossible to deny that the focus of contemporary problems had shifted. Few, however, grasped just how profound these historical upheavals were.

Not only Marxists but almost all influential social scientists and historical thinkers had for long assumed that secularization, in the sense of the decline of religion, is a necessary corollary of modernization. We need only glance at the world around us to find this assumption seemingly confirmed at every turn. There have always been exceptions, such as Poland and Ireland, but these were quickly explained away with handy theories. The most difficult case has always been the United States. Nobody could deny that it is a modern society, yet religion has remained a vigorous force, not only in the shape of Protestant fundamentalism but in a rich plurality of forms. For this reason the United States has been treated as a very special case, as a modern society in a religious third world, as some commentators have put it. But the perspective of sociologists of religion has changed dramatically even in this respect. As large parts of the world outside those areas molded by Christianity modernize rapidly, a huge experiment is taking place before our eyes. This allows us to investigate empirically the relationship between secularization and modernization. The provisional findings make it more plausible to classify Europe—rather than the United States—as the exceptional case. Secularization as Europe has experienced it is not simply being repeated today on a global scale. Some authors therefore even speak of desecularization. Whatever the precise outcome of this research, there are good reasons to question the assumption that religion in all its diversity is set to disappear—without, however, simply presenting this as evidence that religion is a universal, an anthropological given that can be suppressed only by force.

I think this is a fair characterization of the present historical period, in which we ask: Do we need religion? If those who see religion as superfluous and dangerous, as well as believers who assume that without faith there is only decline and decadence, have both lost their certainty, this could be a favorable moment for a new way of thinking.

I certainly do not believe we can answer our question by pointing to advantages of one kind or another that an individual, society or humankind might glean from religion. Some claim that only believers can be truly happy or consistently moral or psychologically healthy; only if people believe can societies be peacefully integrated and considerate toward minority groups. All this may be true; I personally tend to assume that some of these claims are plausible. But in every individual case, our reason compels us to investigate the alleged causal connections in an objective manner. We must never simply take a causal connection for granted because it chimes with the enthusiastic certainties of belief. Reflecting on the functional advantages and beneficial effects of religion in this way can lead to interesting research. Yet it brings us no closer to the point that those who ask "Do we need religion?" want to reach. For one thing seems to me indubitable. Whatever the results of such research, even the most convincing proof of the utility of religious belief cannot cause anybody to hold such a belief. Nobody can believe because he has been convinced by rational means that believing is useful, that it serves a purpose. If we apply notions of religious utility to ourselves, we end up with Pascal's famous wager. But we all know that the result of such cold, rational calculation would inspire little emotional intensity. What is more, as William James once wrote, God would not be taken in by such rational calculations. "And if we were ourselves in the place of the Deity, we should probably take particular pleasure in cutting off believers of this pattern from this infinite reward."[6] If notions of utility with regard to religion are applied to societies as a whole, this inevitably gives rise to a division between an elite that knows better and the masses who supposedly need belief to pacify them. The famous quip "I am an atheist, but Catholic of course" comes from the radical Right in France more than a century ago (Maurice Barrès) and articulates this thinking in a particularly cynical way.

This means that we have to conceive of the "need" in our question in a different way. "Need" relates not to the external purpose of a belief, its usefulness. It must refer to something inherent in belief. It must be bound up with the experience we call belief. The question is not "Is religion useful?" but "Can we live without the experience articulated in faith, in religion?" If this is the right question, then we have to look more closely at what kind of experience this is and in which forms we might encounter it.

I therefore propose that we reflect on those kinds of experiences that are not yet experiences of the divine, but without which we cannot understand what faith, what religion, is. I call them experiences of self-transcendence. This means experiences in which a person transcends herself, but not, at least not immediately, in the sense of moral achievements but rather of being pulled beyond the boundaries of one's self, being captivated by something outside one's self, a relaxation of or liberation from one's fixation on oneself. We thus initially define this self-transcendence only as a movement away from oneself, as the somewhat antiquated German word *Ergriffensein* expresses quite beautifully.

There is no doubt that we do have such experiences. My book *The Genesis of Values* was an attempt to offer, together with philosophical and social psychological reflections on the precise character of this self-transcendence, a rich phenomenology of such experiences.[7] All human beings are familiar with them. Let us take an exemplary description of such an experience without succumbing to the suspicion that I am merely identifying religious faith with such experiences. Yet we can assuredly *approach* belief through such experiences.

In Knut Hamsun's novel *Mysteries*, a man named Nagel walks into a forest. Here is what he experiences:

> A tremor of ecstasy ran through him. He felt himself carried away and engulfed by the magic rays of the sun. The stillness filled him with an intoxicating sense of well-being; he was free from worry; the only sound

was a soft murmur from above, the hum of the universal machinery—God turning his treadmill.

Not a leaf stirred in the trees—not a pine needle dropped. Nagel hugged his knees in sheer delight; he felt exhilarated because life was good. It beckoned to him and he responded. He raised himself on his elbow and looked around him. There wasn't a soul in sight. He said yes to life once more and listened, but no one came. Again he said yes, but there was no answer.

Strange; he had distinctly heard someone calling him. But he dismissed the thought; perhaps he had imagined the whole thing. But nothing was going to shatter his joyful mood. He was in a strange, euphoric state of mind; his every nerve vibrated; music surged through his blood; he was part of nature, of the sun, the mountains; he was omniscient; the trees, the earth, the moss, spoke to him alone. His soul went into a crescendo, like an organ with all the stops pulled out. Never would he forget how this heavenly music would pulsate through his blood.[8]

Here we have all the attributes of an experience of self-transcendence in an experience of ecstatic fusion with nature. Our interaction with other human beings might involve similar experiences. Think of a conversation that goes beyond the exchange of trivialities, information or argument, during which you suddenly have the feeling that your interlocutor has intuitively understood deep layers of your personality, giving you the courage to talk about the formative events in your life and, perhaps, about stirrings you yourself have as yet scarcely acknowledged. Such a conversation also represents the experience of transcending the boundaries of one's self, an experience you will remember and that leaves behind some affective attachment to one's interlocutor, making it easier to interact next time around. We have the same experience, felt with far greater intensity, when we fall in love or are in love with another person. This strong feeling of closeness has for long and in many cultures been interpreted as a *renewal* of a relationship, as if one had known the other before, or forever, or as if one's ancestors or God had meant it to be thus. This expresses the force—for which no other explanation seems to be available—with which two human beings, often after just a few moments, are drawn to each other, recognize themselves in the other and find themselves accepted by the other. We experience third parties' inquiries about what we find so attractive about the loved partner as inappropriate, because we are not falling in love with specific properties or attributes but with a whole person for whom there is no rational denominator. Sexual experiences, one might say, combine the experience of fusion with another person with fusion with nature: we can experience mutual understanding but also the enjoyment of the beauty of another's body, the joy of knowing that one's own body is experienced as beautiful and loved, and a sensual pleasure that goes beyond the quotidian and is one of the strongest foundations of deeply felt human relationships.

No impenetrable wall separates experiences of selflessness and overcoming of the self, in the context of love for one's fellows and charity, from eros. Here, too, a phenomenology can begin with rather trivial experiences, such as the pleasure of giving and the fact that there is probably nobody who always thinks only of himself and his own advantage, although self-love is frequently extended only to a narrow circle, such as one's family, and the fixation on one's self remains intact. But the experiences of helping and receiving help can be experiences of self-transcendence. This is true of the experience of being shocked by others' neediness, be they our loved ones or even anonymous others. The beggar we ignore on ninety-nine out of a hundred days or to whom we make a small donation to quiet our vaguely bad conscience might suddenly be experienced as our "brother"—although this term is too well-worn to really get across the shattering character of an experience that brings home to you the fact that the other truly is an ego like you and that you could be in his shoes, leading his life in his body.

Here, we encounter the voice of morality in the experience of being deeply moved, although erotic love, which demands a certain permanence, also produces obligations, and even the intense experience of nature has repercussions for how we deal with nature and for our moral conceptions of what constitutes an appropriate relationship with nature. In the shattering of one's self by the other, some thinkers have seen the root of all morality, and there is no doubt that many moral emotions like shame and outrage feature an intense experience of self-transcendence. Finally, we must turn our attention to the experiences of collective ecstasy that arise when groups of people begin to feel fired up, as we say metaphorically: when the individuals' self-control diminishes to such an extent that they become overconfident and engage in activities they would otherwise consider beyond their capabilities. Speakers become funnier when they sense that their words are being well received, or grandiloquent when they sense agreement and support. We feel stronger, smarter or more beautiful, or perhaps, when masked or dressed up, like completely different beings, just as others seem transformed by a mysterious, anonymous force. This transformation might make us generous. We might give away our money, as many did spontaneously in Berlin in November 1989. Or it might make us aggressive and violent, prone to pogroms and massacres, united against those we experience as a threat to our ecstatic union. Clearly, not all experiences of self-transcendence are morally good. But we have to be willing, at least initially, to look in a "value-free" way at all experiences that tie human beings to values, whatever these values are, even if we despise them or find them worthless, dangerous or evil.

However, it is not only disturbing social phenomena of this kind, in which the experience of self-transcendence might occur or to which it might lead, that make problematic what might have seemed for a moment a kitsch and overly harmonious panegyric on the miracles of nature, eros and charity. Not all experiences of self-transcendence are rousing. We can also be shaken by suffering, including our own suffering. For rousing experiences of every type, there exists a "terrible equivalent": we might experience not only enthusiasm about nature but also horror at nature, *Naturgrauen* (Arthur Schnitzler), not only the building of trust and commitment but also the loss of trust and betrayal, not only falling in love but the loss of a loved one through separation or death, not only ecstatic sexual union but also rape. Just as we can feel pulled beyond ourselves into unprecedented joy, we can also be shocked to discover how vulnerable we always are, how finite everything to which we are attached in fact is and how incurably precarious our existence is. Asking whether we need such experiences is as pointless as it is in the case of rousing experiences. We simply have them. Life without them is unimaginable, even were we to rid ourselves of all the havoc wrought by human beings.

Paul Tillich wrote in a particularly sensitive manner of the experience of anxiety as an experience of self-transcendence. Anxiety, says Tillich, is "finitude, experienced as one's own finitude." Note the word "experienced" here. Tillich is explicitly not referring to an abstract knowledge that we have always possessed. What he means here "is not the realization of universal transitoriness, not even the experience of the death of others, but the impression of these events on the always latent awareness of our own having to die."[9] This produces anxiety, naked anxiety, which we can bear only for short moments; rational discourse can gain as little purchase on this as it can on the experience of love. A phenomenology of anxiety is thus a necessary component of any phenomenology of self-transcendence. Following Tillich, we would distinguish between three types of anxiety that haunt us as relative or absolute threats to our feeling of existence. We can be relatively threatened by the blows of fate and absolutely threatened in the face of death. We can experience a relative emptiness intellectually and spiritually, and we can also experience the world as completely meaningless: every aspect of the world that might appeal to us and motivate us to act is lost to us in our depressive state. We might feel relatively threatened in terms of our self-understanding as moral beings because of a feeling of guilt caused by our actions or failure to act. But we can also fall apart entirely because of our tremendous guilt, for which we can never make amends, and because of the prospect of eternal condemnation.

Tillich did not doubt that these experiences of anxiety can lead to faith. "Only those who have experienced the shock of transitoriness, the anxiety in which they are aware of their finitude, the threat of nonbeing, can understand what the notion of God means. Only those who have experienced the tragic ambiguities of our historical existence and have totally questioned the meaning of existence can understand what the symbol of the Kingdom of God means."[10]

Those for whom faith is the result of weakness—like Döblin's alienated political friends mentioned at the beginning of this chapter—might see this as confirming their view. But things are not so simple: apart from anything else, we must bear in mind the rousing experiences that inspire adherence to certain values. These are as capable of forming a bridge to faith as are experiences of anxiety. What these experiences have in common is self-transcendence. We encounter in them a power that wrenches us beyond ourselves, even if this means, as in the case of anxiety, that we become aware of our limits. But this awareness of limits entails the feeling of "absolute dependence" (Schleiermacher's *schlechthinnige Abhängigkeit*): as we undergo rousing experiences, we become the grateful recipients of undeserved gifts.

The matter at hand is less simple than it might seem for another particularly important reason. Faith does not simply *emanate* from either rousing or anxious experiences. Religion articulates such experiences of self-transcendence, but it does so in a specific manner. For the believer, the experience of being deeply moved is the experience of an unconditional and unavailable other. But this does not apply to the nonbeliever. Neither does it apply to all believers in the same way. Therefore, having talked so much about experience, we must now turn to its interpretation. If there is no question that we undergo such experiences, what of their interpretation? Do we need to interpret them religiously?

Nonreligious people will tend to consider all the experiences I have mentioned to be purely psychological phenomena. Whereas the believer will feel grateful for creation as she experiences nature and will see love among humans as reflecting the splendor of divine love and the blows of fate perhaps as punishment or at least God's unfathomable providence, the nonbeliever will classify such experiences as the psychological processing of mere accidents, whether happy or unhappy, or of the inevitable fate of all living beings. There is, at first sight, not much to criticize here because these phenomena certainly are psychological in nature. But the question is whether we are justified in stating that they are *nothing but* psychological phenomena, as if classifying these experiences resolves the question of their origin. But just as the believer cannot compel the nonbeliever to accept her religious interpretation on the basis of logic, the nonbeliever cannot advocate his nonreligious interpretation as the only rationally defensible one. Here, a gap opens up between experience and interpretation, which we must look at more closely.

Three observations might be helpful. First, subjectively, specific interpretations of our experience frequently appear to be the only possible or plausible ones. Although the observer might perceive a difference between experience and interpretation, this is not always so for the experiencing subjects themselves. We might have the experience of a (subjective) "revelation" when, for example, we suddenly find the right word that turns the sense of a gap in what had been said before into a specific experience. With regard to all the other interpretations of our experience, even our own descriptions, we might have had a nagging sense of inadequacy. But now, suddenly, everything has become clear to us; experience is completely transformed into expression. When we have this experience, interpretation and experience are indissolubly fused for us. We are then very hesitant even to discuss our interpretations.

Second, the process of articulating experiences can start at both ends. Sometimes we encounter the right word that allows us to admit for the first time that this is the experience we once had. In this sense, languages, cultures and religions are rich repertoires for the articulation of experiences. The existing interpretive models are permeated with experience, just as our experiences are dependent on interpretations and expectations.

Third, and most important, specific interpretations might be the precondition for certain experiences. In the realm of religious experience, this is absolutely crucial. We might cut ourselves off from certain experiences if we give precedence to skepticism. The classical elaboration of this notion is found in William James's essay "The Will to Believe." Here, too, we should think first of all of such things as falling in love and mutual confidence building. He who waits, cold and aloof, to obtain from the other a sure sign of love usually waits in vain. I have to meet the other halfway and be willing to trust her and at the same time be convinced that I am, in principle, worthy of the other's love. For love to arise, I must consider myself worthy of love and the other capable of love. Love demands a leap in the dark. The same goes for religious faith. The injunction to believe only what we encounter in ordinary experience would cut us off from extraordinary experiences—but why should we cut ourselves off in this way, giving precedence to fear over hope? If our attitude to the world alters how the world is expressed, there is no compelling reason to confront the world without faith. To have certain experiences, we must be willing to believe.

This is immediately evident in the case of prayer. Prayers turn the opening up of oneself toward something higher—the experience of self-transcendence—into an activity. Although we must be able to listen if we want to pray, we are also allowed to speak and to turn toward an Other that transcends every concretely human other. William James thought that nobody abstains entirely from praying, that every human being prays whether or not he admits this in terms of his particular worldview. He came to this conclusion because he thought that every self demands an ideal Other that cannot be found among human beings. I do not know whether this is true. I am not even sure how we would investigate it. But James's statement is certainly true if it means that prayer is that type of religious activity that requires almost no theological foundation. Praying, at least in its elementary forms, is a continuation of an activity of which all human beings are capable.

This does not apply to another type of experience, which I would like to call "sacramental." The Eucharist, or the Lord's Supper, is for many

Christian believers a very intense religious experience, but self-evidently the consumption of bread and wine becomes an extraordinary experience only if the participant has a basic knowledge of the faith and the meaning of this ritual. This ritual clearly picks up on elements of everyday life that point somewhat beyond the ordinary, such as a shared meal and a celebration. But it goes radically beyond the ordinary if we grasp its religious meaning. It would be misleading to treat sacramental experiences as if they were nothing but religious interpretations of universally accessible experiences. Here, interpretations are the preconditions for the experience. If we try to convey these experiences to nonbelievers, we will, of course, compare them with experiences accessible to them; some have, for example, boldly attempted to relate the experience of the Eucharist to ecstatic sexual experiences (André Dubus).[11] Some might view this as scandalous, whereas others will see here the mutual reflection of different kinds of love. But everyone is aware that such attempts at description are never more than approximations of the qualities experienced and that the experience itself depends on having been trained to have it.

If this is so, religious traditions and institutions are not only rich repertoires of interpretations vis-à-vis our experiences of self-transcendence, but they enable us to have such experiences in the first place. They contain knowledge of a physical character relating to how we can prepare ourselves for such experiences—through ascetic practices, through certain bodily postures, such as kneeling, by singing and making music together. More important, knowledge of faith can in fact help us overcome the centering of our experience on ourselves. Experiences of self-transcendence really have to be experiences of decentering rather than attempts made by a self that fully intends to remain itself but would also like to enjoy the titillation of extraordinary experiences.

Some will harbor this suspicion anyway if, as is the case here, we place so much emphasis on religious experience. They might think that faith loses its seriousness, as well as its beauty, when interpreted through the subjective experiences of the believers. This danger of tailoring faith to the logic of an "experiential society" (Gerhard Schulze) certainly exists. The sociology of religion features discussions of increasing religious "bricolage" and "patchwork identities," that is, highly subjective combinations of elements from different religious traditions: a little bit of Christianity, for example, with a pinch of Buddhism and a dash of esotericism. Everybody then has his own belief; all binding force is gone, even in regard to the individual; belief and belonging are decoupled; and there are as many religious persuasions as there are individuals. All the theological objections raised against this complete subjectivism are justified. Faith of this kind fails to cast off the shackles of narcissist self-centeredness and is deployed only in specific situations, like a hobby for which there is never enough time because of the constraints of everyday life. A private language merely allows dialogue with oneself;[12] intensification of belief is a more earnest undertaking than its extensification. But we should not overdo this criticism. Such combining can entail creative and productive potential. We should bear in mind that the history of Christianity is far from a linear and homogeneous tradition. Religious virtuosi have always enriched the spiritual heritage of Christianity. Meister Eckhart was inspired by elements of Judaism; Saint Francis probably drew on elements of Islam. Both integrated these into Christianity. Neither should we forget that religious patchworks are not as new in religious history as they might seem. Denominational boundaries have frequently been rather blurred in the minds of believers, and one can often identify the traces of pre-Christian and non-Christian religiosity in the regional variants of this faith. We should therefore exercise caution before rushing to condemn, remaining open to the potential of individualism to help vitalize religious life.

How do these reflections on the relationship between interpretation and experience in the sphere of religion help us answer our original question? We have discovered that all human beings are in principle capable of having experiences of self-transcendence. Believers interpret these experiences in light of their beliefs. For them, this must mean that God can be experienced even by those who do not attribute their experiences to God—those who hear something different than believers do when they hear the word "God." Moreover, we have seen that faith makes certain experiences possible, experiences from which nonbelievers cut themselves off. But all of us have to cut ourselves off from some interpretations and experiences; criticism is a part of interpretation, not external to it. It therefore behooves us to be modest in our relationship to other religions. At least to some extent, we have to consider them attempts, often very impressive ones, to interpret human experiences of the divine. The belief in Jesus Christ is thus grounded in a relationship to God accessible to all humans. "If we were Atheists without Jesus, Jesus himself could not liberate us from our atheism, because we would not have an organ to receive him."[13] But this modesty must also extend to those who are not followers of another religious belief but who profess no faith at all. There certainly exists a profound kind of atheism, an attitude of unbelief that develops into a fervor for the love of others and the world as a whole. Our reflections lead us to conclude merely that those ways of thinking are harmful that allow no interpretation of experiences of self-transcendence, forcing us to remain silent about them and preventing us from entering into communication with the divine. These are harmful because they hinder human profundity and keep us fixated on ourselves. Religious faith thus increases the probability that an individual will have experiences of the kind here described and, if she has them, does not repress them. It increases the probability that one will grow beyond a mere morality of prudence, respect that which is unavailable and find the strength and stamina to change the world. But this is a falsifiable empirical statement, not triumphalist self-adulation. Religion in general and the Christian faith in particular cannot be made logically compelling. Christians can only offer their faith and invite others to follow Christ. We are more likely to succeed in converting others if we convert ourselves, if we live the faith that we are proclaiming, and that we need—rather than explaining to others why they *ought* to need it.

Thus, although there is such a thing as profound atheism, there is also superficial faith or, worse, faith as a false comfort. Some people have difficulties with faith because they assume that being a believer obliges them to see a beneficial act in every blow of fate. They protest against pseudo-rational consolation precisely because they wish to protect the authenticity of their feelings. Even some believers praise their faith and our dependence on religion by arguing that this is the only way to resolve questions for which science and philosophy have no answers. Even great thinkers like Max Weber thought that religions must be understood mainly as attempts to solve the problem of theodicy, that is, the question of why God allows evil and suffering.

But is such an understanding of religion appropriate, particularly with regard to Christianity? Everyone, in Germany at least, knows Paul Gerhardt's wonderful hymn "O Sacred Head Sore Wounded." Consider the following verse:

My Savior, be Thou near me when death is at my door;
Then let Thy presence cheer me, forsake me nevermore!

> When soul and body languish, oh, leave me not alone,
> But take away mine anguish by virtue of Thine own!

The sensational thing about this, if this colloquialism is allowed, is the last line. When push comes to shove, the Christian believer does not expect consolation and help from a great hero who was himself persecuted but who easily triumphed over his enemies by dint of his superior powers. Rather, the Christian turns to one who has been through the whole ordeal himself and thus finds consolation in this very fact. Why though, fearing death, should we find consolation in remembering another's fear of death? Why does this lessen our own fear? It does not simply disappear and make way for a feeling of foolhardy invincibility. Yet my belief that God himself suffered my fear when he took human form enables me to integrate my fear or anxiety into my courage to live. Faith enables me to articulate my experiences of fear and anxiety and to experience afresh salvation through divine love again and again. The emphasis in this sentence is on this "freshness." If we see faith as a fixed source of rational consolation, as the definitive answer to our questions, we deprive it of the dynamism bound up with this freshness.

What has been said here with regard to the experience of fear and anxiety and all experiences of self-transcendence is also true of morality and history. Moral dilemmas do not disappear by virtue of faith, as if God had decided that there can be no conflicts between values or between moral obligations among believers. Neither do the tragic aspects of history vanish, as if there were only one grandiose history of salvation in which all the horrors and failures make perfect sense.

Biblically, this is expressed in the Psalms, among other things. Jesus's cry, "My God, my God, why have you forsaken me?" clearly underlies Paul Gerhardt's hymn. But this cry itself refers back to Psalm 22, which begins with these words. This lamentation of godforsakenness is directed at God, a God, in fact, addressed as "my God" through a specifically personal grammatical form. Is it a contradiction in itself to lament through prayer that one has been forsaken by God? Can such lamentation take the form of prayer in the first place?

At the present time, when people tend to doubt that God exists rather than question his love and affection for us, lamentation as prayer might seem paradoxical. But for the believer, the psalm offers the opportunity to communicate with God about one's very doubts and to implore him to help us reconstruct our shattered confidence in him. For the believer, this means that God does not expect blind obedience from us and constant tacit consent. In fact, the tone of Psalm 22 changes dramatically after the lengthy verses of lamentation:

> But be not thou far from me, O Lord;
> O my strength, haste thee to help me,
> Deliver my soul from the sword,
> My darling from the power of the dog.
> Save me from the lion's mouth;
> For thou hast heard me from the horns of the unicorns.
> I will declare thy name unto my brethren;
> In the midst of the congregation will I praise thee.

After this change of tone, the psalm goes on to praise God and features a declaration of intent to make sacrifices and to tell everyone about God.

Paul Ricœur, the great French Christian philosopher, interprets this passage—in the book *Penser la Bible*[14]—as a means of balancing things out subsequent to the narrative of salvation and the prophets' moralization of our actions. This idea seems to me an exact parallel to my own thesis that morality and history look different if we eschew thinking about them holistically and make room for value pluralism and historical tragedy. We will certainly always have to work to achieve moral consistency and to narrate a comprehensive story. But the vantage point from which we do so will always be a new and unique situation of action and suffering. To deal with this situation, without false certainties, believers trust in God. They cannot live without the experience of being able to offer to God all their rejoicing, all sorrows and even all their doubts, receiving help that might not always come in the form they originally expected. In this sense, believers need their belief. And they offer nonbelievers the opportunity to discover the same thing for themselves.

5

Faith or Self-Optimization?

On the Cultural Role of the Church

The name Jürgen Klinsmann is familiar to many people in Germany and far beyond it, who know him as one of the best German football players of the last few decades. One of his finest moments was his presence on the German national team when it won the World Cup in 1990. After his active time as a player, he became coach of the German team (from 2004 to 2006) and then its American counterpart (from 2011 to 2016). For a short time, during the 2007–8 season, he coached FC Bayern Munich. It was shortly after he had taken up this post that he took a particularly striking step. In collaboration with the club's architect, he had four Buddha statues erected in its training ground, two in gold and two in white. Buddha statues in a symbolically charged site in the middle of traditionally Catholic Bavaria? If I try to imagine this happening there during my childhood and adolescence in the 1950s and early 1960s, I can only conclude that the reaction would have been one of outrage. Klinsmann's action would have been perceived as an attack on the national identity of the Bavarian people, and since, as the saying goes, the residents of Bavaria, at least of the Bavarian heartland, think of themselves as having been Catholic before the birth of Jesus Christ, it would have been seen as an attack on Catholicism itself. In the new millennium, however, this is no longer the case. The spokesman for the archbishop of Munich merely commented very diplomatically that every coach has his own personal style and that football clubs are not the centers of a country's intellectual life. The Protestant Church, which traditionally represents a minority in Bavaria, extolled the ideal of religious freedom and warned against forcing a specific religious faith on football players. Reactions from the ruling Christian-conservative CSU (Christlich-Soziale Union or Christian Social Union) were mixed: some of its representatives expressed skepticism, but none were strident or polemical. The strongest opposition, remarkably, came from some of the players, most clearly from the deeply Christian Brazilian Zé Roberto, who commented: "This won't help me; I already have a faith." He received backing from Frenchman Franck Ribéry, who had converted to Islam.

In the face of this resistance from some of the players and ironic remarks from journalists and others, Klinsmann sought to defend his initiative by explaining that for him the Buddha statues really had nothing to do with religion: he had merely been trying to improve the flow of energy and help the players relax. When he left the club a year later, the statues were soon removed. In November 2014, Klinsmann went so far as to deny that he had ever vigorously supported the idea, which had supposedly been the architect's brainchild.

In my opinion, this anecdote—the details of which I am not in a position to authenticate—vividly highlights some of the most important religious trends of our time: the advancing process of secularization in Europe, which is increasingly calling the equation of European and Christian culture into question; the globalization of Christianity and the impact on Europe of the intense religious life of Christians in the so-called Third World, as well as that of Muslims; the eclectic combining of elements from different religious traditions and the reduction of religion to a technique of relaxation and self-optimization. If we wish to adequately grasp the cultural situation of the present, we need to look at all three tendencies simultaneously.

I think the key concept that allows us to attempt this is "option." It is one of the core terms in my account of the present-day religious situation.[1] In using it, I draw on two great thinkers on religion, one contemporary and one whose oeuvre was written more than a hundred years ago: Canadian Catholic philosopher Charles Taylor and American psychologist and classical pragmatist William James. For me, Charles Taylor's most important achievement in his monumental work *A Secular Age* is his investigation and portrayal of the rise of the so-called secular option.[2] He focuses on the eighteenth century but also discusses the prehistory of its rise, its further entrenchment and long-term influence. Taylor shows vividly that this emergence of the secular option has fundamentally changed the conditions of faith as well. Following this epoch-making shift, believers no longer have to justify their specific faith, such as Christianity, primarily vis-à-vis other confessions or religions, but as such. They are asked why they are believers in the first place and do not embrace the "secular option," which first appeared merely as one legitimate possibility and then, I argue, increasingly became the rule, in other words, was "normalized" in certain countries and milieus.[3] Of course, the rise of the secular option as such must not be understood as the cause of later secularization processes. It merely made them possible but does not itself explain why people take up this option. In the first instance, then, the optionality of faith consists in the fact that it has in principle become possible—in a conscious and publicly visible way—not to believe.

Under conditions of growing religious and ideological pluralism, this optionality is becoming even more pronounced. I believe this calls for the use of conceptual distinctions originally put forward by William James in his influential 1896 essay "The Will to Believe." Options, James states, can be of very different kinds: living or dead, forced or avoidable and momentous or trivial. For James, only those options that are forced, living and momentous are *genuine* options. I limit myself here to the "living" aspect. "A living option is one in which both hypotheses are live ones. If I say to you, 'Be a theosophist or be a Mohammedan,' it is probably a dead option, because for you neither hypothesis is likely to be alive. But if I say, 'Be an agnostic or be a Christian,' it is otherwise: trained as you are, each hypothesis makes some appeal, however small, to your belief."[4]

I think this distinction is of crucial import if we wish to understand what I call "genuine pluralism." By this I mean that it is not *genuine* religious pluralism if, for example, as is the case today in many European societies, a Muslim minority lives side by side with a Christian or agnostic majority, but the majority is no more attracted to Islam than the minority is to the religious or secular views of the majority. In the past, too, there were many cases of the mere coexistence of different faiths. I would like to distinguish these from cases in which a fair number of people can at least imagine converting to the faith of others. The precise extent to which we can refer to genuine pluralism and optionality in different countries or milieus today can, of course, only be determined empirically. But given our current state of knowledge, I consider it certain that in today's Europe most

Christians are constantly confronted with the option of secular worldviews. In this respect, we are experiencing *genuine* pluralism. In the traditionally bi-confessional societies of Central Europe, it should be added, not only have firmly established confessional milieus dwindled in recent decades, but we can make out signs of an emerging interconfessional Christian milieu. In any case, the institutional differences and processes of delimitation between the Christian churches are no longer reflected in matching differentiation and demarcation of families, friendship networks or sociocultural milieus. Far more than in the past, then, people experience their own confession in light of another confession that no longer has the air of the alien; in other words, they see their own faith as an option. Similar developments have occurred in the United States, where many believers are ever less interested in the theological differences between the various branches of Protestantism. Instead, it is individuals' political and moral affinities with certain religious communities that are proving decisive to their affiliation. In the United States, too, religiously defined milieus have long since ceased to be hermetically sealed:[5] more than half of new marriages are "interfaith."[6] The religious map of the United States is also subject to perpetual change because new Christian churches are constantly emerging that cannot be assigned to any of the historical denominations.

The meaning of "optionality" is not limited to the field of religion.[7] Many sociological analyses show that people today often feel the same way about their most important social relationships centered on love, family but also career and political affiliation. This may, of course, cause some to feel overwhelmed by the growth in options, triggering orientational crises and the aggressive destruction of options. Yet orientations may also be adapted to increased contingency. For example, when fixed gender and age roles break down, the need for coordination and discussion increases. Individuals must then become more sensitive to the character of given situations and to others' needs. From the institution to "companionship" is how Ernest Burgess, a Chicago family sociologist, expressed this as early as 1945.[8] The loss of "static" stability may be offset by a higher form of "dynamic" stability.

But today's world is also one of options in another sense. I am thinking here of the consequences of what is generally called globalization. Perhaps the most important sociological trend with respect to Christianity in our time is its tremendous globalization. Serious observers such as British

American historian Philip Jenkins refer to our present age not as characterized chiefly by secularization but by one of the greatest periods of Christian expansion in history.[9] The increase in the number of Christians worldwide is in part a matter of demographics; in other words, it is due to strong population growth in certain Christian countries. But this is not the whole story. There are also impressive trends toward mass conversion to Christianity in Africa, but also in South Korea and parts of China. Through migration and a fundamental geographical power shift both outside and within the churches, this will, sooner rather than later, affect Christians in Europe and North America in a wide range of ways.

All these processes also have profound intellectual, and that includes theological, implications. One of the first theologians to understand this was Karl Rahner. In a 1979 look back at the Second Vatican Council,[10] the great theologian, who had been heavily involved in drafting many of its documents, recognized that this event represented a "qualitative leap" on the Catholic Church's path toward becoming a true world church. What it had always been *in potentia*, Rahner concluded, it was now becoming *in actu*. One of the reasons why the Council became an experience of collective "effervescence" (Durkheim), that is, a source of shared euphoria that engendered unprecedented deeds, seems to have been the intensity of the encounter between bishops and theologians from all over the world. Rahner saw this as the beginning—and only the beginning—of a completely new era in church history, comparable for him only to "the radical new creation" of Saint Paul when he transcended the boundaries of a Jewish sect and turned the Christian community into a magnet for all the peoples of the Mediterranean world of his time.[11] More perhaps even than Rahner had anticipated, this development is leading to a new constellation of "genuine pluralism" across much of the world today. Christianity is becoming a living option for people for whom it was previously either entirely unavailable or tainted by the abuses often entailed in the colonial powers' missionary activities. Yet, at least for Christians in Asia, the ancient intellectual and religious traditions of their own cultures also remain a living option. In the words of David Thompson, a Cambridge-based church historian and Asia expert,[12] "Asian Christians have therefore sought to understand all world faiths as being in some way vehicles of God's self-revelation; in this respect they asked questions similar to those asked by western missionaries. Almost inevitably this has raised questions about Christology. . . . Comparisons between Jesus and Krishna or Buddha seem to require abandonment of any Christian claim that God is uniquely revealed in Jesus Christ. This in turn raises the question of whether Christianity was distorted as it was expressed in Hellenic culture." These are not new questions, but they are now being asked in non-European contexts and in novel and challenging ways.

The two main new scenarios of optionality I have outlined here—the confrontation of Christian faith with, on the one hand, widespread irreligiousness in Europe and a few non-European countries and, on the other, with Asian and African cultural and religious traditions on other continents—bear a striking similarity. Both pull the rug from under the fusion of the Christian faith with particular European cultural traditions. The crucial question is what this means for the contemporary rearticulation of the Christian faith. Any theology that fails to take these challenges seriously seems to me obsolete. We need a new language for Christianity in the sense that this language must be permeated by an understanding of the achievements of secular worldviews and a deep understanding of non-European cultures. In the words of long-standing Catholic Bishop of Erfurt Joachim Wanke, we find ourselves called upon to "elementarize" the imparting of faith, that is, to take the idea of a hierarchy of truths in the Christian faith very seriously.

The main question at this point is how we should envisage the Christian faith in a culture in which self-optimization has become a dominant value. In such a culture, faith is often touted, even by believers and churches, as representing some kind of superior technique of self-optimization. When prominent individuals are interviewed in the media about their faith, they often talk about the strength and comfort they derive from it and recommend it to others as a source of psychological support. Of course, there is nothing wrong with strengthening one's personal efficacy, increasing one's satisfaction with life or fulfilling one's need for solace. Nevertheless, I feel that something is missing when the truth claims of the Christian faith are entirely absent from such statements, which foreground its psychological effects alone. There is a concealed trap here, or perhaps several traps. If the psychological effects of, say, Buddhism happen to be greater in a given desirable sense than those of Christianity—who would expect an improved "flow of energy" at the training ground after the installation of a crucifix?—then why not simply replace the traditional faith with the more effective one? I would even hesitate to call such a change of religious identity "conversion" because this term has always referred to the sudden or gradual experience of a subjective "revelation," that is, to seeing or recognizing a truth. When such experiences occur, it becomes clear to the persons involved that they have been living in the wrong way, that they have to change their ways, and not because it helps them more successfully pursue goals that were already valid beforehand. Instead, they have become convinced that they now know how to live in the right way or regard this as self-evident and believe they must change their habits and life goals. This is in no way a matter of improving strategies: it requires a change of fundamental objectives.[13]

Still, the line between conversion in the strong sense and a change of religious identity centered on self-optimization may not always be easy to draw. Fasting during Lent may be a good example. If the religious framing of fasting falls away, can even renunciation and sacrifice become means of self-optimization? Purification and cleansing then lose their reference to morality and are reinterpreted pseudo-physiologically, as if all that mattered was to purge and detoxify the body, to remove and eliminate superfluous, harmful, toxic substances. These tentative reflections are not meant to sound like a critique of culture delivered as a sermon of penitence. I have nothing against the value of self-realization. In fact, I vigorously affirm it; I am not enamored of the culture that existed prior to the rise of this value at the end of the eighteenth century, before Romanticism,[14] so to speak. I just do not believe that self-realization should be considered the highest of all values. Above all, though, there is a paradox in the fact that one of the preconditions for successful self-realization is to open oneself to something that transcends the self. The question, then, is how we can shield this openness from egocentric instrumentalization.

One of the most interesting philosophical attempts in the twentieth century to develop an appropriate terminology for this fraught predicament is to be found in the writings of German philosopher and sociologist Max Scheler from the 1920s. In his philosophy of religion and sociology of knowledge he distinguished between three types of knowledge and the transmission of such knowledge.[15] The first type is the knowledge we need to control natural processes and all other processes, such as those of an economic nature, that we wish to regulate. This knowledge is produced and made available by the natural sciences and parts of the social sciences;

Scheler calls it *Herrschaftswissen* (mastery knowledge or knowledge for control). For the second type, he uses the word *Bildung* and refers to *Bildungswissen*. *Bildung* is a highly charged term in German and is notorious for its untranslatability. It does not imply goal-oriented education but is based on the individualized pre-Romantic and Romantic transformation of the Aristotelian idea of a telos, a developmental goal inherent in living beings. But the telos is not the same for every human being. It is a specific developmental goal characteristic of each individual, which, moreover, can be achieved only if the individual finds it within himself or herself and actively pursues it. *Bildungswissen* then accrues to the individual from the study of history and culture, such as art and literature. Self-realization is an important aspect of such *Bildung*, but this is self-realization with a communitarian dimension. While self-realizing individuals in this sense must distance or even liberate themselves from conventions, their self-realization will ultimately serve the community—more effectively, at any rate, than if they had not taken this seemingly roundabout route and had simply remained within the framework of conventional expectations and norms. For Wilhelm von Humboldt, the ultimate purpose of freeing individuals to engage in processes of *Bildung* was to produce far-sighted, independent public servants; Friedrich Schleiermacher envisaged the production of similar figures to lead the church. *Self-optimization is what becomes of self-realization when it has lost its communitarian dimension.*[16]

The champions of the idea of *Bildung* in Germany were often ardent advocates of the cause of the Prussian state and later of German nationalism. At least at the institutional level, the ideas of *Bildung* and those of German national identity were closely interwoven, typically, for instance, in the classical gymnasium (academic high school) and the university. Only in the aesthetic "bohemia" on the fringes of society did self-realization become a purely individualistic, noncommunitarian goal. But what might replace the nationalist counterweight today? Could a cosmopolitan orientation devoid of an institutional basis, as some think, be a strong enough countervailing factor, or must we resign ourselves to the fact that such a thing no longer exists?

Scheler, at least, had another possibility in mind. Thus, he needed a third type of knowledge that goes beyond not only mastery knowledge but also mere *Bildung*. He called this type either "salvific" or "redemptive" knowledge (*Heilswissen* or *Erlösungswissen*). As long as he conceived of himself as a Catholic Christian, this type of knowledge was embodied for him by the Christian faith, by respect for the sacred, by love of that which transcends one's own person, be it another human being or another living being, be it God or the whole of creation. When he became a pantheist in the last few years of his life, he transformed his ideas about salvation and redemption in the direction of a meditative, noninstrumental relationship to the world as a whole, a reversal of the will, for which he found inspiration chiefly in the traditions of Indian spirituality. He believed that the Europe of the 1920s was in the grip of a profound cultural crisis, such that the entire continent would benefit from conversion to Asian spirituality. He would never have treated the Buddha as a mere relaxant. But he would surely have accepted the challenge of shifting European culture away from its focus on the mastery of nature and people.

"Salvation" and "redemption" as counter-concepts to "self-optimization"—we might call this the quintessence of Scheler's message. I am unable to pursue this idea further here in a systematic philosophical sense or in terms of intellectual history. But I will allow myself two brief remarks in this vein. First, Max Scheler was not the only one with this sort of thing in mind at the time. He himself had already interpreted Edmund Husserl's phenomenology as an attempt to free human beings to perceive things as they are in themselves through reflection on the world as it is given to us. Jewish philosopher Martin Buber's famous reflections on dialogue and the authentic I–Thou relationship are an equally powerful articulation of the ideal of a noninstrumentalist interpersonal relationship.[17] German Italian theologian Romano Guardini put forward similar ideas under the rubric of "encounter" but did not limit this to interpersonal relationships.[18] At least the later writings of philosopher Martin Heidegger, with their emphasis on "releasement" (*Gelassenheit*),[19] became an important inspiration for the dialogue between European and Japanese thinkers and for ecological thought. Yet it would be barking up the wrong tree to suggest that Scheler was out to devalue the sciences and supplant them with the third type of knowledge. According to him, both Europeans and Asians should in fact learn to switch from one attitude to the other where appropriate.

The second point I want to make concerns Jürgen Habermas. As a young thinker, he presented his influential book *Knowledge and Human Interests* (*Erkenntnis und Interesse*) in 1968, in which—without mentioning Scheler—he too developed a typological triad of "interests" constitutive of knowledge, which is markedly reminiscent of Scheler's with regard to the first two types and thus the distinction between the natural sciences and the humanities. Tacitly, however, he replaced the third type, salvific or redemptive knowledge, with that of the emancipatory epistemological interest. For him, then, it was not religious education, as in Scheler's work, but an education in psychoanalysis and "critical" social science, especially Marxism, that was to embody the dimension that transcends the natural sciences and humanities. A few years later he dropped this third type, but without putting anything in its place. His earlier book can therefore be read as a typical expression of the exuberance of 1968, as influenced by emancipatory utopianism and secularization, while the later development looks like an expression of his growing perplexity about the place of religion in modern culture. The position of faith in the modern world has in fact been central to Habermas's intellectual development in recent decades. In spite of all the changes in his views, he continues to regard "metaphysics" as a defense of a pre-Kantian worldview, whereas in Scheler this term is an attempt to illuminate questions that arise even after the turn toward the self-reflexivity of the knowing subject.

But what do these considerations mean for the role of the churches with regard to *Bildung*, education and culture? If we take Scheler's typology as a basis for answering these questions, it is obvious that the natural sciences and their type of knowledge will not be in the foreground. But this certainly does not mean that their importance should be underestimated or that the challenges they pose, including to traditional religious worldviews, should not be taken seriously. The second type of knowledge, *Bildungswissen*, which grows out of engagement with culture and its history, has always played a crucial role in the Catholic tradition. An institution like the Catholic Church, with its long tradition and its high regard for the importance of tradition to faith, cannot and should not forgo this rich heritage. The Christian confessions differ significantly from each other in this respect. Lutherans in particular did much to increase literacy among large segments of the population and contributed a great deal to the musical culture of the countries in which they had a significant presence, while more radical Protestant currents such as the American Baptists, because they did not academicize the ministry, made it easier for the rhetorically talented among the lower classes, including blacks, to become pastors. For

Catholics, imagery and theater played a much greater role in the so-called Counter-Reformation than for Protestants—with long-lasting effects on mentalities. However any of this may look in the detail, my point here is that there has always been a connection between the specific character of a religion and the quality of the *Bildung* associated with it. Even under highly secularized conditions, one cannot become an educated individual in the sense of *Bildung* if one has no understanding of religious traditions. European art is simply inaccessible if one is unable to recognize biblical scenes or the attributes of saints.

But the church's educational task from a *Bildung* perspective cannot be chiefly concerned with this or limited to preserving the culture of the past and transmitting it to new generations. This brings us to the point where the second and third types of knowledge merge. It is the point at which we confront a religiously inspired culture not only in a historicist sense but in an existential way, that is, when we take seriously the truth claims of a religion, the values inherent in it. The churches are often praised for their role in transmitting and inculcating values, and I too am in no doubt that they can and do play an important role in this regard. But the extent to which they can play this role depends on at least two conditions. First, values cannot be transmitted if they are not articulated in ways that make them accessible to people today. This is more than a matter of language, let alone didactics. It is bound up with the intellectual penetration of one's message. Elsewhere, I have described it as a key intellectual challenge for Christianity today to make the specifics of its ethos of love, its understanding of the person, its special forms of spirituality and its relationship to transcendence understandable in novel ways.[20] Christians must be able to make their faith comprehensible in nontraditional as well as traditional ways. Second, however, there are institutional prerequisites for the credible transmission of values. The church can be credible only if it embodies the values it preaches in its own structures. The sexual abuse scandals have made it abundantly clear that there is a huge gap between, on the one hand, the church's self-image and its claimed authority in preaching and defending the ideal of universal human dignity and, on the other, its true character and institutional mechanisms. In order to evangelize the world, as Pope Paul VI already stated in *Evangelii nuntiandi* and as Pope Francis never tires of repeating, the church must first evangelize itself. All experienced parents and teachers know that their personal example weighs more heavily than the teachings they proclaim, and this applies just as much to institutions.

But faith is more than values and morals. It can be perceived as an alternative to mere self-optimization only if it opens up a sphere of experience in which individuals can go beyond a fixation on the limits of their selves. (Catholic) British anthropologist Victor Turner coined the term "anti-structure" for this sphere of experience.[21] People always and necessarily live a life that is structured in many ways, but they also need a temporary loosening of these structures. For Turner, this happens in rituals that live up to their purpose. Rituals, as I have argued elsewhere,[22] create a controlled environment that temporarily suspends the mechanisms of everyday life. This makes it possible to experience ideal states—and in such a way that they remain in the memory as intense experiences after people have returned to everyday life. This means that participation in rituals has or may have a tremendous effect in terms of both education and *Bildung*. Religious education must therefore prepare people for the liturgy because this provides access to a sphere of experience that goes beyond structured, everyday life. But rituals are not the only form of anti-structure. Sacred spaces are another example. Being able to step inside the church they have just noticed while walking along the street gives individuals an opportunity to leave their everyday lives behind for a short time, to relate more easily to God in prayer and meditation and to take that relationship with them into their profane activities. Pilgrimages are currently being rediscovered as a form of life in which the structures of everyday life are left behind. In Germany, the so-called Catholic and church congresses (*Katholikentage* and *Kirchentage*), that is, gatherings of tens of thousands of believers, are opportunities for Christians to reaffirm the presence of their fellow Christians and their large number but also to experience what Turner called "communitas," that is, intensely experienced, spontaneously generated communality. The rational forms and contents of religious education depend on the vitality of a religious life to which they contribute but that they cannot produce themselves.

God moves in mysterious ways. I began with a sporting anecdote, and I would like to conclude with another. During the communist period, there were two major football clubs in East Berlin. One of them, Dynamo, enjoyed the goodwill of the security organs and all sorts of privileges, which helped ensure frequent victories in the East German championship. The other, Union, was beloved by the very people who supposedly held power in a state that invoked the dictatorship of the proletariat. Both clubs, like everything else in East Berlin and all of East Germany, were profoundly secularist in worldview and style. Neither Christ nor Buddha played any role for them or their followers, so to speak. But something remarkable has happened in the last twenty years. In 2003, on the evening of December 23 to be precise, eighty-nine Union Berlin fans, calling themselves the Crazies (*die Verrückten*), secretly gathered on the pitch of their beloved "An der Alten Försterei" stadium. They had brought with them biscuits, cake and mulled wine and began to sing traditional Christmas carols—as well as the club's anthem. This pre-Christmas gathering then took place every year prior to the COVID-19 pandemic. Attendance grew from the original eighty-nine to four hundred in 2004 and one thousand in 2005, until it reached twenty-eight thousand in 2016, the maximum number allowed in the stadium. At this event, many attendees light the freely distributed candles, the choir from a nearby high school sings and a pastor reads from the Bible. There is a collection, the proceeds of which go to the club's children and youth section. The event can now be watched on regional television in Berlin and throughout Brandenburg. Similar initiatives have sprung up in Cologne, Aachen, Dresden, Gelsenkirchen-Schalke and Schweinfurt. Here we can observe the spontaneous emergence of a ritual tradition. It is in clear continuity with the Christian tradition, or, to be more precise, it has overcome the discontinuity imposed by communist rule. Yet it by no means represents a renewal of Christianity in its institutional structures. It is a scenario replete with ambiguities. In Erfurt, with its magnificent medieval churches (the cathedral and Sankt Severi) atop a hill in the middle of the city, we find a parallel. Years ago, the Catholic bishop and his auxiliary bishop decided to offer a separate Christmas celebration for non-Christians. Increasing numbers of people had been attending the Christmas Eve Midnight Mass at the cathedral without being baptized or familiar with the rituals. Some Christians felt disturbed by them as mere visitors rather than participants. Now the two groups celebrate in adjacent churches.

These examples demonstrate the power of ritual, the power of the sacred, even in deeply secularized societies. They also remind us that Christianity, for all its esteem for cultural tradition—particularly in the Catholic case—must not become the religion of the "cultured." The goal must be to strike a balance between the highest educational and intellectual aspirations, on the one hand, and accessibility to all people through genuine experience, on the other. This is what the third type of knowledge, which goes beyond expertise and *Bildung*, is and should be all about.

6

A Christian through War and Revolution
Alfred Döblin's Narrative Work November 1918

Like suicide, religious conversion may appear to us as an individual act in the purest sense. It is often assumed that shattering existential experiences are the crucial factor when individuals no longer wish to continue their life or change their deepest, identity-defining convictions. Certainly, more superficial considerations or coercion may play a role in the mere joining of a different faith community, such as tax benefits, obtaining a marriage license or political loyalties. In these cases, however, we hesitate even to apply the term "conversion." When it comes to suicide, one of the pioneering works to emerge during sociology's founding phase as a discipline demonstrated impressively that we can discern social patterns even in highly individual, existential acts. Protestants, as Émile Durkheim, the French founder of sociology, claimed in a major study in 1897,[1] committed suicide more often than Catholics and Jews, unmarried people more often than married people, childless married couples more often than those with children. Suicides, he contended, increased at times of economic crisis but also during periods of rapid economic growth. As a rule, he went on, revolutions and wars tend to reduce the frequency of suicide. What is important here is not the details of these findings but the insight that, in light of their social distribution, individual acts, without becoming less personal, point to forces that cannot be traced back to the individual dimension. Research after Durkheim has also made it clear that even the statistical recording of a death as a suicide involves definitional processes that differ by culture and milieu and thus reduce the comparability of the data.[2]

All of this applies to conversions as well. Every person who breaks away from the religious community in which they grew up, every person who finds their way to a new conviction and community, perhaps in the face of resistance from their environment, may experience this as a dramatic break that divides their life into a before and after. But social patterns apply here too—as evident, for example, in the huge surge in people leaving churches in Western European countries since the 1960s, the mass conversion to Protestant groups in Latin America and among North American Hispanics and present-day Christianization in South Korea and parts of China. These statements will probably have made clear what I would nevertheless like to emphasize explicitly: in the social sciences, "conversion" is a value-free term; in other words, it does not denote the finding of a higher or objective truth but foregrounds a subjective change of conviction. Hence, the term may, for example, be applied to the path *to* the Christian faith just as much as the path *away from* it. Further, it may encompass not only *religious* faith but all deep-seated and far-reaching belief systems. In this sense, people convert to Marxism or fascism or Islamist fundamentalism, but also to liberalism, secular humanism or a passionate commitment to social equality or human rights. As it did in the research on suicide, here too it has emerged as vital to recognize conversion narratives as a genre rather than assume that individuals reinvent the narrative form through which they report their change of conviction. In some traditions, there are ready-made model narratives that preform individuals' expectations and experiences. For instance, the narrative about loss of faith in James Joyce's *Portrait of the Artist as a Young Man*—when a student in a Jesuit-run college suddenly realizes just what he wants to break away from when he sees a girl paddling on a beach in summer with her skirt bunched up—also has the structure of the classical Christian conversion narrative. In individual cases of this kind, experience and the articulation of experience are nearly impossible to disentangle.

I would like to develop some ideas that are particularly important to me in this context with reference to a literary text: Alfred Döblin's four-volume *November 1918*, which he described as a "narrative work." In my opinion, and much to the author's chagrin (and in this case partly due to an unfortunate publication history), like all his books except for his one immortal success, *Berlin Alexanderplatz*, this text never quite received the attention it deserves. The lack of interest is surprising, at least in Germany, since this is largely a Berlin-centered novel. In his French and American exile, where he wrote the book between 1937 and 1943, Döblin returned imaginatively to the "proliferation of buildings" "sprawling low and somber across the sand of Mark Brandenburg," traversed by a "shabby excuse for a stream" called the Spree, featuring "an iridescent black from the sewage emptied into it," and to which the houses turned their backs while sheds and coal depots covered the banks of the "murky, proletarian waters" (II, 9/5).[3] In today's postindustrial Berlin, where the river's edge is home to artificial beaches, countless cafés and pseudo-Bavarian beer gardens, and where tourists from all over the world and young people with plenty of time on their hands enjoy themselves ostentatiously, the poor, gray, industrial Berlin evoked by Döblin seems almost exotic. In his chronology, closely based on historical events, which begins on November 10, 1918, the day after the fall and flight of the kaiser, and ends on January 15, 1919, the day on which Karl Liebknecht and Rosa Luxemburg were murdered, the topography of Berlin is a constant and palpable physical presence. We feel it beyond the historical center stretching from the police headquarters on Alexanderplatz to the Reich Chancellery on Wilhelmstraße, and beyond the Landwehr Canal in the Tiergarten—where the book portrays the gruesome murder of Karl and Rosa. This felt topography in fact takes us all the way from the Cemetery of the March Fallen (victims of the Revolution of 1848) in Friedrichshain to bourgeois Wilmersdorf, for example, to Mannheimer Straße, where Liebknecht was arrested in the flat where he had been hiding out, and on to Heidelberger Platz, through which the defeated frontline troops entered Berlin, marching along streets black with people, accompanied by cheers and yet painfully aware of their defeat and the huge number of fallen comrades. Above all, however, this is a *book of conversions*.

By this I do not mean that it was written when Döblin, the secular Jew, was moving ever closer to Catholic Christianity—until finally being baptized on November 30, 1941, in Santa Monica, California. The connections between Döblin's biography and the inner logic of his literary work are not so straightforward: an author of this stature does not use his book as the mouthpiece for a preconceived missionary project. The notion that Döblin became a Christian out of weakness, through a breakdown of his personality—an interpretation put about from Brecht to Grass—is also quite inadequate and must be dismissed as an expression of prejudice.[4] The same goes for attempts to place Döblin within the genre of "renegade literature," that is, the writings of former revolutionary socialists who later find a substitute for their political utopia, for example, in the form of an afterlife.[5] Döblin's *November 1918* does in fact contain a classic conversion narrative in one of its plot lines, which tells the story of war-traumatized officer and Berlin gymnasium teacher Friedrich Becker. But I intend to show that Döblin also places the war as a whole in the light of conversion issues. In addition to military, political and economic aspects, he opens himself up to "psychiatric" questions linked with the personality-altering effects of the experience of violence. New light is also shed on the revolution, which is the subject of the novel not just as a political event but also as something imaginary, as a mythical representation of the dream of the new man and a new world. Only by grasping conversion in this sort of depth can we understand the courage with which Döblin unfolds his second conversion story in this book, that of Rosa Luxemburg. It is when we link together all these strands, and others, that an answer begins to emerge to the two questions Döblin poses in this text and that I seek to express with the aid of the ambiguous word "through" in the title of this chapter: How can a person become a Christian in the face of the World War, which laid bare the bankruptcy of Christian Europe, and how can a Christian live through the revolutionary period as a Christian? How should Christians have related to the war and the revolution if, for them, being a Christian does not mean belonging to a confessional milieu and matching voting behavior but devotion to the Gospel?

The multiperspective narrative work *November 1918*, comprising about two thousand pages, features a large number of interconnected story lines—more than fifty, as a careful count has revealed.[6] From this gripping but also confusing narrative web, I will first separate out the story that most clearly constitutes a conversion narrative, one long enough to have been a novel in its own right. In an autobiographical retrospective ("Epilogue"), Döblin describes the figure of Friedrich Becker as a "probe" that he wished to insert into his old stomping ground of Berlin, "so that he could test and experience himself (me)."[7] Through the medical metaphor of the "probe," the physician Döblin aptly expresses this figure's function as an investigative device that enabled him to write an experimental form of biography. The story, however, does not begin in Berlin, nor in Kiel, scene of the sailors' revolt, but in Alsace during the final days of its existence as part of the German Empire, chiefly in a small-town military hospital, presumably in Hagenau. Lieutenant Becker, who had previously taught ancient languages at a Berlin gymnasium and had been decorated with the Iron Cross, was admitted there to recover from a serious back injury. He has no clear memory of the moment when he was wounded. He only knows that everything in his life changed abruptly: "I'm lying in the trench with my company. When the moment comes and we leap out and run, after barely ten meters I hear it hit nearby and then it's over. It's another one of those strange leaps from being into nothingness or into something else. I have no memory of a transition. Suddenly and simply, I wasn't there" (I, 167). These sentences are indicative of a total, traumatizing rupture in his life, one that leads to the full-scale devaluation of everything that seemed to make life worth living before the war. Becker falls into paralysis and depression, a state in which only one issue matters: who was responsible for his suffering, but above all for the countless human lives wiped out by the war.[8] Döblin's "probe," rather than a seeker of meaning in an abstract, metaphysical sense, is an investigator of causes amid the undergrowth of political and military events. The apolitical world of art and *Bildung* in which Becker, a member of the "educated classes," lived in the prewar period cannot be excluded from this search for causes. The previous description of the moment of his injury, as related by Becker to his closest war comrade during the train journey from the Alsatian military hospital, which had to be evacuated after the entry of French troops, to Berlin, is followed one page later by a lengthy reminiscence on one of the greatest aesthetic experiences of Becker's earlier life (I, 168): Wagner's opera *Tristan und Isolde*, especially Isolde's love-death. We might initially get the impression that Becker is sinking into pleasant memories of the peacetime enjoyment of art, but he breaks off any such inclination with a "dismissive wave of the hand" (I, 170), contrasting the romantic transfiguration of death with his real-world experience of being wounded and his proximity to death: "No supreme pleasure, no undulating suspension, just a uniformly gray, flat plain that knows no end, a rigid lunar crater over which light and shadow alternate" (ibid.). Döblin finds a potent image for the break with aestheticism and *Bildungshumanismus*, the humanism of self-edification, when he allows Becker no sigh of relief after his return to his Berlin home and his reunion with his once beloved bookshelf, his busts of Sophocles and Kant and paintings of Goethe and Kleist. On the contrary, Becker can no longer stand this *Bildungswelt*, this world of knowledge and erudition, prompting him to nail a large gray cloth to the shelves to hide the books from his sight; Kant and Sophocles are rammed under the chaise longue, while Goethe and Kleist are "laid . . . out flat on the floor [with] two dictionaries [piled] on top of them" (II, 61/45). His caring mother is quite happy to see the back of the tragic Kleist but does not understand why the others needed to go, too. But her son cannot allow their voices to drown out those of his dead and maimed comrades: "Although all of them, Goethe, Kant, Sophocles, even Kleist, want to argue with me. I'll not forget what was so unutterably naked and indescribable about it" (II, 62/46).

Many interpreters have recognized that here Döblin, influenced by Kierkegaard, is depicting a human being's shift from the merely aesthetic to the ethical stage of existence. Plenty of people today will have little difficulty grasping this step. But of course, Kierkegaard talks about a third stage, a step beyond the ethical into the religious, and many people find this more difficult to comprehend. Döblin leads his character into this religious stage, a process that had already begun during the long train journey to Berlin: medieval Alsatian mystic Johannes Tauler appears to the dreaming Becker and teaches him to see a potential form of grace in suffering. The religious awakening then continues in Berlin, to which nurse Hilde, who had cared for him in the military hospital, has followed him out of love. She is portrayed as a simple Catholic Christian and as a "voluptuous" woman who wishes to comfort the man she is falling ever more deeply in love with, leading him out of his despair—through utterances such as, "You're tormenting yourself, Friedrich. We are all sinners. Don't weigh yourself down so much. If I were all alone, I could not have helped myself either. But the Savior has appeared and shown us mercy. I've experienced his grace and help" (III, 80/354). But Becker cannot, not yet, fit what he hears into his schemas for interpreting the world and himself. This diminishes the erotic tension between the two: "But it sobered Becker. He stared at Hilda. Was she joking with him? What were these trite phrases supposed to mean? She was smiling to herself and her eyes were closed. Gioconda. 'I know, Friedrich, that that doesn't help you if I say it. You have to find it out for yourself and you will find it. I'll help you. Believe me, it's not so difficult'" (III, 80/355).

What Becker must find his way to is not simply faith in the Savior but the insight that even the most intensive ethical self-examination and evaluation of the world still leaves us shackled to our own ego—if the goal is to trace our ethical standards back to our choices or our own rationality and if the only answers we will accept amid this search for meaning render the ego "higher, prouder still" (III, 198/441).[9] The only way out of the egocentricity that typifies even the ethical conduct of life is to open ourselves to something that takes hold of us with uncompromising force. This opening of the self cannot, of course, be a merely intellectual process. Through a blend of psychiatric knowledge and wild narrative fantasy, then, Döblin first describes Becker's path into ever-deeper despair. This is the despair of a suffering human being but also of a thinker who is no longer persuaded by the meaning offered by aestheticism, by an amoral, power-centered worldview or by the psychoanalytically influenced reduction of the moral conscience to a "sensitivity that you learned, that was drummed into you," a mere form of "training" (III, 248/476). It is the despair of a man who can find no way out that convinces him intellectually *and* heals him spiritually. Having reached this nadir, Becker tries to hang himself from one of the hooks left unused following the removal of the paintings and busts. The hook holds, but the knot does not, and the loving nurse, sensing that something is wrong, finds Becker still alive, "unconscious from strangulation" (III, 259/484), still despairing, but also oddly relieved, peaceful, open to appreciating her prayer and what is described as "mankind's king of thoughts" (III, 287/508), the notion of a suffering and compassionate God.

Döblin by no means simplifies the character's path after this turning point. The emerging possibility of conversion to Christianity does not mutate instantly into a stable faith. Nor are Friedrich Becker's psychological problems and intellectual questions suddenly resolved as if by magic. Above all, though, new questions arise, especially the question of how someone who has become a Christian *through* the war and its consequences is now supposed to continue on his path while avoiding taking Christianity too lightly, as if he owned it and could "walk around with it as if it were a book I'm carrying under my arm" (IV, 557–58/459).

Just as I could recount Becker's conversion only through a few excerpts, I can describe the new convert's path *through* the time of the revolution with reference to just a few scenes. When Becker, having regained his strength of spirit, resumes teaching at the gymnasium, his class is initially looking forward to meeting their teacher: despite the defeat of the German Empire, they are expecting this fighter with frontline experience, a man highly decorated for his bravery, to speak stirringly and impressively about war, state and nation. The pupils are to study Sophocles's *Antigone*, and the chasm between their expectations and the new perspective of their teacher, who has been transformed by the war, soon becomes apparent. They are dismissive of Antigone, who, defying the king's prohibition, buries the body of her fallen brother and is walled up alive as punishment, and sneer at her reference to an unwritten "law about funeral practices" handed down from heaven (IV, 221/191). Becker, meanwhile, cannot let go of the question of why none of the men who went into the field in 1914 even raised the question of "divine right versus civil right" (IV, 222/192), criticized the state or hesitated to go to their death for it. This teacher believes that the next generation is following the same wrong track and feels "for the first time as a Christian among heathens, . . . compelled to make his profession of faith, even if it [leads] to martyrdom" (IV, 223/193). For him, classical tragedy is about more than "emotion versus duty," more than "duty to the state versus duty to heaven." It is also about death: "How is the world of the living to treat the world of the dead?" (IV, 224/194). But his star pupil, articulating the attitude of the entire class, brushes this aside with the rousing statement that what matters now is something quite different, namely, "whether one has a clear concept of the nation and what one owes it. We have no need for spiritualism these days. The nation just needs men who will take up its cause" (IV, 226/195). Conversely, Friedrich Becker's new existence as a Christian is deeply marked by skepticism toward the state and by antinationalism. He is first put to the test beyond the classroom when the staunchly nationalist and virile pupils revolt against the headmaster, an antinationalist aesthete who is accused of making homoerotic advances toward pupils. The situation escalates, and the father of one of the children beats up the headmaster, who dies of his injuries, throwing up the Antigone question for Becker when he is laid to rest. He decides to attend the funeral against the wishes of the school staff, who demonstratively stay away. As a Christian, he refuses to take the lead in demonizing a homosexual, instead adhering to the unconditional obligation of brotherhood toward the dead. Forced to resign from his teaching post, Becker soon finds himself facing another dramatic decision, this time in connection with the revolutionary events. Döblin portrays the revolutionaries as often leaderless and aimless, driven by rage rather than strategic plans: "The revolutionaries' hatred of the bourgeois press was immense. The lies and the malice of such stupid, mercenary journalism infuriated them; and thus it happened that their first attacks had not been directed against military targets but against the strongholds of the hue and cry, the newspaper offices" (IV, 469/381). Explicit mention is made of the building housing the SPD-aligned *Vorwärts* newspaper. The Mossehaus and the Ullsteinhaus, also home to organs of the press, are referenced as well, as are their occupation and the heavy losses suffered when they are shelled by government troops, who also fire on the workers from the tower of the nearby Jerusalem Church. Although the Christian Becker does not share the revolutionaries' utopian hopes and abhors all violence, during the occupation of the police headquarters he is forced to decide whether to side with the rich and powerful or with the poor, who seem to know no other way: "And whatever they do, whether they're mistaken or not, they are my brothers and sisters, they are like me, and I am no better a man than they" (IV, 502/410).

I will break off the retelling of the Friedrich Becker story at this point. In Döblin's work, too, the character's path following the revolutionary period is merely summarized in a kind of coda. After his release from prison and the death of his mother, abandoned by his girlfriend, Friedrich Becker leads a wandering existence as an itinerant Christian preacher and is finally killed in a mugging. The ending of this particular narrative strand has been interpreted in two quite different ways, which shed a great deal of light on the topics we are grappling with here. Some see it as Döblin's vision of a Gospel-oriented way of life. While all the "professional Christians" in the novel, such as a German military chaplain, are subjected to ridicule in light of their blinkered fixation on possessions and prosperity, Döblin has presented us with an "uncompromisingly lived Christianity beyond all confessional limitations and institutional sclerosis."[10] Others, however, view this interpretation as underestimating the intellectual complexity of this enormous narrative work. I agree with them.[11] If the Becker figure were a role model and the conversion story the entire novel, the above interpretation might make sense. But Döblin portrays Friedrich Becker highly critically in his Christianity. He recognizes that his attitude entails a turning away from realistic politics, embodying a desire to exit real history and thus exhibiting an unfortunate continuity with the power-backed cultural inwardness of the prewar period, along with a religious hubris that is anything but Christian. For this dialectic in Christianity and Buddhism, the term "salvific egotism" (*Heilsegoismus*) has taken hold, and I believe it applies in this case. Yet the principle of *unus Christianus, nullus Christianus* was already enunciated in ancient Christianity: no one can be a Christian alone, and no criticism of the institutions and social forms of Christianity can reasonably disregard this dependence of individual faith on a community of believers.[12] In the novel, however, Friedrich Becker becomes a fanatical disrupter of church services, warning against church attendance and calling for the starvation of pastors, which Döblin explicitly describes as a "pitfall" of his Christianity.

I could not have reasonably called Döblin's narrative work *November 1918* a novel of conversions if it contained just this one conversion story. Conversion as a result of the experience of violence may also lead in completely different directions, away from Christianity for good, for example. In his account of frontline troops' return home, Döblin presents us with fictitious letters from these returnees to their wives. One of them states: "Does the pastor still visit your parents? Give him my greetings. I've had to dig graves for several dozen corpses with my own hands, and what they looked like I'll save to tell you later. We had to use a spade to scoop some of them up in pieces. Just dumb luck that I wasn't one of them. According to your pastor, God once said, 'It's all good.' Dear Elsa, if that's good" (III, 191/436). This is presumably a case of final disillusionment with the churches loyal to the state, a conversion away from something rather than toward something. Above all, though, Döblin is interested in those whom the experience of violence turns into habitual perpetrators and ideological glorifiers of violence. One chapter, titled "The New Wolf-Men," refers to a new kind of man "formed by the war" (III, 350/557). In a conversation with Lenin's emissary Karl Radek, Karl Liebknecht expresses concern that the war "has brutalized people, wrecked them" (III, 358/563), and that some of those returning from it had come to resemble predatory beasts. Radek dismisses them as counterrevolutionaries, but Liebknecht fears they are spreading through the ranks of the revolutionaries as well. This type finds its most concise embodiment in the figure of Friedrich Becker's best friend, Johannes Maus. Closely interwoven with Becker's conversion story is that of Maus, another wounded officer, but one who is now addicted to violence, who is violent toward Hilde, the nurse he covets, in the military hospital, who sympathizes with the idea of a revolutionary dictatorship for a short time in Berlin but then joins the emerging Freikorps, the paramilitary militias. He goes so far as to denounce his friend to the authorities and perceives Becker's commitment to the gay headmaster as a major reason for breaking off their friendship (IV, 556/458). The multiple plotlines feature numerous converts to violence from all walks of life. The officer corps is consistently portrayed as viewing the fight against internal enemies as a chance to escape the ignominy of defeat in war. The "stab-in-the-back myth," the idea that an undefeated army was betrayed by communist insurgents and Jewish war profiteers, far from arising spontaneously, is launched deliberately even before the kaiser's abdication. In the novel, Maus explains this to his friend Becker at a time when Maus himself still backs the revolutionaries and rejects the slogan "Down with Bolshevism" and "Down with the Jews" (III, 69/346). An aged countess who mocks the general staff for failing to produce a new Wallenstein, that is, for missing the chance to replace the emperor with a military dictator, descends into an ecstatic fantasy of violence in her chambers (II, 267/201). With these tales of conversion to violence, the novel sets a clear counterpoint to the conversion story of the new Christian Friedrich Becker.

Yet even this contrast does not exhaust the theme of conversion in Döblin's novel. Hanging above all the historical and fictional events portrayed in *November 1918* is a word of the greatest imaginative potential: "revolution." Since the eighteenth century, when this term ceased to denote the mere rotation of celestial bodies and began to refer to an upheaval giving rise to something new, it has elicited the idea of radically new political and social conditions, but above all of a new human being, a better human being, one free of petty self-interest and the striving for power.[13] The mythical dimension of the concept of revolution entails at least the hope of such a new world. In our context, we might refer to the conversion of individuals that turns them into revolutionaries, and of revolution as a whole as the vision of mass conversion to a new humanity.

However, Döblin does not write about the German November Revolution of 1918 in order to transfigure it and incorporate it into humanity's remembered treasure trove of historical advances toward freedom. He is writing in exile, aware of the victory of Nazism in Germany barely a decade and a half after the revolution, which he declares botched or betrayed, a revolution that has tragically petered out or run out of steam. He asks what elements of the revolution facilitated the later victory of reactionary forces within the state, economy and military and whether this was a revolution without revolutionaries. In one of the places in the novel where the narrator addresses the reader directly—titled "The Author Takes Stock"—we are told: "So far no actual revolutionary masses have come into view. This might be considered sufficient reason for reproaching someone who has set out to describe a revolution. But it is not our fault. This is, after all, a German revolution" (II, 242/186). His view of events is thus marked by bitter cynicism, while his portrayal ranges from the ironic to the satirical. No social class or milieu is exempt. Even his account of the first few days after the collapse of the military and political order in Alsace features little in the way of organized efforts to build a new reality. Instead, in the words of contemporary observer Ernst Troeltsch in the first of his "Spectator letters," a "jolly holiday feeling" holds sway.[14] The relations between the upper and lower classes are reversed in carnivalesque fashion, sexual escapades become possible, thievery goes unpunished. With regard to the dismantling of the military hospital in which Becker and Maus had been treated, we read: "Since yesterday evening, the nurses and every other female in the military hospital have been helping themselves to bed linen on a grand scale. They had the generosity to bring in women from outside and looted so thoroughly that the storerooms were 'sold out' by noon. Our quiet old lady, the pastor's doorkeeper, where might she be?" (I, 140). She, too, joins in the looting and even helps take "the marble slabs from the surgical ward out of the hospital on prams." "What a transformation at such an advanced age, a revolution in miniature," the narrator comments (ibid.). An entire chapter of the volume describing the second half of November 1918 in Berlin is titled "A Private Revolution." Here we meet a young printer who dresses up the theft of bread stamps and their hawking on the black market as a revolutionary act. Bleak too is the account of a meeting of the Prussian Academy of Sciences. In the days of the revolution, under the leadership of Max Planck, it adopts a business-as-usual approach, defiantly declaring this its contribution to defending the empire against its enemies (II, 100–101/78–79). These scholars and intellectuals either perceive the events as an irritating distraction or pose as astute leaders who are nonetheless incapable of providing concrete advice. The functionaries of the Social Democratic Party, but also the members of the soldiers' councils, are caricatured as straightjacketed by the mind-set of the organization or club: "And they were discussing what to do with the five hundred crates of gas masks that were stored in the warehouses, how much they cost to make, how much they wanted to sell them for; they could still make a pretty penny. Oh my goodness" (I, 218). Döblin reserves his greatest scorn for Friedrich Ebert, the new Reich chancellor, whose secret collaboration with the Supreme Army Command he assails just as much as his inability to do anything to counter the Freikorps or to ensure that the republic is protected by its own police force rooted in the workers' parties and rebellious soldiers.[15]

Many have interpreted Döblin's portrayal of the revolution here as an indication that, as a Christian, he had turned away from all that is revolutionary, in which he himself may have believed earlier, as if the message of his entire narrative work is that individual conversion to Christianity must supplant radical social change. But we find many elements that run counter to this widespread interpretation, such as how and where the voice of God is heard in Döblin's text. After a long silence, God speaks on the day of the armistice: "I did not reveal myself as long as you waged war. I have nothing to do with the raving mad and the obstinate. I have long known that people have fallen away from me. . . . But because you feel gratitude, I listen to you. You feel how good this is for you. I do not trust you. I do not trust you. . . . I do not trust you" (I, 208). And in the last volume we read: "War and revolution were the rousing calls of a supernatural voice. Who heard them, who noticed them? In these weeks of revolution, the voice gradually dwindled away" (IV, 351/309). All those who seek to apply the schema of Christianity *or* revolution, religion *or* social change to Döblin and his work are bound to end up confused, unless they consider him a writer lost amid a web of contradictions. Conversely, I argue that his picture of the German November Revolution was shaped by intuitive insights into two of the most important consequences of war and the mass experience of violence, both of which have since been broadly confirmed by social-scientific research. Wars test people's loyalty to the political orders in which they live. Victories bolster their legitimacy; defeats rattle it. And the unleashing of violence in war changes those involved in such a way that the level of violence also rises significantly within postwar civilian life.[16] The tragedy of the November Revolution was that, having stripped the old order of its credibility, war had made a revolution possible, but at the same time the potential revolutionaries, brutalized and numbed by the conflict, were miserably equipped to usher in a new social order.[17] The pettiness and opportunism of the new leadership, coupled with the country's precarious international position, further contributed to making a revolution impossible. Certainly, Döblin's narrative work does not embrace the communist utopia and willingness to use violence characteristic of Lenin and those who take their lead from him. In line with the tenets of Christianity, he does not see an earthly paradise as an achievable goal. But he criticizes the German revolution not because it was a revolution but because it was not a real revolution. It is a mistake to understand Döblin as if he is presenting itinerant preacher Friedrich Becker as a role model and the revolution as a calamity. In Döblin's portrayal of the revolution, it is the actors' *lack* of conversion—as manifest in their inability to seize a historical opportunity—that becomes the object of ridicule and the source of sorrow.

It seems to me that it is only against this background that we can understand the portrayal of Rosa Luxemburg, which takes up a great deal of space in the last volume of the narrative work and represents the second major individual conversion narrative alongside that of Friedrich Becker. It is highly controversial because Döblin portrays the most intellectually and rhetorically significant figure among the revolutionaries not only with the associated qualities but also as a loving woman, a person engulfed in profound grief and (almost) as a mystic. No one can deny that in the letters from the prison to which she had been sent for agitating against the war, Rosa Luxemburg did indeed show sides that Döblin could take as the starting point for his portrayal. Her much younger lover, Hans Diefenbach, had been killed in the war, and Döblin depicts how the imprisoned Rosa is driven into a state of obsessive grief by sexual fantasies of union with her dead lover and hallucinatory perceptions of his return and physical presence. This portrayal has stirred disapproval among some radical left-wingers and feminists, who feel that it turns a powerful political actor into a weak woman. This seems unfair to me. Döblin leaves the reader in no doubt about Rosa Luxemburg's leadership abilities (although in the novel she is ever less optimistic about the prospects of a revolution). Nor is her mourning a private phenomenon, so to speak: this is mourning for a person who died in the World War, a beloved figure who represents all the other dead who are loved and mourned by others. Döblin has Rosa herself declare: "I'm locked in like Antigone in her bridal chamber, buried alive within these walls" (IV, 16/8), thereby building a bridge to the far-from-apolitical Antigone tragedy and to one of the pivotal points in Friedrich Becker's conversion story. Döblin's Rosa does not convert to

Christianity like Becker, but neither does she convert to violence like Johannes Maus and so many others, on both right and left. In this respect, she differs profoundly in Döblin's text from Karl Liebknecht, who, reluctantly at first, allows himself to be pushed into a Lenin-like role that he then seeks to play. Rosa's mourning, conversely, leads away from violence, we might say to anti-Leninism. As is well known, Rosa Luxemburg was a trenchant critic of Lenin, of the unbridled violence of his revolutionary practice and of the party dictatorship that emerged from it. Döblin, however, exaggerates the real differences,[18] and he thus turns the fictional character of Rosa into the symbol of "socialism with a human face"—if it is not too anachronistic to quote this expression coined by Alexander Dubček to convey his hopes for the Prague Spring of 1968. The rejection of violence has far-reaching consequences for the vision of the order to be established. Rosa—in both novel and reality—is by no means self-evidently ready to deal with these consequences. The novel presents us with a broadly depicted inner struggle, which in literary terms emerges as "the grand experiment of renewing the religious epic, of which, Klopstock aside, there is no tradition in Germany."[19] Döblin describes Rosa's inner struggles as battles with Satan and between Satan and the angels for Rosa's soul. For Döblin, there was more to the fascination with Lenin than admiration for the organizer of a successful revolution. Now that Lenin has been bid farewell in Berlin and beyond, this is no longer universally understood. Lenin himself also speaks in Döblin's novel, for example, in the section "A New Man Must Be Created," and this is what he has to say: "Man, in his present state, is worthless. People are dumb and soft, sentimental idiots with a bourgeois love of comfort; mystics, pious and lazy, and, as a result, criminals. We must declare war against them, destroy them root and branch. The remnants of the old tyranny must be smashed. Not just its army, its administration, its legal system, but also, and above all, its hidden bastions in people's minds, in their ideas, ideals, faiths, religions, metaphysics, emotions" (IV, 63–64/50). For Döblin, this Lenin is the incarnation of a violently rational will to change the world, while his "new man" is a vision not of liberation but of subjugation. The hopes that gave rise to the myth of revolution are thus transformed into a nightmare. Yet in the figure of Rosa Luxemburg Döblin maintains the vision of a democratic socialism that is not hostile to religion, a notion that was vibrantly alive in part of the left.

The only way to do justice to Döblin's vast narrative work on the German November Revolution of 1918–19 is to refrain from pulling out one of its numerous strands, looking at it in isolation and believing it conveys the message of the entire work. The various conversion stories are reflected in each other in the most surprising ways. Thus, the Christian Friedrich Becker moves closer to the revolution, while revolutionary socialist Rosa Luxemburg shifts away from it.[20] Friedrich Becker's story is mirrored in his friend Johannes Maus's turn toward the extreme right-wing, pre-fascist Freikorps, while Rosa Luxemburg's conversion finds its contrastive counterpart in that of Karl Liebknecht, which takes him into the vicinity of Leninism. At the same time, all the conversion stories are contrasted with stories of failure to convert. The most extensive of these—and hitherto unmentioned here—is that of playwright Erwin Stauffer. If we fail to consider Döblin's mirroring intention, this narrative strand, almost as extensive as the Becker story, must inevitably seem functionless within the book as a whole. Hence, though surprising, it is at least explicable that the translator of Döblin's narrative work into English simply removed this plotline completely. In the style of a light novel, here Döblin demonstrates what happens when there is no break with the aesthetic way of life and an individual postures as a "poet" who has no need to concern himself with politics and is fully absorbed in the enjoyment of himself.

But does this mean that this novel of conversions has no message at all and that, however much we might admire the virtuosity of its polyphonic construction, it ultimately leaves us confused? If we look back over it, we can see that this narrative work does in fact entail a coherent political ethics, at least *ex negativo*. The Friedrich Becker story teaches us that mere self-transformation will remain self-centered if it fails to engender a commitment to institutional improvements. The recounted history of the revolution also shows that Lenin's and the Freikorps's violent actions, as well as Noske's and Ebert's bloody repressive measures, merely perpetuate a time-worn history of perdition. Depending on their sympathies, interpreters tend either to separate the history of the revolution and the conversion narrative or to prioritize one over the other. The conversion stories then appear to them as foreign bodies in a historical novel or as an alternative to the revolution propagated by Döblin. But Döblin has no such alternative in mind. His visions of social change go beyond the horizon of the actors involved in the events depicted. In the book, both Friedrich Becker and

Rosa Luxemburg break with the hubris inherent in the desire to dominate the world. But rather than exoticize this as an American or Soviet ideology alien to Europe, Döblin had addressed it as the core of Europe's global expansion in the work preceding *November 1918*, the *Amazon* trilogy. Also relevant here is the one historical figure in the novel who is portrayed in an unreservedly positive light, American president during the World War era, Woodrow Wilson, the "great voice of reason." He meets with Döblin's approval because he had advocated the establishment of a League of Nations, in other words, peaceful forms of international conflict resolution and a way out of the seemingly eternal conflicts between the European states. How far this picture matches the real Wilson need not concern us here. My goal is to dispel the impression that Döblin's Christianity is an apolitical one merely because it is difficult to assign it to one of the existing political camps and because his portrayal of the revolution makes a poor fit with conventional political narratives. Certainly, we are expecting too much from a novel or misjudging it if we believe we can retrospectively extract a superior political program for the revolutionary period. Furthermore, Döblin was not an author who embarked on the writing process with a clear message or fixed ending in mind. Still, his book does provide answers to the questions that triggered the writing process. Anyone who interprets European culture before the First World War as Christian must in fact perceive the war as a complete failure of Christianity. The consequence of this may be a definitive break with Christianity. Equally, however, one might question the Christianity of the prewar period and see a way out of the catastrophe of the World War in a fuller embrace of the Gospel. Those who gear themselves toward such a radical understanding of Christianity will lament two things above all in the brutal struggle of the Freikorps and government troops with rebellious workers and soldiers and in the murder of Karl Liebknecht and Rosa Luxemburg: violence and the hopelessness that ensues from dynamics of revenge. And they will look for a way out of them.

"Deep down and immovably," Döblin wrote in a later reflection on his book, "every Christian knows that one ought not to change the state of this world through force of arms."[21] Even in the Cold War era, he reminded his readers that socialism had arisen "from a pure, humane and Christian feeling" and that revolutions were explosions of a cauldron that must always prompt us to ask what had heated up the cauldron so much in the first place.²² The Christian Döblin was thus a bad fit for the Christian Democratic West Germany of the Adenauer era.

In Döblin's works, the Christian dimension is not present in the form of a ready-made interpretation of history featuring clear political alignments but as a tremendous challenge to take moral responsibility within historical life. This challenge applies not only to Christians but to all moral universalists. What makes Döblin's late work so special is that it defies not just conventional liberal, socialist and Christian ideas but also Max Weber's interpretation of history as a process of progressive "disenchantment." The conversions in his narrative work cannot be reduced to the formula of escape from a disenchanted world. Döblin found a literary form that makes it possible, even looking back on the tragedy of the World War and the November Revolution and the failure of the Weimar Republic, for the reader's eyes to be opened to new values and new paths.

7

Christianity without the Church?
The Intellectual Trajectory of Leszek Kołakowski

Probably no other philosopher in recent decades has engaged so intensively with historical research on a church-free Christianity as famous Polish thinker Leszek Kołakowski (1927–2009). This statement will surprise all those who are only familiar with his name and work from other contexts. This thinker initially became famous due to his role as a leading "revisionist" and dissident within Polish communism in the 1960s, then—after his forced emigration from Poland in 1968—through his comprehensive three-volume history of Marxism, which sought to take stock of it. Also significant to his renown were his engagement with important thinkers of the past such as Pascal, Spinoza, Husserl and Bergson and a multitude of sometimes satirical, occasionally aphoristic writings that are also of substantial literary merit. Much of this has been translated into numerous languages and has made Kołakowski a prominent intellectual respected across the world. In Poland—as Adam Michnik wrote in an obituary[1]—he was for decades a moral authority and a symbol of free and independent thought.

Kołakowski's most comprehensive and ambitious book from his Polish period, however, has been translated only into French and has to this day remained almost unknown in the German- and English-speaking worlds. Even when scholars have taken any note at all of his great work on *Religious Consciousness and Confessional Ties in the Seventeenth Century* (to cite the subtitle of the 1969 French translation of the Polish book of 1965),[2] it often made sense to them to read it merely as a kind of parable, as a coded plea not so much for Christianity but for a Marxist thought that should be able to develop free from party control and state dictatorship.[3]

As I argue in the following sketch of Kołakowski's intellectual path, however, this interpretation profoundly underestimates his authentic interest in his seemingly arcane object of study, which led him not only to delve into the existing historical research but also to immerse himself in the sources and primary literature for many years and to compile an eight-hundred-page book, which was strikingly titled *Christians without a Church* in the French translation.

While eschewing the idea that this book was solely a testament to the struggle for intellectual freedom under Polish communism, it is intriguing, in addition to probing the motives for a church-independent Christianity in the period between Reformation and Enlightenment, to inquire into the role of this theme in this Polish philosopher's political and religious biography. Precisely because his interest in a church-independent Christianity ought to be regarded as authentic, it is worth exploring how an initially convinced Marxist thinker arrived at this point and what role this work played in his further development. It will become apparent that, as unusual or perhaps unique as it was in many respects, Kołakowski's path itself has much to teach us. Since the philosopher provided detailed rationales for his stances and assessments at each step of his intellectual journey, while indicating in the next step which new insight compelled him to change them, his readers may struggle to keep abreast of his numerous transformations. Yet there is no need to discern a compelling logic at work in Kołakowski's intellectual biography or declare him a role model for others to consider his case instructive and productive.[4] It is productive because the gradual appropriation of Christianity by a thinker who began with a position sharply at variance with it shines a new light on the assimilated content, provided that the process of appropriation is guided by genuine and rationally controlled conviction rather than a forceful will to convert. Part of what is at play here, then, is exploring a new language for Christianity and a new understanding of the meaning of the church. At a time when interest in Kołakowski seems to have waned along with interest in Marxism, this perspective could prove fruitful.

So let us begin with a brief look at the philosopher's early intellectual and political biography.[5] Kołakowski grew up in a "free-thinking," politically left-leaning family and, as an eleven-year-old grammar school pupil in Łódź, was already refusing to attend religious education class. In deeply Catholic Poland, then, he did not engage in a youthful rebellion against the faith passed on to him by his family but held an aversion, shared with his family, to a faith that they perceived as a concoction of intellectual narrow-mindedness, nationalism, clericalism and anti-Semitism.[6] During the war and the German occupation—to which his father fell victim— he was already thinking about communist ideas, and he began to engage with them politically and journalistically immediately after the war. Looking back in a later interview, he stated that communism had sparked his enthusiasm as a "human universalism," as *the* alternative to nationalism and fascism.[7] In his *first* phase, that is, from 1949 until his first significant turning point in the mid-1950s, the (extremely) young and highly gifted philosopher focused on criticizing the Christian, in his case Catholic, philosophy of his time. "Criticism" in this context meant polemics and the unmasking of religion, as evident in a list of the titles of his early publications: "Neo-Thomism versus the Progress of Science and Human Rights," "'The Rights of the Person' versus Human Rights," "The True Meaning of 'Christian Personalism,'" "Science before the Tribunal of Obscurantism."[8] It was not just Polish Catholic philosophers whom he assailed, but to an even greater extent their foreign (French) inspirers such as the founder of personalism Emmanuel Mounier, eminent neo-Thomist Jacques Maritain and leading historian of medieval philosophy Etienne Gilson.[9] In order to defeat his opponent, the Catholic Church, Kołakowski acquired considerable knowledge of all the writings on which the latter claimed to rely, in other words, the Bible, the church fathers, scholasticism, papal pronouncements and contemporary Catholic philosophy.[10] One gets the impression that Kołakowski conceived of the Christian faith as a doctrinal edifice analogous to Marxism, with the writings of the founders at its core and what amounted to official party resolutions and elaborations as supplementary sources. Hence, his true goal was to refute the doctrines and attack the institution of the church, which championed this doctrinal edifice and used it to justify its claims to power. Christianity itself in terms of its possible contrast to the church does not even appear in this context. The church, meanwhile, is viewed chiefly in terms of power, the internal power of the priestly hierarchy and the support afforded the ruling political and economic power holders outside the church. The teachings and morals of the church, he asserts, were always tailored to these power interests, and they served primarily to turn people into subjects who were to be deterred from improving their situation in this world by the promise of an afterlife. Due to the wholly irrational nature of its teachings, beginning with the purely mythological character of its alleged founder, Jesus, Kołakowski tells us, the church is bound to be the enemy of any kind of free intellectual life and scientific progress. He thus provided the communist state and party with justification for the harshest repressive measures against the church; despite the brutality of their efforts, his writing tended to imply even more severe steps than party and state were—for tactical reasons—prepared to carry out.

If Kołakowski had stuck to this initial position, we would remember him today, if at all, as one of the most trenchant of Stalinist ideologues and church opponents of his time. In two respects, however, a dramatic change was already in the offing in the mid-1950s. One took place on the political level, while the other was the inevitable result of an inner weakness in his antireligious struggle. Politically, Kołakowski seems to have revised his image of the Soviet Union and the predictable consequences of its sociopolitical model not in reaction to the workers' unrest of 1956, the so-called Polish October, but earlier—such that he should be viewed as a precocious exponent of this turn rather than having adapted to it after the event.[11] In light of his ideas about socialism and what it ought *not* to be, Kołakowski became a hero to those opposed to the Polish regime. Socialism, he contended, should not mean a state in which people are forced to lie, where there are more spies than nurses, which produces excellent missiles but miserable shoes.[12] For him, this also meant seeking to deliver Marxism from its dogmatic rigidity and thoroughly rethinking it, above all with regard to the freedom and responsibility of the individual and in opposition to a deterministic understanding of history—as well as the absurd hubris inherent in the idea that Marxism had recognized the laws of historical development once and for all and turned them into a scientific guide for politics.

In religious terms, due to its innate character, Kołakowski's struggle was bound to fall short. Even the most powerful or convincing refutation of theological and philosophical doctrines fails to address lived faith, which is, of course, more than a mere derivative of such doctrines. This error was summed up by the great Catholic thinker and priest Józef Tischner:

> Kołakowski learned about the church from texts instead of looking at what was happening in the church across the street. . . . He did not see the concrete dimension—the concrete reality of a popularly rooted faith. He did not share in the experiences of a simple peasant and worker who, kneeling before the altar on a Sunday, in no way felt compromised in his humanity and sense of self-worth by the associated hopes. . . . While Kołakowski lived in Poland, he looked at it from a great height, from a great distance.[13]

It was to be some time, however, before Kołakowski himself grasped the weakness of his intellectualist understanding of faith.

Instead, his *second* phase revolved around taking his shift away from Stalinism further toward a consistent revision of Marxism, insofar as Marxism had legitimized the development of Stalinism and made it possible in certain forms. As mentioned above, this made it particularly vital to dismantle the pretensions of a philosophy of history that—with communist goals in mind—seemed devoid of all mercy for opponents or of any room for individual morality and responsibility outside involvement in the party's project. "Skepticism," "responsibility," "rationalism" and "commitment" became key terms within the envisaged alternative;[14] for good reasons, a young Jürgen Habermas claimed that Kołakowski was close to French existentialist philosophers Sartre and Merleau-Ponty.[15] Yet none of this weakened Kołakowski's commitment to Marxism. The great project of human self-redemption now seemed far more genuinely within reach thanks to the radical insight into the false path of Stalinism and the revision of its philosophical foundations, along with its political and economic concepts.

The details of these theoretical developments within Marxism need not detain us here. As far as religion is concerned, Kołakowski's position initially remained largely unchanged. Even in his first phase, he had been interested in possible "progressive" currents in the history of Christianity, as typical of Marxism. For him, however, all of them ultimately failed. Kołakowski described the Catholic Church's expressions of understanding for the situation of the proletariat as "crocodile tears," dismissing Catholic social teaching as an attempt to achieve "reconciliation with the factory owners" under "the merciful patronage of the pope" rather than pursue serious change and as the "sacralization of relations of oppression."[16] In the second phase of his development, Kołakowski continued to impute to the Catholic-Christian conception of freedom an opposition to human autonomy, seeing it merely as a means of subjugation to the "spiritual dictatorship" of the church.[17] Hence, for the now anti-Stalinist and still anti-Catholic thinker, his two opponents, despite their mutual enmity, moved closer together as parallel historical phenomena that could be characterized and attacked with the same vocabulary.[18] Church and party appear as organizations that have become ends in themselves and that mercilessly persecute "their heretics, dissidents, apostates and renegades."[19] In this view, standing in opposition to both religion and the totalitarian "political religion" is the human being, who insists on his freedom in the sense of autonomous self-determination and works to change social conditions—both in order to increase his own self-determination and to lay the ground for that of others. Unlike a philosophy of history that ignores the finitude of the individual human being in favor of collective progress, this view underscores the necessarily tragic character of the individual life, which never proceeds without irretrievable losses and inevitably ends in death. Yet with great pathos, the otherwise rather sardonic Kołakowski maintained that the human being, with her capacity for autonomy, must never surrender to the consolations on offer—neither those of the sacralization of history nor hopes of an afterlife. In this phase and beyond, then, Kołakowski the revisionist Marxist remained a decidedly atheist "humanist" who claimed to be "authentically areligious"—in full awareness that there is also a "false," "inauthentic" form of areligiosity. He thus wrote:

> Authentic areligiosity always grows out of an awareness of the needs to which religious symbols are a response, and out of a conscious refusal to countenance the religious ways of satisfying these needs. [Authentic areligiosity] is thus the affirmation of the human situation in the world, a situation in which reintegration into the animal world is impossible and any other kind is illusory—that is, conscious renunciation of self-deception coupled with knowledge of the situation that produces this self-deception. This kind of self-consciousness is possible only through a humanistic culture: it can illuminate the need for religious symbols, their meaning and their value, while simultaneously conveying the conviction that the values extant in human life are greater than the values of these symbols and cannot coexist with them.[20]

It is no great surprise that Kołakowski's avowal of "authentic areligiosity" is accompanied by proud declarations that access to religious experiences is closed to him; in this respect, he stated, he was talking about religion like a person with no ears talks about music.[21] From his perspective, such experiences appear as something that is in itself an aberration, an evasion of the seriousness of existence, a defeat in the struggle for autonomy. Yet from the perspective of the faithful, the very idea of a separate realm of religion is the fundamental error that inevitably leads to the exoticization, if not pathologization, of the faithful by those who lay claim to a clearer and more rational awareness of the *condition humaine*. The question is whether it would make more sense to refer to an experience of transcending the boundaries of the self, one common to all human beings, for example, through love or oneness with nature. These are experiences that may be interpreted as merely psychological or even physiological but that may also be taken seriously in their broader meaning.[22] In the shape of death and the fear of death, however, experiences of and at the limits of the self appear in a shocking rather than exhilarating form, and in the second phase of his development Kołakowski also scoured the history of philosophy to establish, for example, what advice and existential succor the ancient Stoics might offer present-day human beings, what "authentically areligious" persons might learn from them about coping with their existential lot. But another aspect is more important to Kołakowski's further development than this ultimately aporetic endeavor.[23] In his work, the hiving off of the dimension of experiences of self-transcendence and insight into the limits of an intellectualist understanding of religious faith combine to form an intellectual interest in those thinkers who emphasize experience in religion. This means the mystics and above all those among them who made their mystical practices the object of reflection, taking them into a field of tension between religious institution and doctrine, on the one hand, and their practice, along with the articulation of the associated experiences, on the other.

Kołakowski's engagement with the history of mysticism in this more specific sense, it seems to me, constitutes the *third* stage in his development.[24] This is the phase in which he devoted himself to the research that led to his great book on Christianity without the church. It is undoubtedly a Marxist book on the history of religion, but one with no intention of declaring religion a mere epiphenomenon, that is, a lesser reality than the struggles of social classes and one that must therefore be traced back entirely to and explained in light of them. In this respect, it most closely resembles the incomparably more famous study by Lucien Goldmann from the 1950s on the history of Jansenism, the philosophy of Pascal and the tragedies of Racine.[25] But Kołakowski explicitly dissociated himself from this text with an argument of much interest in our context. Goldmann, he contended, had tried to derive the Jansenists' religious ideas straightforwardly from a specific class situation, namely, that of the nonhereditary nobility under the absolutist regime of Louis XIV. But, he goes on, this attempt at derivation failed because religious ideas are never a direct expression of interests but are inevitably articulated and championed via collectives and ecclesiastical organizations ("collectivité ecclésiastique") as well as confessional struggles.[26] Kołakowski himself was much interested in the fields of tension between different organizations and forms of organization within Christianity and between a religion's proclaimed ideals and its institutional realities. He sought to create a rich typology of the variants that emerge in the Christianity of a specific era and a particular country to negotiate this tension, variants that distinguish themselves from one another, motivate individuals to convert and eventually die out. In his drive to typify, he seems to borrow from Max Weber's "ideal types," though he does not mention him in this context, despite referring to "ideal models" to characterize his own approach.

The more specific methodological questions, as fascinating as they are, need not be pursued further here, with one exception. This relates to the distinction between Kołakowski's thinking and the phenomenology of religion pursued by Max Scheler and Rudolf Otto. For the Polish philosopher, the latter approach seems to commit an error that is the mirror image of the Marxist reduction of religion to material needs. The aforementioned thinkers, he argues, assume an anthropologically universal religious need or an experience of the sacred that is in itself substantively sacred—and this, of course, is not something that a Marxist is going to concede (47, 68). In line with his eschewal of this perspective, Kołakowski sees no need to foreground religious experience in history in the manner of Otto, Scheler and the briefly mentioned William James (32); instead, we should probe the history of religious teachings about experience, the "histoire doctrinale" as he calls it in the first sentence of his book (8). His text thus offers a panorama of developmental possibilities for an institutionless

Christianity; each chapter focuses on a historical figure who is put forward as the epitome of a theoretically coherent means of resolving the aforementioned tensions. The first substantial chapter looks at Dutchman Dirk Camphuysen (1586–1627), who is presented as an "ideal model" of a radically nonconfessional Christianity, followed by, among others, Cardinal Pierre de Bérulle (1575–1629) as a mystic within the Catholic Church and Angelus Silesius (1624–77) and his mystically imbued path from Lutheranism to the Catholic Church. These figures are certainly known today, while Kołakowski's analysis saved others from oblivion. The philosopher was unfazed by the fact that the representatives of a nonconfessional Christianity and a radical concentration on mysticism were always small in number and that almost all of them played only a marginal role even in their day. He was not out to paint a representative picture in a quantitative sense but to argue that religiosity finds its purest form of expression when distanced from its institutional manifestations and must therefore be studied primarily in this form.

If it is wrong to conceive of history as the step-by-step realization of ideals, then historiography must focus on those who were most intensively seized by these ideals and most consistently oriented their lives toward them—and on Kołakowski's premises, these are certainly not the holders of institutional power within the churches but institution-skeptical religious seekers. The disappointment of (Dutch) Protestants at the development of the Reformed churches plays an important role in his account. He was therefore interested in their attempts to reform the Reformation, a "second Reformation"; he was equally preoccupied by attempts to reform the Catholic Church in the aftermath of the Reformation and schism, a process only inadequately described as the Counter-Reformation. Since he believed he could discern in mysticism the pure form of religion, he thought it crucial to distinguish between its many forms. He thus divided mysticism into theocentric, egocentric and pantheistic kinds, as exemplified by Jean de Labadie (1610–74), Antoinette Bourignon (1616–80) and Angelus Silesius. In his hands, these types never descend into ossification. He manages to produce lively portraits of historical personalities in all the contradictoriness of their situations and ideas.[27] Alongside and through these portraits, a picture also emerges of institutional reactions to anti-institutional endeavors, from the fight against the religious "subjectivism" inherent in them to attempts to grant them a place within the institution, whether sincerely or on purely tactical grounds. Kołakowski concluded that the more hierarchical and disciplined an ecclesiastical organization is, the easier it is for it to make space for the anti-institutional aspirations of mysticism (620–21), while weaker organizational structures easily lose their flexibility and capacity for action entirely under the pressure of these anti-institutional currents. In reaching this conclusion, Kołakowski is trying to deal with the fact, which seems paradoxical at first glance, that it was not the Reformed churches but the Catholic Church in which mysticism found a favorable setting in the pre-Enlightenment period (556–57). This sounds paradoxical in light of the impulses that propelled the Reformation, which were of course originally mystical in nature. But Kołakowski went so far as to refer to the "génie incomparable" with which the Catholic Church had shone in this respect (ibid.). It had, he stated, enriched itself with ideas whose initial impulses had grown out of a critique of its structures and had in fact used them to enhance its own luster.

Of course, a wealth of empirical questions arise in relation to Kołakowski's accounts and interpretations. Specialist historians have made important corrections, for example, to his interpretation of Cardinal Bérulle and Angelus Silesius,[28] while some have criticized the geographical limitations of his study and called for the inclusion of "Christians without a church" in Russia, England and North America.[29] But the key issue is of course whether a changed research situation would place a question mark over Kołakowski's conclusion that all these efforts ultimately failed. This is the deeply sobering finding with which he ends his impressive study. All paths had been explored, Kołakowski tells us, but none led to the desired goal. According to him, embedded within the attempt to establish an institutionless Christianity, a Christianity without the compromises and half measures inherent in institution building, is a contradiction that necessarily emerges as it proceeds. Those who renounce institution building eventually founder. But those who move in an institutional direction must compromise. The renunciation of institution building may preserve the ideal in a purer form for the moment. But those who take this approach will be all at sea when it comes to transmitting and collectively realizing this ideal beyond the present and small circles. This insight into the self-contradictoriness and tragedy of these attempts certainly applies not only to seventeenth-century Christians or solely to Christianity but to all religions and secular movements guided by ideals that go beyond existing social forms. Kołakowski acknowledged this failure, which in a sense also signals the failure of his own scholarly efforts, with no scorn or air of superiority. He did so with a sense of respect for those who had made heroic attempts in this vein, only to find themselves inevitably entangled in contradictions. We will, however, search in vain for the enthusiasm engendered by the uncovering of the utopian dimension of religious and political movements as embodied by Ernst Bloch.[30]

At this point, only a radical revision of Kołakowski's premises can propel him further. This, it seems to me, takes place in the *fourth* phase of his development, immediately after the conclusion of his great historical study on attempts to achieve a nonconfessional Christianity. I would characterize his new perspective as the recognition of the immanent validity of the mythical.[31] Whereas in all previous phases, despite his engagement with religion, the intellectualist and rationalist constraints on his thought were unmistakable, and even his analysis of mysticism was less about the testimonies of mystics than theological statements on mysticism, Kołakowski is now ready to acknowledge the legitimacy of questions for which there can be no scientific answer. He refers to "an indelible mythogenic situation," in which "both the role of myth in forging social ties and its integrative function within the organizing process of individual consciousness seem irreplaceable, and above all not interchangeable with beliefs governed by the criteria of scientific knowledge."[32] During this period Kołakowski was clearly engaging—though he did not document this in detail—with some of the key figures in the twentieth-century theory of religion "after Hegel and Nietzsche."[33] The influence of Mircea Eliade, Paul Tillich, Karl Jaspers and others is unmistakable. He was not suddenly asserting the anthropological necessity of religion, which would have constituted a complete turnaround in his thinking. But he recognized that rejecting a teleological or deterministic philosophy of history does not free us from the need to identify meaningful continuities in history. He saw that we cannot live an active life unless we see meaning in our endeavors and experience the world as one in which that meaning is grounded in some way beyond our own, ultimately arbitrary imposition of meaning. It was not through religion but the concept of value that he groped his way toward an understanding of the inherent validity of myth. For him, the presence of mythical consciousness comes into play whenever people think in terms of value-guided action and of history as a meaningful framework. Anyone who feels bound by a value, we might add, will want to tell stories about the discovery of this value and about how it has or has not been realized over the course of history.

It is only consistent, then, that Kołakowski vigorously opposes all moves toward radical "demythologization"—whether of Christianity or culture as a whole—from this phase of his intellectual journey onward. Yet even this plea for the indispensability of the mythical-narrative dimension within the realm of personal conduct and in a culture's understanding of both history and the present cannot escape the question of the legitimacy of a single, specific narrative. At this point in his development, however, Kołakowski was so intensely focused on distancing himself from the rationalist rejection of the mythical as such that he was unable to come up with a truly satisfactory way of illuminating the "truth" of myth. Against all irrationalism, he argued that it was vital to maintain a "permanent suspicion" toward myth, just as it was crucial to ensure its transmission. Cultures, he contended, need both "custodians of myth" and "critics of myth," a distinction reminiscent of that between priests and prophets in the history of religion and of that between priests and fools in the author's own writings.[34] What was missing from Kołakowski's work at this point—an element vital to resolving the issue of the truth of myth—is reflection on the historical decoupling of this very issue from myth in what Karl Jaspers called the "Axial Age." We can never do justice to a religion such as Christianity, which is based on this decoupling, if we describe it solely as myth. Christianity does indeed make a claim to truth, although not in a way that diminishes truth to the status of rational-argumentative truth.[35]

As mentioned in the Introduction, in the second half of the 1960s Kołakowski was not only ejected from the Polish Communist Party (PVAP) and then his chair at Warsaw University, but he was also forced to leave the country permanently (rather than formally emigrate). After some turbulent years of transition, he found excellent academic working conditions at Oxford University and on the Committee on Social Thought at the University of Chicago. When Theodor Adorno died unexpectedly in 1969, Jürgen Habermas proposed him as his successor at the University of Frankfurt, but this was scuppered by the resistance of far-left philosophy students at that institution.[36] A year at Berkeley at the height of the student movement prompted Kołakowski to permanently abjure its aspirations.[37] These experiences resulted in his final departure from Marxism in all its variants, including the Western ones. This marked the beginning of the *fifth* phase of his development with respect to religion, one characterized by a complex dilemma. His book on myth could already be read as a plea for the functional necessity of religion in an anthropological sense. Kołakowski's emphasis on the high value of European cultural traditions and the indispensable contribution that Christianity, and especially the Catholic Church, had made to this culture became ever stronger following his permanent departure from Poland. He now recognized not just Jesus and not just "Christians without a Church," but the church itself. Of course, this has a different ring to it when it comes from believing Christians rather than an "authentically areligious" scholar. While a fair number of important nineteenth- and twentieth-century thinkers forthrightly promoted Christianity as a cultural force, even in the present, despite having no personal Christian faith, Kołakowski was too smart and honest for that. He criticized all those intellectuals who—as nonbelievers—defended faith as an educational and moral force. Of course, he did so not in order to assail their lack of religious faith but to throw cold water on their assumption that they could contribute to the change they propagated, "because to spread faith, faith is needed and not an intellectual assertion of the social utility of faith."[38]

Yet even the clear recognition of a dilemma does not free one from it. Kołakowski's texts during this phase are deeply ambiguous. He frequently sounds like a conservative or even reactionary cultural critic, yet often playfully and elusively undoes this impression in the same text. In the turbulent era of the Solidarność movement and the collapse of communism, Polish Catholic intellectuals especially—with some exceptions—increasingly attacked this ambiguity. But even those among this circle who continued to live and advocate Kołakowski's authentic areligiosity now found his ideas hard to swallow.[39]

In the West too, however, irritation with Kołakowski grew in two key areas. One was centered on the self-reform of the Catholic Church; the other, on Europe's role in the world. Many found it more than passing strange that this former opponent of the church, far from nodding in approval at the *aggiornamento* initiated by Pope John XXIII and the reforms subsequently introduced by the Second Vatican Council, instead penned a polemic in 1973,[40] which dismissed them as a mere adaptation to the zeitgeist, as the church's renunciation of its key role as bastion of the sacred in an increasingly shallow, merely profane culture. Here Kołakowski stood up for the "real existing" church more than many of the Christians did who professed loyalty to it. As they were by his views in this regard, many were understandably surprised by this former communist's repeated and polemical rejection of the burgeoning critique of the European "subjugation of the world" (Wolfgang Reinhard) within the history of colonialism and imperialism, which he consciously countered by composing a paean to Eurocentrism—albeit one that foregrounded the capacity for self-critique in Europe.[41]

In both cases, it seems to me that the views he advocated were not simply those of a "renegade" who was now overshooting the mark in rejecting his former convictions much as he had previously done in defending them. In both cases, Kołakowski's convictions point to deeper problems. When it comes to the churches, few will deny that we can indeed discern cases of "self-secularization" (Wolfgang Huber), of superficialization and adaptation to the zeitgeist. But it is too simple to take these phenomena as representative of the whole. The emancipation of women and homosexuals are epoch-making phenomena, not passing fads that can be ignored or weathered. Rather than the result of a weakening commitment to values or rampant relativism, they are fruits of an increased orientation toward the "sacredness of the person" and thus a core aspect of Christianity. No one has captured this as concisely as Polish Catholic intellectual and politician Tadeusz Mazowiecki: "For what has happened in Christianity is more than just . . . the desire not to be left behind, to be equally enlightened and no less modern. This was certainly the case. But something else was happening before our eyes. An act of truth was taking place, the recognition of values once negated, of the secular origin of values that had arisen outside the church and Christianity. The history of the church's relationship to human rights is a prime example of this."[42]

When it comes to the just assessment of Europe's historical role in the world, Kołakowski's turn away from the communists' anti-imperialist propaganda and its rehashed version in the student movement may be understandable. But with each step toward overcoming the mere equation of "Europe" and "Christianity," the need to measure Europe by Christian standards increases—we cannot simply celebrate Christian Europe but must glean from Christianity the driving force for a European self-critique.[43] It is true that, in light of his experience of totalitarianism,

Kołakowski expressed skepticism about a future European superstate and rejected the European constitution put forward in 2004–5. But we should also carefully consider the legitimacy of a critique of Europe or the West that takes seriously the experience of, for example, the colonized countries and all the victims of European expansion.

It is not obvious to me that Kołakowski truly found a way out of the dilemma I have described at this or any later stage of his development. What I mean, of course, is a philosophical or theory-of-religion solution to the problems he raised. As I see it, the prerequisite for such a solution would be greater differentiation between "morality" and "religion" or, perhaps better, between the "restrictiveness" of norms as opposed to the "attractiveness" of values. Only then does it become understandable that secularization in the sense of a weakening of religion does not lead, let alone inevitably leads, to moral relativism or moral decay.[44] Only then do we gain a strengthened awareness of new impulses toward the universalist sacralization of the person. The elements of this solution can certainly be found in Kołakowski's writings. For example, he recognized the inner connection between pragmatist epistemology and mysticism early on. In one of his most famous texts, "The Priest and the Jester," we read: "Pragmatism stands in opposition to realistic epistemologies just as mystical theology stood in opposition to speculative theology."[45] But these elements are never truly linked in Kołakowski's work. This may be due to his oft-stated aversion to highly systematic thinking. In any case, though we find flashes of deep insight scattered throughout a miscellaneous range of texts in his late work, even when these are combined into books,[46] Kołakowski, intentionally or unintentionally, fails to truly clarify the connection between them. He does not declare his thinking to be "post-metaphysical" as does Jürgen Habermas: he does not evade the need to grapple with metaphysical questions. But he answers them only in fragments.

The question of whether he ultimately found his way to the Christian faith itself was put to Kołakowski in countless interviews. He always refused to answer it, and when asked why, he explained that any response he might give would reveal how he would answer the "Gretchen question" itself. As early as 1989, however, he stated in a Polish interview that God already knew the answer.[47] In the case of any other thinker, this would induce a compelling logical conclusion about his personal faith. Delighting in the role of "jester," however, Kołakowski keeps us guessing.[48]

8

Human Dignity

The Religion of Modernity?

My argument begins with reference to a key event in the intellectual and political history of Europe, which occurred in the last few years of the nineteenth century. The year was 1898; the location, France. This year saw the birth of both the French Human Rights League and the ultranationalist, proto-fascist and anti-Semitic Action Française. Both movements were outcomes of the same conflict, which rocked the country and almost split it into two camps—the so-called Affaire Dreyfus. In December 1894, the Jewish-Alsatian artillery captain and general staff officer Alfred Dreyfus was accused of high treason, that is, of passing defense secrets to Germany, dishonorably discharged from the French army and sentenced to lifelong deportation to Devil's Island. In the years after his conviction, more and more doubts arose regarding the evidence adduced against him and the rightfulness of the court's decision. In 1897, the judgment was appealed, and from then on (but particularly after the sensational open letter by Émile Zola addressed to the president of the republic, published January 13, 1898, with its blaring headline "J'accuse") what had been a matter for the judiciary turned into a political affair of the highest order. On February 20, 1898, the Human Rights League was founded. Initially, its sole aim was to achieve a retrial and prevent the "honor of the army" or latent anti-Semitism from tipping the balance against the probably innocent captain. In early September 1898, the chain of events reached its dramatic climax when it emerged that the director of the military secret service had been arrested in late August and confessed to having falsified a decisive document incriminating Dreyfus. A day after his confession, he took his own life in jail. After this sensation, Dreyfus's conviction was, of course, no longer tenable. It was at first annulled, then commuted to a mere prison sentence, for which Dreyfus received an amnesty enabling his immediate release. It was only years later, in 1906, that Dreyfus was finally acquitted, but in such a way that some remained unconvinced of his innocence despite all the evidence.

The enormous emotion and polarization triggered by these events have been documented in innumerable writings, including works of great literature, ranging from Marcel Proust to Roger Martin du Gard. In her book on totalitarianism, Hannah Arendt claimed that late nineteenth-century France prefigured the political cleavages of the twentieth century in much the same way as the French Revolution foreshadowed nineteenth-century history.[1] This certainly applies to the Dreyfus affair. It also applies to the spread and intellectual penetration of the belief in human rights and to the radical rejection of this belief.

The most intellectually consistent argument produced thus far concerning why we should regard belief in human rights and universal human dignity as the "religion of modernity" resulted from this conflict. The author of this text was the greatest French sociologist, one of the classical figures of the nascent discipline, Émile Durkheim. He was a founding member of the Human Rights League and secretary of its Bordeaux chapter.[2] Articles such as Charles Maurras's "The First Blood,"[3] which agitated for struggle against the Dreyfusards even if Dreyfus should be innocent, resulted from the same context. For Maurras, the rights of the individual or human dignity are minor concerns when an institution such as the army or the well-being of the nation is at stake. A violation of these rights, even a lie or falsification, is then justified in a higher sense—or, rather, requires no justification. Just as Mussolini later encouraged his fascist militias to engage in violence without even maintaining the facade of instrumental or moral justification, this entails crossing a line, one that twentieth-century fascist movements were to scornfully and systematically ignore. It is important to underline the twofold character of the intellectual reactions to the Dreyfus conflict, because awareness of this ambiguity helps guard against the drawing of unfounded optimistic conclusions on the basis of certain affinities between the structures of modern societies and the belief in human dignity, affinities to which I shall now turn.

Durkheim kicks off his argument, which is intended to demonstrate the "sacredness" of the individual in modernity, by highlighting the profound ambiguity of the term "individualism." He considers this a pressing matter because the so-called anti-Dreyfusards accused all those willing to accept the weakening of the army's authority and who "obstinately refuse to bend their logic before the word of an army general" of promoting "individualism."[4] In this view, such individualism would mean the end of all social order and sense of commonality; it was the "great sickness of the present age" (43). Durkheim concedes that such a destructive, anarchic individualism does indeed exist. According to him, it can be found whenever individuals lack a higher goal than maximization of egotistical pleasure or economic utility. He yields to no one in his criticism of such individualism. But he regards it as completely unacceptable to identify this type of individualism in any way with the moral philosophy of Kant or Rousseau or the individualism "which the Declaration of the Rights of Man attempted, more or less happily, to formulate" (45).

Such sentiments suggest that this second type of individualism is more or less the opposite of the egotistical variety; interests of a merely personal nature are viewed with skepticism or, as in Kant, almost as the source of evil. Such individualism has nothing in common with "that apotheosis of well-being and private interest" and "that egoistic cult of the self for which utilitarian individualism has been rightly criticized" (45).

Individualists of this second type, far from abandoning themselves to the impulses arising from their pregiven nature, gear themselves toward an ambitious ideal, that of acting in a way of which all human beings might in principle approve or, to put it philosophically, such that the maxim underlying their action is amenable to universalization. Durkheim wrote:

> This ideal so far surpasses the level of utilitarian goals that it seems to those minds who aspire to it to be completely stamped with religiosity. This human person (*personne humaine*), the definition of which is like the touchstone which distinguishes good from evil, is considered sacred in the ritual sense of the word. It partakes of the transcendent majesty that churches of all time lend to their gods; it is conceived of as being invested with that mysterious property which creates a void about sacred things, which removes them from vulgar contacts and withdraws them from common circulation. And the respect which is given it comes precisely from this

source. Whoever makes an attempt on a man's life, on a man's liberty, on a man's honor, inspires in us a feeling of horror analogous in every way to that which the believer experiences when he sees his idol profaned. Such an ethic is therefore not simply a hygienic discipline or a prudent economy of existence; it is a religion in which man is at once the worshiper and the god. (45–46)

Following this long quotation, we should pause for a moment for the sake of conceptual clarification. I find the distinction between two types of individualism convincing, although one would have to pin down more precisely what constitutes purely egotistical individualism. Even the utilitarian paradigm that Durkheim clearly had in mind here cannot be dismissed as readily as he implied. Moreover, we would have to add a third version of individualism that goes beyond the Kantian moralistic version, a Herderian variety for which not moral duty but self-realization is the guiding value. This expressivist-romantic alternative does not occur to Durkheim at all.[5] But his own distinction between types of individualism is certainly important even today and is an advance on his own earlier attacks on the destructive effects of individualism.

Furthermore, Durkheim speaks of the "sacrality" or "sacredness" of the person. He does not refer to Kant here, although he could have done so, because Kant speaks of sacredness at precisely the point where he introduces the concept of *dignity* (in his *Grundlegung zur Metaphysik der Sitten*). For Kant, dignity is that which is and must be priceless; it is "exalted above all price and so admits of no equivalent."[6] It is impossible to compare the mode of thought characteristic of the concept of dignity with that relating to the prices of goods "without, as it were, violating its holiness."[7]

But that which is a mere momentary conceptual intuition in Kant's work is for Durkheim the point of departure for his developing theory of religion and for the idea that the person himself has become the sacred object of modern societies. I will return to this point shortly.

Two additional conceptual clarifications are necessary. Durkheim speaks alternately of the sacredness of the individual and of the person, as if these two concepts were interchangeable. If there is no risk of the concept of the individual being misunderstood along utilitarian and egotistical lines, this is unproblematic. Durkheim can then interpret the cult of the individual for the sake of the individual as a superstitious and decadent form of authentic individualism. I refer to the sacredness of the *person* rather than that of the *individual* to make completely sure that the belief in the irreducible dignity of all human beings is not conflated with an egocentric self-sacralization of the individual, a narcissist inability to transcend one's self-centeredness.

Durkheim thus articulates the belief in human rights and human dignity as the expression of a process of the sacralization of the person. In this sense, his ascription to the person of the same aura characteristic of all sacred objects is understandable and apt. But Durkheim characteristically overstates his case when he calls the morality of human rights a religion "in which man is at once the worshiper and the god." By demonstrating the fruitfulness of his idea of the sacredness of the person, he has by no means shown that human beings are the source of their own sacralization. Durkheim, the rabbi's son, allows his programmatic atheism to distort his argument here. If we take this lacuna in his argument to be symptomatic, we can say that his atheism was dogmatic. Durkheim fails to open himself to the possibility that belief in the sacredness of the person can have competing origins; he is closed to the idea that religion might in the future support human rights. This will become even clearer in what follows.

Durkheim's next step is an attempt to demonstrate that such a belief, which he calls, following Auguste Comte, "la religion de l'humanité," the religion of mankind or humanity, is assuredly capable of integrating whole societies. In his book on the division of labor, he had still defended a different assumption: "the cult of the individual" is an anomaly among beliefs and values because it directs the will toward a common goal that is not social and thus cannot contribute to the formation of authentic social bonds.[8] Durkheim has now overcome his earlier skepticism: he has recognized the difference between glorification of one's own ego and the sacralization of the human person as such. "It springs not from egoism but from sympathy for all that is human, a broader pity for all sufferings, for all human miseries, a more ardent need to combat them and mitigate them, a greater thirst for justice" (48–49). Durkheim then briefly rejects the possible objection that freedom of opinion leads to anarchy by demonstrating how scientific discourse, given absolute freedom of thought, is fully capable of generating consensus and rational authority. He then goes one decisive step further. For him, the sacredness of the person is not just one possible belief system with socially integrative effects but the only system of beliefs that can "ensure the moral unity of the country" (50) in the future. This far-reaching claim imposes on Durkheim a dual burden of proof. On the one hand, he must show that modern societies have certain structural features that make it functionally necessary to generate social integration by means of moral individualism. On the other hand, he must delineate the relationship between this moral individualism and traditional religions. His contribution to the Dreyfus debate, of course, fails to cover either point in real depth.

Nonetheless, his basic line of argument is fairly clear, and it is to this that we must now turn. There can be no doubt that Durkheim, the alleged functionalist, has no time for those who champion the strengthening of religion in order to increase social harmony. And it is indeed true that nobody can become a religious believer just because it would be socially advantageous were she to do so.[9] Although it is a sociological truism that "a society cannot be coherent if there does not exist among its members a certain intellectual and moral community" (51), pleas for community do little to bring it about. Moreover, it might be that in new circumstances old forms of community are no longer viable so that pleas for a return to old forms of social integration frequently involve the articulation of a problem rather than a solution. For Durkheim, the only solution is the sacralization of the person, because it is the only way of reconstituting the social bond that avoids flying in the face of the very structural tendencies that made maintenance of the traditional bonds impossible. Two such structural tendencies are mentioned: the territorial expansion of societies and the advancing division of labor. The larger a society is in a spatial sense, the more difficult it is, according to Durkheim, to achieve uniformity of traditions and practices. One might add that this remains irrelevant as long as there is no interaction between the inhabitants of different parts of a country. But as soon as this interaction, and commerce, increases, differences must be tolerated or systematically repressed. If they are tolerated, there will be many variants rather than one unitary culture. The increasing division of labor reinforces this tendency even in small regions. Professional specialization, for example, gives rise to different skills, competencies, attitudes and perspectives. Division of labor and territorial expansion thus lead to a state of affairs in which people are less and less able to identify with one another on the basis of particular features they have in common. The only source of a shared culture is then "this idea of the human person . . . the only idea which would be retained, unalterable and impersonal, above the changing torrent of individual opinions" (51–52).

And what is the relationship between this idea and the Christian faith? Durkheim assumes that this conception of the human person is a contemporary articulation of the impulses that originally brought Christianity into being:

> Whereas the religion of the ancient city-state was quite entirely made of external practices, from which the spiritual was absent, Christianity demonstrated in its inner faith, in the personal conviction of the individual, the essential condition of piety. First, it taught that the moral value of acts had to be measured according to the intention, a preeminently inward thing which by its very nature escapes all external judgments and which only the agent could competently appraise. The very center of moral life was thus transported from the external to the internal, and the individual was thus elevated to be sovereign judge of his own conduct, accountable only to himself and to his God. (52)

Christianity's importance to the cultural prerequisites for the emergence of modern individualism thus cannot be exaggerated. Durkheim took a great interest in these cultural processes, with regard, for example, to the concept of the *soul* in Christianity and its continuity with ideas found in "primitive" religions,[10] the role of Christianity in the history of education in the Occident and legal history. In his political-moral declaration of 1898, he consequently rejects any assumption that he favors breaking with the Christian tradition. On the contrary, he presents his plea for human rights as a continuation of that tradition. But for him, to continue a tradition is to overcome it. From this viewpoint, Christianity is a form of "restrained individualism" and now has to be replaced by "a more fully developed individualism" (53). The belief in human rights is thus not embedded in Christianity; it is to take the place of that religion, which is claimed merely to have laid the ground for this modern faith.

Sociology after Durkheim has produced a wealth of studies and reflections on the potential functions of a belief in human rights and human dignity under modern conditions and on the expression of this belief in everyday social interaction. In the main, Durkheim emphasized the division of labor or functional differentiation between actors and societal subsystems as the main feature of modern societies. His reference to territorial scope played only a secondary role because he generally considered size and density prerequisites for setting in motion processes of differentiation. The sociological literature after Durkheim goes further than he did in emphasizing the importance of cultural pluralism in general—a pluralism that is not necessarily the result of functional differentiation but that might also come about in other ways, for example, through migration, value change and cultural diffusion. But there is no doubt that functional differentiation increases the need for integrative resources—what Talcott Parsons called "societal community," an expression that must sound paradoxical if one assumes that there is a dichotomous distinction between "community" and "society." In our time, Niklas Luhmann (in his book *Law as a Social System*) has radicalized Durkheim's approach. For Luhmann, a strict causal connection exists between increasing functional differentiation and the codification of subjective rights; the former leads to the growing autonomy of the individual subsystems and increasingly reduces human beings to mere elements of the environment of systems rather than assuming that they are constitutive of them. The individual, according to Luhmann, "is provided with subjective rights as a compensation for the loss of all that was certain before": the legal system thus "functions largely . . . to cushion the consequences that the restructuring of society towards functional differentiation has on the individual."[11] For Luhmann, this functional relationship makes it entirely predictable and plausible that human rights would be codified for the first time during a period when functional differentiation was advancing with particular vigor, namely, during what is called the *Sattelzeit* around 1800. For Luhmann, it also stands to reason that today at a time of so-called globalization—another step forward in the global division of labor—the institutionalization of human rights is also advancing.

But one might object that such a bird's-eye perspective completely fails to bring out the concrete historical processes that led to the emergence and dissemination of human rights. The alleged functional relationships, as plausible as they might be, were certainly not evident to the historical actors. It would be terribly reductionist, therefore, to assume that questions such as whether human rights spring from religious or nonreligious roots can thus be declared settled or irrelevant. Durkheim himself paved the way for an additional and alternative view. The individualism he was talking about was—in his eyes—not so much a philosophical system but one of a "practical and not theoretical nature. If individualism is to be what it is, it must penetrate the mores and the organs of society."[12] Like every religion, the religion of humanity should be judged not by its dogmas but by its practices, its rituals. In two areas, Durkheim himself undertook pioneering efforts to apply these insights. First, he had a strong interest in how the role of punitive justice had changed on the way to modernity.[13] Killing, which we moderns take to be the most abominable of crimes, particularly if it is arbitrary or cruel, was not always thought of in this way. In premodern societies, whose sacred core does not revolve around the human person, this evaluation is absent. There, the worst crimes are violations of the transcendent or mundane incarnation of the sacred, such as blasphemy, sacrilege or regicide. It is not only the evaluation of actions that changes dramatically within the framework of these processes but also ideas about punishment. Torture as a means of producing confessions or as punishment in public is increasingly experienced as incompatible with the dignity of humans, including criminals. The whole system of punitive justice changes, becoming more oriented toward imprisonment or resocialization; it undergoes a process of humanization. This is a far from simple or linear process. One need think only of the persistence of "lynching" in the racist milieu of the US South well into the twentieth century. Opinions on whether the death penalty as such is cruel or only certain forms of execution are differ markedly not only between Europeans and Americans but also among Americans. Many contemporary readers learn about this process from Michel Foucault's famous book *Discipline and Punish*, which uncovers the downside of modern forms of punitive justice in impressive fashion, but in a way that practically negates the civilizational progress that this process nonetheless entails.[14]

The other field of research to which Durkheim himself contributed in this regard is concerned with the changing culture of rational argumentation. Science, for him, is one aspect of the development of moral individualism—not the most fundamental aspect but an important one. Science, too, is based on a belief in the essential worth of each individual. A "dogma" of this faith is the autonomy of reason, its "rite" the freedom to verify all claims to validity (49). The American pragmatists developed this insight even further, concluding that since no one can predict where cognitive innovation might arise, the social status of the speaker is irrelevant; each proposition must be examined according to the validity of its truth claims.

Durkheim's own research methods, however, focused on the *institutions* of law and science rather than on their *practice*. He did not deal microscopically with topics such as the legal knowledge of actors, the structures of legal discourse or the dynamics of scientific argumentation. Since Durkheim, both sociology and history have moved in this direction. This microscopic analysis is particularly important when dealing with the sacralization of the person in everyday life, in rules of greeting, interaction rituals, mutual face-saving in conflicts, politeness and so on. Erving Goffman's writings can be read as Machiavellian guidebooks for strategic impression management but also as studies of the sacralization of the person in everyday life.[15] An abundance of other examples exists. The interaction between doctors and patients is changing, as the latter increasingly demand respect. One generation ago, medical paternalism allowed or even recommended keeping patients in the dark about certain diagnoses (as in the case of cancer) or therapies. Today, surgery without the informed consent of the patient is considered a crime. Increased public awareness of sexual harassment, child pornography or sexual abuse of children by pedophile priests is not the result of an increase in these offenses but of increasing sensitivity to the destructive character of such acts. All public discourse on loss of values must be balanced by taking into account these examples of increasing moral sensitization.

The connection I have in mind between the sacralization of the person and intense experiences can be illustrated by turning to the field of sexuality. In an almost unknown text, the summary of a debate in Paris in 1911 on problems of sexual education, we can detect Durkheim's position on this matter.[16] He found himself confronted by medical doctors for whom sexuality was nothing but a bodily process and who propagated the radical dismantling of what they saw as a web of prejudices, norms and fantasies surrounding this process. Although Durkheim was firmly in favor of sexual education, he was against such a reductionist conception of sexuality. As a sociologist, he could not disregard the fact that in all cultures sexuality has an aura of the "mysterious"; a truly rational interpretation, he thought, should never consider such an aura a mere prejudice. Sexuality, he states, has a double character, being anti-moral and constitutive of morality at one and the same time. I am aware of the risk of being misunderstood here. Reference to the anti-moral character of sexuality sounds like prudishness today. But if we accept—against Norbert Elias—the finding of cultural anthropologists that shame is culturally universal and sexual activity does not take place in public even in cultures in which nakedness is the norm, then Durkheim is right to describe the transgression of the boundaries of shame as one of the features of sexuality. Insofar as shame is not only an empirically verifiable psychological phenomenon but also a virtue in all cultures, though certainly not to the same extent, we might state that sexuality always negates this virtue to some degree. But as I have said, sexuality is also constitutive of morality; the sexual act, in Durkheim's own words, is "foncièrement moralisateur,"[17] "profoundly constitutive of morality." This might sound even stranger today than the notion of the amoral character of sexuality. Sexual experience is constitutive of morality because it is one of the most important sources of deep-seated affective ties among human beings. A merely biological perspective fails to do justice to the way in which shared sexual experience generates social bonds, distorting the specifically human character of sexuality.

All cultures therefore fence in sexuality with specific institutions and ideas. In an age of increasing sacralization of the person, this "fencing in" is growing in importance. This might sound implausible, given all the talk of sexual liberalization today. But the term "liberalization" fails to capture the increasing sensitivity to sexual abuse and harassment referred to previously. If we take seriously the parallel between the aura of sacred objects and the aura of the person under the condition of sacralization, we can see why physically approaching another person without following certain prescribed rules is experienced as profanation. Respect for the sacredness of the person entails respect for the free will of the other. Physical distance is an expression of such respect, and sexuality tends to abolish this distance. It might lead to the experience of communion, a fusion with another person that negates, for an ecstatic moment, the boundaries separating our identities. This is the experience of self-transcendence that gives rise to attachment to others as well as to values. It is not surprising then that sexual relations change under the influence of the sacralization of the person.

This example leads on to the complex question of how the different levels of the sacralization of the person interconnect. When Durkheim speaks of the belief in human dignity as the "religion" of modernity, he is thinking of a belief system but also its manifestation in law and other institutions and in everyday practices of public and intimate interaction. But it is far from clear that he successfully analyzes the interconnection of these levels and identifies the historical and existential foundations of the ideal of moral individualism. There is much disagreement over whether the notion of the "religion" of modernity is appropriate in the first place. It is true that human dignity is not simply a moral and normative imperative but an ideal with an intense affective charge. But this "religion" lacks a cult in the sense of special rituals or a genuine church, a community of the faithful. This is not because this individualist ideal has no need of such practical and institutional supports. Durkheim himself had no real answer to the question of which institutions might undergird it. He was forced to tackle this question precisely because his original progressive optimism gradually came to seem implausible. His study of the elementary forms of religious life, primarily totemism, was clearly motivated by these questions. But in a sense he never really returned from his imaginary research trips among the Australian Aborigines and North American Indians. He ascribes to the democratic state and professional associations, revitalized on the model of the guilds, a key role in embodying and maintaining this ideal. But this cannot be the last word on this, not only because his political objectives with respect to professional groups remained ridden with aporiae but also because his solution was overly abstract. We need to grapple far more concretely with existing religious and national traditions and historical experiences if we wish to do justice to the interplay among state, civil society and values in the history of human rights.

With regard to national traditions, Durkheim focused on the case of France. He saw a continuity between the principles of 1789 and the struggle for human rights in France in his own time:

> And if there is a country among all others where the cause of individualism is truly national, it is our own; for there is no other which has created such rigorous solidarity between its fate and the fate of these ideas. We have given them their most recent formulation, and it is from us that other peoples have received them. And this is why even now we are considered their most authoritative representatives. Therefore we cannot disavow them today without disavowing ourselves, without diminishing ourselves in the eyes of the world, without committing a veritable moral suicide. (54)

As impressive as this plea might have sounded in France, the fusion of universalism and French nationalism can only be perceived skeptically beyond its borders. US missionary universalism is a parallel phenomenon; in both cases, national interests are frequently couched in universalist terms. But in both countries, there are indeed public rituals, symbols, myths and institutions that support moral individualism in the Durkheimian sense.

Durkheim's ideas with respect to religious traditions were far less compelling. He was right to claim that such traditions must be continued in creative ways; that new forms of moral individualism exert a certain pressure on them to express and articulate themselves anew. We tend to think of Islam in this respect today, but we should not forget how difficult it was as well for Catholicism and much of European Protestantism to develop a positive relationship to human rights, religious freedom, democracy, market economics and world peace. From 1791 on, the official doctrine of the Catholic Church assailed human rights because they were perceived as an aspect of the anticlerical and antireligious heritage of the French Revolution; the church supported the anti-Dreyfusards in the Dreyfus affair. This changed only in the mid-twentieth century. Durkheim's attempt to describe Christianity as an obsolete forerunner of the secular religion of modernity is, in my view, the flipside of an antimodernist self-understanding of the church.

But we do not have to choose between these two options. It is possible for religion to be individualized if the churches accept individuals' increasing demand for moral self-determination and self-realization. The spirit of the Gospel could thus support the struggle for human rights; and this support is needed, because this struggle is not over. My emphasis on the complex interplay of values, institutions and practices is intended to underline that the realization of these ideals is never guaranteed. Durkheim's historical optimism is untenable if we take the experiences of the twentieth century seriously. For him, the structure of modern societies makes the institutionalization of human rights inevitable. "For in order to halt its advance it would be necessary . . . to contain . . . the tendency for societies to become always more extended and more centralized, and to place an obstacle in the way of the unceasing progress of the division of labor. Such an enterprise, whether desirable or not, infinitely exceeds all human capability" (52). After the twentieth century, we have to make clear that Durkheim was too optimistic in this respect. The proto-fascist Action Française might have shown little creativity and enjoyed little success, but Italian fascism and German Nazism were not simply antimodernist.

They were attempts to develop alternative modernities without the values articulated in the human rights catalogues. We do not know whether the twenty-first century will see new attempts of this kind. Thus, the institutionalization of human rights remains dependent on the active support of each new generation.

9

Is Human Dignity Still Our Supreme Value?

Are human rights and respect for human dignity secure in today's world, or do they face new threats? This question was put to me at a dinner to which the financially powerful sponsor of an American university had invited me at his house following a lecture. "There are certainly threats," was my answer. Nothing is historically certain in the long run. As a German with the history of National Socialism and the Holocaust burned into my consciousness, I explained, I am incapable of thinking otherwise and feel an absolute obligation to affirm this historical contingency. Yes, came the reply, but do these dangers exist in the old democracies of the West as well? Carefully, so as not to spoil the atmosphere at dinner, I spoke in quite abstract terms about the tensions between values, for example, between national security and human dignity, in the United States as elsewhere. Only after further insistence did I utter the word "Guantanamo." "We're defending our citizens' human rights at Guantanamo," replied the host, raising his voice.

This statement has been echoing through my mind for some time. How is it best answered? Is it inherently contradictory, because as soon as we talk about human rights, we can no longer think only of "our citizens"? Is it justified when the lives and rights of one's fellow citizens are in fact threatened by terrorism or war? Does this statement show that the use of these terms has become or always has been arbitrary?

Many people today have no time for references to human dignity. What appears to some as the epitome of an embryonic global ethics, as perhaps the only possible means of agreeing on a concept of the good in culturally plural societies, is denounced by others as political hypocrisy, waved aside as an empty, nonbinding notion or (as in a commentary on the German constitution) viewed with suspicion as a "gateway [through which] certain particularist ethics or political views" can infiltrate the rational systematics of constitutional law. None of these fears is entirely groundless. Yet a look at the history of the term "human dignity" reveals a different picture.

Historically, the term "dignity" typically served to assign a specific rank to certain individuals or social groups and thus place them in a hierarchy, whereas "human dignity" is an attempt to convey a quality inherent in all human beings and in humanity as a whole, that is, the idea of the person as the bearer of subjective inalienable rights. "Human dignity" is an attribute of all human beings without exception. It is not acquired through achievements and cannot be forfeited through a loss of capacity or violations of others' human dignity.

Because of the centrality of the postulate of human dignity in German constitutional discourse, the concept's history has been thoroughly researched. While views may differ on some of the details, we can discern an overall consensus. After its beginnings in Roman antiquity (Stoicism), the major roles in this context have been played by Christian notions of human beings as made in the image of God and as the children of God; ideas within Italian humanism about human beings' self-creative potential; debates in colonial ethics following the "discovery" of the New World; and later, increasingly, a philosophical understanding of reason. Here the thought of Immanuel Kant plays a preeminent role.

For Kant, the dignity of humanity is rooted in the moral nature of the human being. He makes a sharp distinction between "dignity" and "price," foregrounding unconditional validity to counter any tendency to relativize.

Kant himself occasionally referred to "sacredness": according to him, dignity is that which is and must be priceless; it is "exalted above all price and admits of no equivalent." For him, it is impossible to relate dignity to the prices of goods "without, as it were, violating its holiness."[1] This idea, which is also inherent in the term "inviolability," became the starting point for a new perspective in the late nineteenth century—in the work of Émile Durkheim, founder of French sociology. From this vantage point, philosophical justification is one thing, while attention to the manifold processes through which people ascribe supreme value in the first place—to nation, church or scholarly endeavor—is another. Within this framework, the history of human dignity is the history of social and cultural processes through which the person as such, each and every person, is ascribed such supreme value. We might call this the sacralization of the person.

Torture and slavery, for example, which were long justified, including by many Christians, thus become recognizable as intolerable offenses against human dignity. This diminishes the significance of the terminology used in specific instances. Some may refer to human dignity but are not really driven by this sacredness of the person. Others are driven by it but use other terms to articulate their sense of value. No religious or secular tradition, then, has a monopoly on human dignity. Many traditions, both religious and secular, can interface with something that has been conceptualized as human dignity in the European tradition.[2]

More than in most philosophical literature, the social preconditions for realizing the postulate of universal human dignity came into play when the workers' movement of the nineteenth and twentieth centuries took up the struggle against conditions unworthy of human beings and sought to achieve an "existence worthy of the human being" (Ferdinand Lassalle). Experiences of human disenfranchisement and degradation—through National Socialism and fascism, communism, colonialism and imperialism—have increasingly turned the idea denoted by "human dignity" into a symbol of hope. Warnings against its inflationary use or legal vagueness fail to do justice to attempts to articulate the sacredness of the person.

Such attempts at articulation are inherently expansive in nature. They sensitize us to grievances and injustices that we might otherwise fail to perceive or perceive insufficiently. When, for example, gay people demand thoroughgoing equality and do so with reference to human rights and human dignity, they are certainly acting in a way not foreseen by the authors of many a document in the history of human rights. But this as such does not diminish the legitimacy of their demands. When people in Bangladesh die in the workplaces where they produce our garments, it rouses us from the complacency with which we refer to securing decent working conditions in the Global North. The discourse on human dignity contains a prophetic potential that always points beyond existing law. It must not be silenced by Western triumphalism[3]—any more than by a detached, cynical realpolitik asserting that the only factor shaping history is the ruthless struggle for power and advantage. Of course, the notion of human dignity is not immune to hypocritical use. But this is true of all values and rights.

And what of Guantanamo, an extraterritorial political prison where people are held without trial for well over a decade with no prospect of getting one and force-fed when they express their despair through hunger strikes? I should have replied to that genial and generous American host that his comments embody a failure to grasp the very thing on which the West bases its pride.

10

The Church as Moral Agency?

The churches in Germany cannot currently complain about a lack of public attention. Amid the so-called refugee crisis from the summer of 2015 onward, they made a huge splash with their eye-catching campaigns and appeals. Of course, not all the attention they receive is propelled by benevolent motives. Although the reactions of the media and many people in Germany to Pope Francis's personal style and initial actions and statements were extremely positive, we all know how quickly the popularity of public figures can nose-dive. Signs of a shift, then, should not be overlooked. In the Protestant realm, for years Wolfgang Huber was astonishingly successful at combining the highest church offices with perceptive statements on diverse aspects of public political and moral debates. He thus became—alongside staunchly church-critical theologian Friedrich Wilhelm Graf—the most high-profile public intellectual in German Protestantism in our time. Heinrich Bedford-Strohm, Huber's later successor as EKD (Evangelische Kirche in Deutschland) Council president, very consciously followed in the footsteps of his academic teacher and role model, while Margot Käßmann, addressing needs other than those for intellectual argument, has won over different sections of the public.[1]

Alongside this receptive, highly person-centered form of attention, however, a skeptical attitude can also be observed, especially toward the institution of the church, which finds expression in a propensity to focus on scandals. The Catholic Church in particular has experienced a lot of this in recent years—deservedly and undeservedly. The revelation of numerous cases of sexual abuse and their habitual cover-up has deeply shaken many people, whether believers or not. The full extent of these incidents, and the way they were handled, is only gradually coming to light and has unsettled even the most faithful of the faithful. The financial conduct of the bishop of Limburg, Franz-Peter Tebartz-van Elst, which was exposed in 2013, and the institutional enabling of this behavior, have turned many people away from the institution of the church. Further revelations, about the Vatican's inner workings, for example, seem possible at any time. During Benedict XVI's pontificate, some commentators went so far as to speak of the greatest crisis in the Catholic Church since the time of the Reformation. This, however, is greatly exaggerated and indicates a surprising lack of historical awareness, for example, of the crises that threatened the church's existence during the French Revolution, the impact of secularization, Bismarck's *Kulturkampf* and especially the churches' predicament during the Nazi and communist eras. Still, there is a widespread and not unfounded sense that the social anchoring of the churches has been weakened as a result of milieu erosion as well as an aging and shrinking membership, and that therefore any shift in public sentiment is likely to have a major impact on church members and their willingness to sustain their membership. There is a danger that the public role of the two large churches in Germany is increasingly out of proportion to their actual strength. I believe the present situation calls for some fresh thinking, from both a social-scientific and theological perspective, about what church means. This process of reflection will be of interest to all those for whom religious faith is more than a pick-me-up and source of comfort. This is how it is generally experienced by those who define themselves today as "unchurched but not unreligious." But if faith is to have any implications for action toward other people, and if faith cannot, perhaps, be lived in a sustained way without others who share it, then we must inevitably ask how best to organize believers. Critical distance from the church as it is, then, is not enough. There may be superior forms of social organization that it behooves us to discuss. Because biblically based doctrinal or theological definitions of what the church is often merely establish an ideal while failing to focus enough on the extent to which this ideal has been realized, the social sciences too must come into play as a corrective force.

Guiding the following reflections is the question of how the churches relate to the morality of the societies in which they find themselves and how they see the role of morality in the propagation of their message and in their public presence—whether the church is a moral agency of society, whether this is its task and whether it ought to regard itself as such an agency. My answer is essentially skeptical. This may surprise some, given that my argument comes with a strong emphasis on moral universalism in Christianity and thus a normative frame of reference. This was, however, related in part to the key characteristics of the contemporary religious situation, namely, increasing "optionality" through individualization and globalization, and to reflection on the social form of the church, which is so central in our context. The result of my reflections is that the moralization or politicization of the Christian message and the churches' tasks are an inappropriate response to the challenges of today.

The church I tried to describe in my book *Kirche als Moralagentur?* is, in short, a missionary church. It is enthusiastic about the faith alive within it, globally oriented, and does not sacralize its own structures. It is capable of compromise because its faith provides it with a compass, and it learns from other Christians, other religious traditions and secular universalists.

Such a church cannot define itself as a moral agency because its message is not primarily a moral one and because it does not offer itself as an agency to anyone. It is difficult to evangelize with morality; mission must be undergirded by enthusiasm and spark off the same kind of enthusiasm in others. Morality may be understood as restrictive: it limits our potential actions and prohibits certain goals and means. Ideals, meanwhile, are attractive and "enabling": they increase our potential for action by opening up to us routes and experiences that were previously closed off.[2] While we can imagine morally guided persons as high-performance athletes—to paraphrase William James—who concentrate on their will, religious persons, or persons guided by ideals in general, are borne up by a passion. Of course, such passion may then motivate the joyful fulfillment of moral duties, but that does not render it itself morality. And of course the term "agency" refers to a willingness to take up a task and become active for another because the latter desires this. But if the churches saw themselves in this way, whose moral agencies might they be? It might seem obvious to view them as agencies of the state, but since the Third Reich both churches in Germany, despite their dependence on the state, are keen to avoid any suspicion that they are too close to it. So, while they refer to "society," or to "civil society" like Wolfgang Huber in his groundbreaking book *Kirche in der Zeitenwende* (The church in changing times),[3] I would surmise that any attempt by the churches to interpret themselves as central to the moral cohesion of society is intended to justify their existence and legitimize state subsidies. I believe it is only the specific conditions in the Federal Republic of Germany and its distinctive state–church arrangement that point to such a definition in the first place. Neither in the case of a sharp laicist separation of church and state (as in France) nor in the case of diverse and "genuine" religious pluralism (as in the United States) would this definitional approach make sense. Inherent in it is the notion of a deal that offers institutional recognition in exchange for self-limitation to morality.

This focus on morality, however, fails to honor not only the intrinsic character of the religious sphere but also that of the political dimension. We might call this the trap of an ethics of conviction (*Gesinnungsethik*). Those who intervene in political debates exclusively with moral arguments will appear either helpless or arrogant: helpless if they take a stand without considering the complexity of a political problem and without thinking through the foreseeable effects of a policy advocated on moral grounds, and arrogant if they sweepingly claim moral superiority for their own political position while failing to recognize that others may come to a completely different conclusion out of no less moral impulses. This is a key angle of attack in Friedrich Wilhelm Graf's polemical critique of the church. One of the seven vices of the churches in Germany he enumerates is that of moralism: he assails the "cheap, trivial morality" of Christmas sermons, the (alleged) "paternalism" of those who express ethical reservations about a person's "right" to end their life and the (alleged) claim to exclusive validity of an ethics-of-conviction-based pacifism as a supposedly Christian stance.[4]

Christians may hold a wide range of legitimate political opinions. This is essentially beyond dispute and can easily be illustrated in light of attitudes to social inequality, war and peace and immigration policy. Although I am personally in favor of the option for the poor, a defender of nonviolent conflict resolution and an advocate of human rights, I know that this does not make all social inequality, military deployment, border controls and immigration restrictions un-Christian. In the political debate among Christians, there is always a risk, on all sides, of denying one's opponent's Christianity.

German Protestantism is frequently subject to intense debates on these issues, which are in fact of fundamental importance. In the Catholic Church and outside Germany, however, the battle lines are often drawn quite differently than in German Protestantism.[5] American Catholic bishops, for example, voiced sometimes withering criticism during the Obama presidency, warning of the looming risk of a "secularist tyranny" and declaring philosophical secularism the "greatest threat to democratic freedom." The fight against abortion and the equality of gay couples set the agenda here. The tone of the American Catholic bishops is also highly moralistic, though their political message runs counter to that of German Protestantism. Yet the current debate not only raises traditional questions about the legitimacy of such forceful moral interventions by the churches in democratic societies' political decision-making. The correct understanding of Christianity's moral universalism is also at stake. If churches see themselves as the moral agencies of a society, or, even if they reject such a definition, de facto behave as such, then their understanding of what constitutes Christian morality becomes central to assessing their role.

"Look at the individual. There is no such thing as the refugee crisis, as hordes or a glut of refugees. There is only ever Aishe and Ahmed."[6] These are the words of Irmgard Schwaetzer, chair of the Synod of the Protestant Church in Germany (EKD), in her speech to the Central Committee of German Catholics (ZdK or Zentralkomitee der deutschen Katholiken), which she viewed as a cross-confessional appeal to all Christians to "always take action against hard-heartedness and selfishness in the public sphere." Here, with a rare lack of ambiguity, a moral call to individual charitable action is taken to the point that a political problem no longer seems to exist and any reference to such a problem is bound to appear as a deficient willingness to act morally. In a quite taken-for-granted way, here the radical ethos of the Gospel would appear to inform the political action of Christians and their churches. Yet any reasonable observer is bound to wonder about the selectivity with which this ethos is mobilized to political ends. Would a genuine belief that there are only ever individuals, only "Aishe and Ahmed," not mean rejecting all organized military action? Can a church even be organized on the basis of such a yardstick? The question that arises here is whether the universalism of the Christian commandment of love truly compels such apolitical conclusions. I believe this is far from being the case.

In one of the most important texts on the tension between the Christian ethos and concrete social orders and on possible means of coping with this tension within the individual and collective conduct of life, the book *Christ and Culture*,[7] American Protestant theologian H. Richard Niebuhr pointed out that while for the Christian faith all people have the same dignity and value *before God*, people live in relationships. They are "relational" beings, so naturally they have differing value for other people. "In Christ there is neither Jew nor Greek, bond nor free, male nor female; but in relation to other men a multitude of relative value considerations arise." He also invokes Luther's argument that an individual may refrain from resisting perpetrators of violence, but not if he is also a protector of others. The greater sin then, he argues, is to fail to live up to one's responsibility to those others out of an individual desire for holiness.[8] This certainly raises complex moral questions about which nothing more precise can be said at this point. My only goal for now is to make it clear that a relational or even community-oriented, that is, communitarian understanding of the individual may have different moral consequences than a purely individualistic understanding that disregards people's social relationships, community ties and institutions.

If we think of people as necessarily embedded in particular relationships and communities, it follows that this embedding endows them with moral obligations that exist alongside the obligations they have toward all people, including those who are distant from them. We have good reasons to feel a special obligation to our children, for example. It would not be morally better of us to cast off this sense of obligation and—like Mrs. Jellyby in Charles Dickens's novel *Bleak House*, as the embodiment of "telescopic philanthropy"—neglect our own children because of our commitment to the children of Africa. Even moral universalists live with highly particular obligations that are of no lesser moral quality than the obligations that follow directly from moral universalism. There is not and cannot be a formula for offsetting or ranking these obligations. Particular and universalist obligations coexist in an incommensurable way. They must be balanced against each other—both in terms of individuals' concrete decisions about how to live and in collectives' democratic decision-making processes.

With regard to immigration policy, American political philosopher Michael Walzer has set out the dilemmas that need to be resolved here in terms of concrete deliberation and decision-making.[9] For him, there is no doubt that collectives with membership regulations, and thus also states with citizenship laws, may in principle determine who is newly admitted as a member. This certainly does not mean, however, that they are completely free to make decisions, stipulate criteria for new admissions or impose quantitative regulations or that they are subject to no normative guidelines—arising from a universalist morality as well as from particular obligations. Universalist morality may result in an obligation to admit people who are in particularly great need of protection. Particular obligations can result in regulations in favor of members of one's own ethnic group (as in the case of the *Russlanddeutsche*, ethnic Germans living in Russia) or the representatives of values with which one feels a particular affinity (persecuted Christians and democratic activists).

In connection with Walzer's book, an intensive debate has taken off on other normative commitments of this kind. In a proposed theory of "constitutive justice," that is, an attempt to clarify what justice means within the constitution of collectives, American Catholic theologian William Barbieri,[10] summarizing the results of this debate, lists ten key criteria. These include states' international commitments and promises of mutual assistance. Again, what matters here are not the details of these normative ideas, only their fundamental underpinning. This lies in the fact that the great universalist ethos of love presented in the Gospel, if it is to be made the yardstick for political action beyond its fundamentally apolitical character, in no way compels us to negate specific particular obligations.

It is a misunderstanding of the Christian commandment to suggest that love invalidates the demands of justice and political prudence. Even in the New Testament, the principle of justice is not *replaced* by that of love. In the Gospel of Luke (6:20–49), Jesus's "Sermon on the Plain" famously places the Golden Rule alongside the commandment to love one's enemies. Certainly, this new message goes beyond the Golden Rule as the moral expression of the principle of reciprocity. But it would be a mistake to conceive of this new aspect of the commandment of love simply as an alternative moral principle. To do so is to become entangled in the difficulties and paradoxes, which have been discussed since Kant, thrown up by the question of how love can be commanded in the first place. The solution is to attribute a "supramoral" dimension to love;[11] once again, the distinction between the attractive and the restrictive is crucial. What this means is that Christians are not subject to an unfulfillable commandment that demands obedience from them and feelings of love they do not have but must talk themselves into having against their spontaneous inclinations. Christians are people whose sense of life is permeated by the experience that God loves humans and his entire creation, that Jesus Christ embodies this divine love in human form and that his example invites us to follow and emulate him within the scope of our human capabilities. However, since love comes under this kind of "supramoral" rubric, it can never replace the organizing principles of social life, such as the principle of justice in the configuration of a polity but also in its very constitution. It can only reinterpret the rules of morality in a given case, enable us to act morally, stabilize our commitment to morality, make grace, generosity and humility possible and prevent us from pursuing mere calculatory reciprocity. Only at its sectarian fringes was Christianity ever what Max Weber, in his comparative studies on the economic ethics of the world religions, called the "acosmism of love," that is, a radical "worldless" (*weltlos*) devotion to the ethos of brotherhood without regard to the inherent logic of political and economic life.[12] The churches have never taken that path. It did nothing to help their credibility when they suddenly acted—with respect to a single, nationally and internationally controversial issue such as keeping the German borders open—as if there could be no doubt at all that backing this was the correct stance both for them and the individual Christian.

The starting point for all these considerations is how to appropriately understand the church in our time. There seems to be a need to clarify anew what the church is, can or should be at a time when ever more people see no point in belonging to one, yet the churches play a considerable and self-confident role in public moral and political debates. I have attempted to depart from well-trodden paths and neither simply perpetuate a church-internal and theological understanding of the church nor deploy the social sciences to critique church and religion. In order to clarify the normative frame of reference, it seems vital to go back to the basic definition of the church produced by an important council of late antiquity, one repeated in Christians' creeds ever since and that unites them across confessional differences. It turns out that the formula agreed at the Council of Constantinople (381), that the church is *una, sancta, catholica et apostolica*, can be related to and translated into contemporary terminology in such a way that it takes on an electrifying topicality.[13] This form of words expresses the sense of enthusiasm generated by placing a universalist ideal on a permanent basis and having found an institutional form for it. The topicality of this perspective is especially palpable at a time when the Christian faith has in many ways lost its cultural self-evidence. Faith has become an optional matter in two respects. This has occurred, first, through believers' inevitable encounter with others who do not share their confession or Christian faith, and here I have underlined the importance of distinguishing between mere coexistence and genuine optionality or "genuine pluralism." Second, faith has become optional by virtue of the globalization of Christianity, through its new inculturation in East Asia, for example, and the repercussions of these developments on traditionally Christian-influenced cultures. Hence, at a time when faith has become an option and nonbelief has largely become the norm in Europe, the message of the Christian faith can be articulated anew only through a new language and a courageous push to propagate the core elements of its message.

But what does this mean for the churches? Under contemporary conditions, I am trying—certainly not as the first or only commentator—to highlight the astonishing fact that Christianity, in the shape of the "church" as institution, has produced and preserved for two millennia something that rises above the sum of shared symbols of sacredness or the worldview characteristic of a tribe, people or state and places a universalist ideal on an enduring basis. This insight is in no way meant to gloss over troubling realities. Without a doubt, a de facto merger with people or state has taken place in the church or in various churches time and again, the church's own forms of corruption have been laid bare and the institution has moved far away from the ideals it proclaims. Those who now emphasize the astonishing if not miraculous aspects of the church's tremendous historical continuity avoid sounding mawkish and triumphalist only if the church is relativized in two respects. First, the church has never been the only form of social organization among Christians. There have always been Christians who, for example, felt that the compromise-oriented churches were failing to embody their radical understanding of the Christian message and thus created alternative forms of religious life by founding what we can, without pejorative intent, call a "sect," or by entering into loose forms of association with others with whom intense religious experiences are shared. Second, other forms of universalist ideal formation, for example, in East and South Asia, have also led to institutions independent of peoples and states, though these have often relapsed in ways reminiscent of the churches. Today, the historical and social-scientific understanding of the church must present the pluralism of Christian forms of social organization as expressions of the richness of Christianity and tease out the special features of all these forms by comparing them with other religions. This makes new kinds of institutional synthesis within Christianity conceivable, but even beyond it—through dialogue between all universalistically oriented religions. Against this background, it is extremely interesting to probe learning processes of this kind that may have taken place in the past, for example, between Judaism, Christianity and Islam,[14] or even between them and the great Asian religious traditions.

Understanding the church in this way puts some present-day phenomena in a new light. Any focus of Christianity and the churches on morality comes to seem highly problematic, let alone any attempt to specialize in moral interventions in the public sphere. This obviously applies to the focus on sexual morality, which so unhappily determined the public image of the Catholic Church before Pope Francis, especially since this rarely seemed to entail serious moral sensitivity. It looked more like perpetual rearguard action on the part of an institution incapable of incorporating women's emancipation and the extension of human rights to sexual self-determination into its worldview and conception of history as epoch-making shifts. Less obviously, however, we also find this problem whenever excessive closeness to the pre-democratic state—as in the case of German Protestantism, which mostly viewed the Weimar Republic, the first German democracy, with the greatest reserve—leads to the conclusion that it is now appropriate to instruct the public on what it should understand by democracy. I have tried to at least hint at an alternative to a Christianity understood exclusively in terms of the ethos of love by putting forward a more complex understanding of love and the morality of justice, while also pointing to a richer perspective on the relationship between universalist and particular moral obligations. It is the supramoral character of love that speaks against any narrowing of faith and the church to morality. The autonomy of the Christian faith, even vis-à-vis the ideologies of the democratic state, and the churches' at least potential independence from the state should make it clear just how perilous it is for the churches to turn into moral agencies. They succumb to this temptation much more often than one might expect given their explicit embrace of an independent role.

Rather than openly or tacitly accept the role of moral agency, the churches might pursue a different, brotherly or sisterly approach, especially with respect to unavoidable differences in political assessments. The churches' charitable activities and welfare services, as well as the work of their educational institutions and schools, can make a greater impact than a demonstrative political presence. Unfortunately, though, there is often little sign of a different way of dealing with each other in the churches. In the Catholic Church, it is ultimately clerical power that traditionally holds sway, and in the Protestant Church controversies can easily degenerate into partisan clashes. I believe a different way of dealing with each other, if experienced as an instantiation of the message the churches themselves promulgate, would itself have a missionary effect. I would thus like to close this chapter with the somewhat forlorn but nevertheless hopeful words attributed to the Apostle Paul in the Letter to the Ephesians (4:2): "Be patient, bearing with one another in love."

11

The Church's Global Responsibility and Particular Obligations

It must be one of the most satisfying experiences in an author's life when others not only read his writings but engage deeply with them. I will never forget how my mood changed while attending the Frankfurt Book Fair for the first time in the early 1970s: my elation at seeing my first book on display was abruptly supplanted by the worry that it would sink without trace amid an ocean of new publications. The attention garnered by my little book *Kirche als Moralagentur?* (Church as moral agency?),[1] published in 2016, came as a positive surprise in three respects. First, because the book is just a small by-product of my work. Second, because the circle of discussants is particularly distinguished, and some of the leading German theologians from the two major Christian confessions, as well as one of the most high-profile Christian politicians in Germany, have commented on it at length. Third and finally, because the initial reactions of leading figures in the German churches to my criticism of their unqualified support for Chancellor Merkel's migration policy amounted to declaring my reservations groundless. After all, they averred, no one is suggesting that churches should be moral agencies, and no one supports the federal government unreservedly. To put it simply, I was supposedly pushing at an open door.

The multitude of other responses to my intervention made that rather difficult to believe. Ultimately, even the German Protestant Church's Chamber for Public Responsibility published a remarkably self-critical "Impulse Paper" in summer 2017 and invited me to discuss it in public.[2] The contributions to the debate sparked off by my book that were gathered in a volume published in 2019 seem to me essentially devoid of this pushing-at-an-open-door notion—Annette Schavan's response perhaps being the nearest thing to an exception. Ulrich Körtner shares my critical stance in any case and has made this very clear in his public interventions;[3] Magnus Striet treats the state of affairs I criticized as fact and discerns a tendency toward the "insincere reduction of complexity" in church leaders' political statements in this context; the late Eberhard Schockenhoff wrote that "it is scarcely possible to deny the danger of making moral appeals to the political realm with an air of superiority based on an ethics of conviction" (61). And Peter Dabrock states generously that while my concerns may not be justified, the "hermeneutics of suspicion toward the churches that shines through" in my commentary and "others' [contributions] should be seen as an important signal that in particular instances the difference between (rather than dichotomy of) religion and morality/politics" is being undermined by the representatives of the religions themselves (52). In light of this evidence that my critique is not completely missing the mark, it seems to me that the ground has been laid for a good debate.

As gratifying as I find such attention, however, the way my arguments were construed and brief glimpses of the motives imputed to me are sometimes quite puzzling. It would be petty and tedious for readers if I attempted to correct every detail. I therefore confine myself to a small number of topics, first setting out why I wrote the book in the first place (1). I then turn to two sets of issues touched on in all the contributions: the role of the distinction between the ethics of conviction (*Gesinnungsethik*) and the ethics of responsibility (*Verantwortungsethik*) (2) and the relationship between morality and religion (3). Finally, I briefly probe what all this means for our understanding of the church today (4).

1.

In her contribution,[4] Annette Schavan surmises that my "starting point and probably also the source of vexation that inspired this text . . . was the churches' behavior vis-à-vis the refugees arriving in Germany since the summer of 2015." The object of my criticism, she goes on, is "an attitude rooted in an ethics of conviction and an approach to political presence that despise doubt" (82). Both these statements are too simple and fail to accurately capture my views. It seems crucial to make this clear. In fact, my text has an unambiguously identifiable and easily documented origin in the conference "Renewing the Church in a Secular Age," held at the Pontifical Gregorian University, Rome, in March 2015. There I had the honor of giving one of the keynote speeches alongside Charles Taylor, José Casanova and Tomáš Halík. In it, I sought to express my fascination with the historical fact that the church exists in the first place—as a community or institution alongside the state that is characterized by an unprecedented, not to say miraculous, continuity. One of my goals was to open the eyes of those who take the church far too much for granted as a given entity in the world, while also addressing the challenge inherent in the church's existence for the historical-comparative study of religion in the social sciences. I believe that the first sections of *Kirche als Moralagentur?* clearly show that I do not see myself as a quasi-professional "church critic," that in reality my aim is to influence church-internal discussions on its self-reform by recalling the meaning and purpose of the church.[5]

When I was invited to the "Seventeenth Consultation of the Church Leadership and Academic Theology" organized by the United Evangelical Lutheran Church of Germany (Vereinigte Evangelisch-Lutherische Kirche Deutschlands or VELKD), held in Eisenach in the autumn of 2015, I decided to turn my manuscript written for Rome into a text of interconfessional relevance. It would have been oddly out of step with the historical moment had I failed to address the specific role of the church vis-à-vis the government's migration policy at the time. The title of the event, not coined by me but by the VELKD, was "Church and Theology as Moral Agencies of Society?"[6] This was the inspiration for the title of my book.

This backstory not only reinforces the point that I do not see myself as a "church critic" but also shows that it is quite wrong to impute to me total skepticism about any form of political participation by the churches in the democratic decision-making process (let alone in the struggle for democracy). My work on the history of human rights is, after all, permeated by sorrow at the Christian churches' long-standing failure to play a more dynamic role in this regard.[7] My skepticism about the German churches' current political role is rooted in a much more specific context. I lament the selective moralizing inherent in basing oneself on the Gospel with respect to migration policy while eschewing such an approach in response to other issues—such as peace and armaments policies. I take issue with the moral rejection of restrictive measures, a stance that tends to entail disdain rather than encouragement for political pluralism within the churches. And, with reference to specific quotes, I have assailed the inclination to reduce political questions to matters of individual morality. Contrary to the assumptions of Annette Schavan, this critique is about more than the "form and style of certain statements" by the churches (91). It is not, however, anchored in a radically antipolitical conception of faith.

2.

Nor can my critique be grasped through a simple distinction between an ethics of conviction and an ethics of responsibility. Yet virtually every chapter in the discussion volume seems to operate on this assumption. It is astonishing to me that—perhaps precisely because of this—not a single contribution addresses the argument I myself consider to be my true contribution to the migration debate.

Building on the insights of H. Richard Niebuhr and Michael Walzer, I view my key argument as the claim that even moral universalists are and must ever remain people with particular obligations who are thus required to balance two incommensurable types of obligation.[8] I believe this is the philosophical way out of the dilemma of either being a moral universalist who obviously advocates equal rights for all citizens regardless of their ethnicity but who must then also favor international freedom of movement as a human right,[9] or, conversely, an exponent of a more restrictive immigration policy who sides with those who treat immigrants as second-class citizens. The distinction between an ethics of conviction and an ethics of responsibility cannot do justice to this issue.

Though not central to my argument, this distinction has its own validity. As I see it, this consists in moralizing the question of what the consequences of a well-intentioned action might be. Like the American pragmatists from whom I have taken inspiration for decades, I see myself as a responsibility ethicist insofar as I consider the deliberate ignoring of the evident consequences of action morally irresponsible. Yet I am also aware that we ourselves can only very imperfectly assess the outcomes of our actions. This means it is sometimes safer to adhere rigidly to the dictates of conviction. The concrete historical context in which Max Weber deployed the distinction between the ethics of conviction and the ethics of responsibility was, of course, his polemical attack on the pacifist opponents of the First World War.[10] But who would now claim that the "realist" advocates of war did a better job of assessing its consequences than its unconditional opponents with their ethics of conviction?

My relationship to Ulrich Körtner's contribution is determined by the fact that while I share many of his aims, his argumentational approach is quite different from mine.[11] I share his skepticism about the role of the churches as "custodians of the Federal Republic's civil religion" (99) and consider highly perceptive his objections to Richard von Weizsäcker's statement that while the churches should not engage in politics themselves, they should make politics possible—words that appear in the title of Peter Dabrock's chapter.[12] Where we differ is not only with regard to the status within our arguments of the distinction between the ethics of conviction and the ethics of responsibility but also in our view of the supposed tendency toward functional differentiation in modern societies and thus in our assessment of Niklas Luhmann's sociology. Körtner finds in Luhmann a basis for his argument about the dangers of moralization. I have put forward detailed reasons at many points in my writings in sociological theory for major reservations about the theory of functional differentiation and the "fascination with amorality" stemming from Luhmann.[13] As Körtner does not go into these differences, my critical analysis, which emphasizes Christianity's moral universalism, appears contradictory to him. Yet my critique of "selective moralization" is simply not rooted in the standpoint of an "amoral sociology."

This is not the right place to continue the debate on the already extensively discussed questions, soon to occupy contemporary historians, about the reasons for Angela Merkel's decision in autumn 2015, its consequences and its legitimacy. But since two of the contributions deal with this issue quite extensively, I cannot avoid commenting briefly on their arguments.

Annette Schavan sees the determining factor in the chancellor's humanitarian motive rooted in her Christianity. The former federal minister of education's personal closeness to the chancellor gives her statement a degree of credibility that I cannot counter as such. I would merely point out very tentatively that for long stretches of time, Angela Merkel did not stand out for her straightforwardness and firm convictions but rather for radical changes of course, for example, with respect to social policy and the peaceful use of nuclear energy. It is also very hard to discern any Christian humanitarian motives at work when, as leader of the opposition in 2003, she expressed support for the Iraq War to the president of the United States in the American press and on American soil, departing from the German government's position with what some regarded as a kind of national disloyalty. Even in the field of migration policy, one might consider whether the emergency at the border arose in part due to a failure to address looming problems—an unlikely state of affairs if the chancellor's views had long been informed by humanitarian motives.

Interestingly, in Annette Schavan's case, Merkel does in fact come across as an ethicist of conviction, whereas Eberhard Schockenhoff put forward an in-depth justification for her decision in terms of the ethics of responsibility—more detailed, in fact, than anything articulated by the chancellor herself. His argument centers on the uniqueness and inescapability of the emergency facing the country.[14] Yet without reconstructing its prehistory, without examining specific actions and their (hyper-)justification afterward and ever since, this focus seems to me a simplification and an attempt to present the chancellor's decision as "the only available option." Also absent here is any attempt to engage with Christian arguments for a more restrictive migration policy—from the statements of Protestant theologian and politician Richard Schröder to those of the Polish church. If the phrase "fundamental opposition to the admission of any refugees" (64) is supposed to refer to me, I explicitly reject it as a misrepresentation of my views. Schockenhoff goes so far as to put forward an argument that I have otherwise encountered only in the form of a critique of motives (64), namely, that the refugee crisis was an opportunity for the Germans if not to free themselves from the guilt of the Holocaust in the eyes of the world then at least to project a new national image and to enjoy a new sense of national pride on valid grounds. Such motives seem to me to amplify the threat to rational policies.

At this point, it might be helpful to clearly separate two distinct issues. My comments so far have focused on the relationship between religion and morality on one side and politics on the other. The following section shifts focus to the relationship between religion and morality. In distinguishing politics from religion *and* morality, I do not intend to deny religion and morality any political significance. Like Ulrich Körtner, I take the view that "the goal cannot be to tear the political realm and faith apart, but certainly ought to be to distinguish the two from each other" (113). Like

Annette Schavan (81), I believe that while the message of Jesus of Nazareth is not political, it is not politically inconsequential either, and that the political realm and the Christian realm, as she quotes the late Catholic Bishop Klaus Hemmerle (92), can provide impulses for each other. It is precisely because of this fundamental agreement that I am perplexed to find multiple passages in the various chapters that make sense only if I am assumed to favor a completely apolitical Christianity.[15] Why does Annette Schavan mention the impressive role of Pope John Paul II in overthrowing communist rule in Poland? Why, in concluding his examination of my views, does Eberhard Schockenhoff express opposition to the idea that "the churches and their official representatives should generally stay out of politics" (79)? Why does Peter Dabrock begin his essay by asking: "Is it permissible for high-ranking church representatives to speak out on political issues?" (35). All these cases could truly be described as pushing at an open door. My criticism of the selective moralization of specific policy fields and the lack of respect for political pluralism within the churches, as evident in the field of migration policy, is—to repeat—way too specific to be illuminated by such abstract perspectives.

3.

In Schockenhoff's and Dabrock's contributions, a staggeringly large role is played by my specific use of the terms "morality" and "religion" and my view of the relationship between the phenomena thus distinguished. For me, the emphasis they place on my choice of terms is astonishing, as I myself am rather dispassionate about it. I would first like to explain my intentions at the substantive—rather than terminological—level before addressing, in light of this clarification, those aspects of the contributions that assume that we are faced here with a fundamental bone of contention.

In essence, I am concerned with the analytical distinction between the restrictive and the attractive within the domains of religion and morality. I believe everyone is familiar with the experience of being attracted by other people or by ideational content, with the vision of becoming a different, fuller, freer person through commitment to these individuals or ideas. Likewise, everyone knows what it is like to be denied something by other people or by what they themselves consider good and right and thus being restricted in one's potential actions. This distinction, based in the human experience, is scarcely my invention. It has a long tradition in philosophy and the human sciences. Yet neither philosophy nor these sciences use a uniform vocabulary in this respect. While certain philosophers have tried to capture this distinction through the "ethical versus moral" framework, for others ethics is a dimension of reflection on morality. While some sociologists seek to convey this distinction by referring to "values versus norms," others talk about the two sides or forms of morality. One could further extend this list of different terminologies and their pros and cons. I am grateful to Magnus Striet for underlining the arbitrary element in the particular choice of terms;[16] we should avoid quibbling over words. I myself have commented at length on both substantive and terminological issues in my writings, particularly in my book *The Genesis of Values*, originally published in German in 1997.[17] American pragmatist and psychologist of religion William James, who parallels my distinction between "restrictive" and "attractive" with that between "moral" and "religious," plays a key role in my phraseology. A kind of anti-Puritan sentiment may have been significant to him here, that is, a desire to liberate himself from a tradition stagnating in moralism or that reduced religion to "morality touched by emotion" (Matthew Arnold). I admit to being sympathetic to this sentiment but do not expect anyone who does not share it to adopt my terminology.

What matters is my emphasis on the *analytical* distinction between the restrictive and the attractive. This is my attempt to underscore that these two modes of experience are not confined to entirely separate spheres of reality. It would never enter my mind to deny the restrictive consequences of the experience of attraction. To put it in less abstract terms: those who fall in love and for whom this leads to a successful, loving relationship naturally assume obligations of fidelity and assistance that have a restrictive character. If all goes well, however, the burden will be light because it is imbued with the spirit of attraction. Similarly, the last thing I seek to do is deny that a system of normative regulations—from the Ten Commandments to a state's constitution—may develop its own appeal, just as the mere phenomenon of conscience, the moral law within us, may, as Kant put it, trigger an experience of admiration and awe akin to that inspired by the starry heavens above.

All this is worth mentioning here because I wish to make it clear that I agree entirely with Eberhard Schockenhoff's pleasing exegetical remarks on the "inclusion of morality in religion" if I base them on *his* understanding of these terms rather than *my* way of using them. There is no competition here, as he thinks, between a dissociative and an integrative model. With all due respect, most of my work on the history of human rights would be incomprehensible if I thought in the way imputed to me here.

Unfortunately, much the same can be said of Peter Dabrock's essay. I am particularly grateful to him because, more than the other contributors, he also draws on other works of mine in his discussion of my short book on the church as moral agency. As always, this is crucial to providing the context needed for a proper understanding. In his case, too, I certainly perceive a terminological difference but not a substantive one. He believes I do myself no favors if I "radically" separate norms and values (50). Yet the "radical" distinction between concepts does not imply the radical division of phenomena. Often, though, we can better conceptualize phenomena by making clear terminological distinctions. That is what I believe I learned from Max Weber.

I find it somewhat ironic that toward the end of his often brilliant essay, Peter Dabrock returns to my notion—which builds on the work of Émile Durkheim—of the "sacredness of the person" when he seeks to determine the most important orientational frameworks in the world of today. My idea, however, is anchored in a conception of sacredness, of the holy, which defines it not primarily as restrictive but as attractive. Still, in the case of the sacred we can discern with special clarity how its appeal is secured through restrictiveness, such as prohibitions on contact or entry.

Several of the contributors to the debate refer to Kant's philosophy when they put forward their definition of the relationship between morality and religion. This is entirely justified in that Kant's (one-sided) definition of this relationship is of epoch-making importance to continental European philosophy and Protestant (and, catching up in recent decades, Catholic) theology. The question of how to interface with Kant's understanding of autonomy without making religion appear as heteronomy seems to me of systematic importance here. Ulrich Körtner's chapter includes some impressive passages on this, inspired by Dietrich Bonhoeffer. A definition of faith that points in this direction also appears toward the end of Magnus Striet's text. He writes that faith "is always partly a struggle and rejoicing in God, gratitude for being allowed to exist and trust that the whole will come to a good end" (134). It is unclear to me how his remarks on prophecy as "autonomy that has not become reflexive to itself" relate to this (129). Does this imply a secularist understanding of autonomy after all? I myself am looking for a persuasive way of thinking about these issues, following Paul Tillich and Paul Ricœur, but cannot pursue this further here.[18]

4.

All of these valuable contributions conclude by generalizing their perspective in attempts to illuminate what it might mean for the church today. Annette Schavan cleaves closely to the Pastoral Constitution of the Second Vatican Council, *Gaudium et spes*, and the renewal of its spirit in the ministry of Pope Francis. She welcomes my call for renewed social-scientific reflection on the church but does not comment on the reasons, which I also addressed in my book, why so much of what the Council initiated has petered out in the decades since. Eberhard Schockenhoff calls for a church that intervenes but leaves the internal problems of this interventionist church completely unexamined in his chapter. Magnus Striet takes a concrete approach, calling for greater decentralization of the Catholic Church. Ulrich Körtner, following Bonhoeffer, speaks of a "waiting church" and a "waiting theology"—both in a spirit of integrity that avoids any need to feign certainty where it is not present. He sees no contradiction between such a "waiting church" and my idea of a missionary church, in which the missionary dimension does not follow from morality and does not become a moral demand. I have no trouble agreeing with this and take it as impetus for deeper reflection. Peter Dabrock develops his understanding of the church most clearly at this point. He speaks of a "responsive understanding of church and faith-based identity" (40). Explicitly agreeing with me, he writes that "a church falls short of the open identity promised to it if it merely trumpets shoulds at the world" (45). He believes, however, that his appealing outline of "the church as a living community of witness to the ultimate and to [the church's] forms of self-reassurance and modes of expression in the penultimate" goes beyond my understanding of the church as it assigns "meaning to action, action orientation and to the associated morality as well" (ibid.). But this assumption of a difference between us follows from the misunderstandings that my specific way of using the terms "morality" and "religion" has evidently helped bring about.

Finally, I would like to underline that my motive for understanding the church in historical-sociological terms points to the need for comparison with other ways in which the religious focus on transcendence has been organized within societies. "Church" is not the only form of social organization among Christians, and other transcendence-oriented religions such as Judaism and Islam have established their own forms of social organization; I have repeatedly pointed this out in this book. This, I believe, is the framework within which a sociology of the church needs to be developed much further.[19] I would also like to lay bare a motive that has not been mentioned so far and does not appear in any of the contributions to the debate. Since I attribute the weakening of Christianity in Germany, especially in its Protestant form, largely to its bourgeoisification in the nineteenth century and to the alienation between the church and the working classes, I react with concern whenever further steps are taken in the same direction. At times my concerns in this regard may be unfounded: in some cases, the alienation may already be so great that further steps make no difference. Still, I would like to point out that as far removed as the Christian educated classes in today's Germany are from the nationalism and anti-Semitism of their ancestors, they often lack the awareness that even a well-traveled, multilingual, staunchly antinationalist and Europhile bourgeoisie may have a poor grasp of the worldview and interests of their working-class compatriots.

Coda

In his late novel *Der neunzigste Geburtstag* (The ninetieth birthday), the great Catholic writer Günter de Bruyn portrays a young (West German) pastor in a Brandenburg village. Her name in the book is Anna Merkel, but she immediately points out unprompted that she is not related to the German chancellor. This clarification is immediately followed by a somewhat cryptic statement: "Like her, she grew up in a Protestant parsonage, but unlike her she is aware of the obligations this entails."[20] This sentence, at least in the opinion of the male addressee of this remark in the novel, becomes comprehensible only in the wake of the church service the pastor holds shortly after a conversation with him and a dozen or so women. The sermon, songs and prayers revolve around the insight that "religion is not a matter of knowledge, but of faith. It is also a moral teaching, but above all it is the herald of the divine and the hereafter, which cannot be reached through rational education. A church that, as sadly too often in its history, makes itself the servant of an ever-changing zeitgeist, is betraying itself. The Good News it was tasked with proclaiming was not that of a welcoming culture [*Willkommenskultur*, in other words, the idea of welcoming refugees into Germany] or climate protection, but that of the Gospel, that is, of God-become-man."[21] Through this experience, the listener feels the "Christianity lying dormant within him [beginning] to bloom again a little."[22]

Notes

PREFACE TO THE ENGLISH-LANGUAGE EDITION OF *WHY THE CHURCH?*

1. Jean Daniélou, *Why the Church?* (Chicago: Franciscan Herald Press, 1975), 15.
2. Ibid., 27.
3. Hans Joas and Robert Spaemann, *Beten bei Nebel: Hat der Glaube eine Zukunft?* (Freiburg: Herder, 2018).
4. Hans Joas, *The Sacredness of the Person: A New Genealogy of Human Rights* (Washington, DC: Georgetown University Press, 2013).
5. Hans Joas, *The Power of the Sacred: An Alternative to the Narrative of Disenchantment* (New York: Oxford University Press, 2021); Hans Joas, *Under the Spell of Freedom: Theory of Religion after Hegel and Nietzsche* (New York: Oxford University Press, 2024).
6. Hans Joas, *Faith as an Option: Possible Futures for Christianity* (Stanford, CA: Stanford University Press, 2014).

CHAPTER 1

1. Hans Joas, *Do We Need Religion? On the Experience of Self-Transcendence* (Boulder, CO: Paradigm, 2008).
2. Pippa Norris and Ronald F. Inglehart, *Sacred and Secular: Religion and Politics Worldwide* (Cambridge: Cambridge University Press, 2004).
3. For a critique, see, for example, Daniel Silver, "Religion without Instrumentalization," *Archives Européennes de Sociologie* 47 (2006): 421–34.
4. Ronald F. Inglehart, "Giving Up on God: The Global Decline of Religion," *Foreign Affairs* 99 (2020): 110–18.
5. John Dewey, *A Common Faith* (New Haven, CT: Yale University Press, 1934).
6. Hans Joas, "Mutter Kirche," *Herder Korrespondenz* 75, no. 12 (2021): 15–16.
7. Joas, *Do We Need Religion?* (see Chapter 4 in this book). Revised versions of this chapter and Chapter 8 are taken from the earlier book.
8. For a more detailed engagement with my research, which is only hinted at here, see Hans Joas, *The Sacredness of the Person: A New Genealogy of Human Rights* (Washington, DC: Georgetown University Press, 2013); Hans Joas, *The Power of*

the Sacred: An Alternative to the Narrative of Disenchantment (New York: Oxford University Press, 2021); Hans Joas, *Under the Spell of Freedom: Theory of Religion after Hegel and Nietzsche* (New York: Oxford University Press, 2024), especially the final chapters in the latter two books.

9. For initial reflections on this, see Hans Joas, *Faith as an Option: Possible Futures for Christianity* (Stanford, CA: Stanford University Press, 2014), 13–16; and Hans Joas, "Wann glauben Religionen an sich selbst?," *Frankfurter Allgemeine Zeitung*, August 3, 2015, 9.

10. See, for example, Joas, *Faith as an Option*, and many shorter texts and interviews.

11. See Philip Jenkins, *The Next Christendom: The Coming of Global Christianity* (New York: Oxford University Press, 2002).

12. For many of the quantitative data that appear in what follows and their statistical interpretation, see Ryan P. Burge, *The Nones: Where They Come From, Who They Are, and Where They Are Going* (Minneapolis: Fortress Press, 2021).

13. Ibid., 4.

14. For a more detailed treatment, see Philip Gorski, *American Babylon: Christianity and Democracy before and after Trump* (New York: Routledge, 2020).

15. A book by a longtime American China correspondent paints an extremely vivid picture: Ian Johnson, *The Souls of China: The Return of Religion after Mao* (New York: Pantheon, 2017).

16. Yu Yingshi, quoted in Ji Zhe, *Religion, modernité et temporalité: Une sociologie du bouddhisme chan contemporain* (Paris: CNRS Éditions, 2016), 46.

17. Thanks are also due to Daniel Deckers for valuable substantive and editorial input on the entire manuscript of the book; to my assistants Emma Sandner and Jan Philipp Hahn for their help in sourcing literature and producing a print-ready text and the Bibliography; and to Christian Scherer for his help in proofreading the text and compiling the index.

CHAPTER 2

1. Peter L. Berger, "A Bleak Outlook Is Seen for Religion," *New York Times*, April 25, 1968, 3. Of course, there have always been exceptions to this division into two camps. In Germany, for example, Franz-Xaver Kaufmann has made outstanding contributions to a sociological understanding of the church. See, for example, Franz-Xaver Kaufmann, *Kirchenkrise: Wie überlebt das Christentum?* (Freiburg: Herder, 2011). In his doctoral dissertation, Reinhard Cardinal Marx made an important contribution from the perspective of Catholic theology to building an unprejudiced bridge to a sociology of the church: Reinhard Marx, *Ist Kirche anders? Möglichkeiten und Grenzen einer soziologischen Betrachtungsweise* (Paderborn: Schöningh, 1990). As far as I am aware, however, this contribution has been completely ignored by sociologists. His explanations suffer from identifying sociology as a whole with functionalist ways of thinking. The same author has produced

another book on the topic: Reinhard Marx, *Kirche überlebt* (Munich: Kösel, 2015). In US theology, the following is a classic attempt to move toward a sociology of the church: James M. Gustafson, *Treasure in Earthen Vessels: The Church as a Human Community* (1961; Louisville, KY: Westminster John Knox Press, 2009).

2. In this respect, the important chapter "Christentum als Kirche," in Karl Rahner, *Grundkurs des Glaubens: Einführung in den Begriff des Christentums* (Freiburg: Herder, 1984), 313–87, here 332–33, also seems to me inadequate.

3. Karl Jaspers, *The Origin and Goal of History* (1949; New York: Routledge, 2010). For an overview of the research that builds on this, see Hans Joas, *The Power of the Sacred: An Alternative to the Narrative of Disenchantment* (New York: Oxford University Press, 2021), 154–94.

4. See Robert N. Bellah, *Religion in Human Evolution: From the Paleolithic to the Axial Age* (Cambridge, MA: Harvard University Press, 2011), 596; Ilana Friedrich Silber, *Virtuosity, Charisma, and Social Order: A Comparative Sociological Study of Monasticism in Theravada Buddhism and Medieval Catholicism* (Cambridge: Cambridge University Press, 1995).

5. Ernst Troeltsch, *The Social Teaching of the Christian Churches* (1912; London: Allen & Unwin, 1931); Max Weber, *Economy and Society* (1922; Berkeley: University of California Press, 1978), passim.

6. Manfred Wichelhaus, *Kirchengeschichtsschreibung und Soziologie im neunzehnten Jahrhundert und bei Ernst Troeltsch* (Heidelberg: Winter, 1965).

7. Romano Guardini, "Zwischen zwei Büchern" (1965), in *Vom Sinn der Kirche / Die Kirche des Herrn*, by Romano Guardini (Mainz: Grünewald, 1990), 105–13, here 106–7.

8. John Locke, *A Letter concerning Toleration: Latin and English Texts Revised and Edited with Variants and an Introduction by Mario Montuori* (The Hague: Nijhoff, 1963), 23.

9. Ernst Troeltsch, "Review of Peter A. Clasen, 'Der Salutismus,'" *Historische Zeitschrift* 115 (1915): 327–30, now in Ernst Troeltsch, *Rezensionen und Kritiken (1915–1923)*, KGA (Berlin: De Gruyter, 2010), 13:84–87.

10. Ernst Troeltsch, *Augustin, die christliche Antike und das Mittelalter* (Munich: Oldenbourg, 1915).

11. Ernst Troeltsch, *Die Soziallehren der christlichen Kirchen und Gruppen* (1912), ed. Friedrich Wilhelm Graf, 3 subvolumes, KGA, vol. 9 (Berlin: De Gruyter, 2021).

12. H. Richard Niebuhr, *The Social Sources of Denominationalism* (New York: Holt, 1929). For a detailed account of Niebuhr and his work, see Hans Joas, *Under the Spell of Freedom: Theory of Religion after Hegel and Nietzsche* (New York: Oxford University Press, 2024), 256–76.

13. David Martin was already putting forward similar arguments at an early stage. See David Martin, "The Denomination," *British Journal of Sociology* 33, no. 1 (1962): 1–14.

14. For more on Stark, see Joas, *Under the Spell of Freedom*, 277–98.

15. Werner Stark, *The Sociology of Religion: A Study of Christendom*, vols. 2 and 3 (New York: Fordham University Press, 1967). Other important works in our context by the same author are "The Place of Catholicism in Max Weber's Sociology of Religion," *Sociological Analysis* 29 (1968): 202–10; "The Routinization of Charisma: A Consideration of Catholicism," *Sociological Analysis* 26 (1965): 203–11.

16. Stark, *The Sociology of Religion*, 3:250.

17. For more detail on Weber (but not Troeltsch), see Otto Gerhard Oexle, "Max Weber und das Mönchtum," in *Max Webers Religionssoziologie in interkultureller Perspektive*, ed. Hartmut Lehmann and Jean Martin Ouédraogo (Göttingen: Vandenhoeck & Ruprecht, 2003), 311–34.

18. Karl Rahner, "Theologische Grundinterpretation des II. Vatikanischen Konzils," in *Schriften zur Theologie*, by Karl Rahner (Cologne: Benziger, 1980), 14:287–302.

19. See Paul Honigsheim, "Religionssoziologie," in *Die Lehre von der Gesellschaft: Ein Lehrbuch der Soziologie*, ed. Gottfried Eisermann (Stuttgart: Enke, 1958), 119–81, here 145–48.

20. Rahner, *Grundkurs des Glaubens*, 342.

21. Here I draw on a comment in H. Richard Niebuhr, *The Purpose of the Church and Its Ministry: Reflections on the Aims of Theological Education* (New York: Harper, 1956), 23–24.

22. The reference is to canon law Can. 215. I am borrowing from Stefan Vesper, "Schlicht privat: Von den freien Vereinigungen in der Kirche," *Salzkörner* 24, no. 1 (2018): 8–9.

23. The classic exception is E. K. Francis, "Toward a Typology of Religious Orders," *American Journal of Sociology* 55, no. 5 (1950): 437–49.

24. See Joas, *Under the Spell of Freedom*, 342–43, with reference to José Casanova's research.

25. Ernst Troeltsch, "Die Kirche im Leben der Gegenwart" (1911), in *Gesammelte Schriften*, by Ernst Troeltsch (Tübingen: Mohr Siebeck, 1913), 2:91–108, here 105. Troeltsch's ideas here are taken up in a remarkable study: Ulrich Schmiedel, *Elasticized Ecclesiology: The Concept of Community after Ernst Troeltsch* (New York: Palgrave, 2017). Also noteworthy is the application of Troeltsch's ideas to the organizational landscape of Christianity in the United States in Steven M. Tipton, *Public Pulpits: Methodists and Mainline Churches in the Moral Argument of Public Life* (Chicago: University of Chicago Press, 2007), esp. "Appendix: Ecclesiology in Action," 425–42.

26. Troeltsch, "Die Kirche im Leben der Gegenwart," 94.

27. Ibid., 100. On this basis, it is easy to build a bridge to Gerhard Wegner's studies, which have made an outstanding contribution to the sociology of the

church. See Gerhard Wegner, *Wirksame Kirche: Sozio-theologische Studien* (Leipzig: Evangelische Verlagsanstalt, 2019); and the anthology by Detlef Pollack and Gerhard Wegner, eds., *Die soziale Reichweite von Religion und Kirche* (Würzburg: Ergon, 2017).

28. See the classic critique of Foucault: Axel Honneth, *The Critique of Power: Reflective Stages in a Critical Social Theory* (Cambridge, MA: MIT Press, 1991), 99–202; and Hans Joas and Wolfgang Knöbl, *Social Theory: Twenty Introductory Lectures* (Cambridge: Cambridge University Press, 2009), 354–64.

29. Otto von Gierke, *Das deutsche Genossenschaftsrecht*, 4 vols. (1868–1913; Darmstadt: WBG, 1954). For an overview, see the works of Gerhard Dilcher, including "Der Staat als herrschaftlich-genossenschaftlich verfasstes Gemeinwesen," in *Staat und Historie: Leitbilder und Fragestellungen deutscher Geschichtsschreibung vom Ende des 19. bis zur Mitte des 20. Jahrhunderts*, ed. Walter Pauly and Klaus Ries (Baden-Baden: Nomos, 2021), 113–42.

30. Here I take inspiration from Mariano Barbato, "Double Bind: Der Synodale Weg und die Entmachtung des katholischen Klerus," *Herder Korrespondenz* 75, no. 10 (2021): 24–26.

31. Daniel Bogner's provocative polemic is a forceful case in point: Daniel Bogner, *Ihr macht uns die Kirche kaputt . . . , . . . doch wir lassen das nicht zu* (Freiburg: Herder, 2019), 98.

32. For an organizational sociologist who attached great importance to this, see Amitai Etzioni, *Modern Organizations* (Englewood Cliffs, NJ: Prentice Hall, 1964).

CHAPTER 3

1. "Die kirchliche Leere" instead of "Die kirchliche Lehre."

2. Grace Davie, *Religion in Modern Europe: A Memory Mutates* (Oxford: Oxford University Press, 2000).

3. According to Philip Jenkins, *The Next Christendom: The Coming of Global Christianity* (Oxford: Oxford University Press, 2002), 56, with reference to the *World Christian Encyclopedia* (Oxford: Oxford University Press, 2001).

4. Sarbeswar Sahoo, *Pentecostalism and Politics of Conversion in India*, with a preface by Hans Joas (Delhi: Cambridge University Press, 2018).

5. Pippa Norris and Ronald F. Inglehart, *Sacred and Secular: Religion and Politics Worldwide* (Cambridge: Cambridge University Press, 2004).

6. Jörg Lauster, *Die Verzauberung der Welt: Eine Kulturgeschichte des Christentums* (Munich: Beck, 2014), 125.

7. His magnum opus is David Martin, *A General Theory of Secularization* (Oxford: Blackwell, 1978). On his oeuvre as a whole, see the discussion volume: Hans Joas, ed., *David Martin and the Sociology of Religion* (London: Routledge, 2018). See also Hans Joas, *Faith as an Option: Possible Futures for Christianity* (Stanford, CA: Stanford University Press, 2014), esp. 37–49.

8. Hans Joas, *Kirche als Moralagentur?* (Munich: Kösel, 2016). See also the recent discussion volume: Jochen Sautermeister, ed., *Kirche—nur eine Moralagentur? Eine Selbstverortung* (Freiburg: Herder, 2019). For a summary of my book and my reply to its critics, see Chapters 10 and 11 in this book.

9. Charles Taylor, *A Secular Age* (Cambridge, MA: Harvard University Press, 2007).

10. Hans Joas, *The Power of the Sacred: An Alternative to the Narrative of Disenchantment* (New York: Oxford University Press, 2021). In the following I rely on a passage from that book.

11. I can claim to have been championing this distinction for a number of years. See Hans Joas, *The Sacredness of the Person: A New Genealogy of Human Rights* (Washington, DC: Georgetown University Press, 2013), 56–57, on the secular/religious pairing versus profane/sacred. On the pairing transcendent/immanent, see my studies on the Axial Age, such as chapter 5 in Joas, *The Power of the Sacred*, 154–94. This distinction is expressed with particular clarity in José Casanova, "Religion, the Axial Age, and Secular Modernity in Bellah's Theory of Religious Evolution," in *The Axial Age and Its Consequences*, ed. Robert N. Bellah and Hans Joas (Cambridge, MA: Harvard University Press, 2012), 191–221. It also forms the basis of the theory of religion in Reinhard Schulze, *Der Koran und die Genealogie des Islam* (Basel: Schwabe, 2015), 109–81.

12. On the genesis of the term "religion" as a phenomenon opposed to the "secular," see the remarks in chapter 1 of Joas, *The Power of the Sacred*; on the emergence of notions of transcendence, see chapter 5 of the same book.

13. For a more in-depth treatment of the concept of the sacred, see chapter 2 in Joas, *The Power of the Sacred*; Joas, *The Sacredness of the Person*, 51–57; Hans Joas, "Secular Sacredness: Rudolf Otto," in Hans Joas, *Under the Spell of Freedom: Theory of Religion after Hegel and Nietzsche* (New York: Oxford University Press, 2024), 52–68.

14. Max Weber, *The Religion of China* (New York: Free Press, 1951), 226.

15. See Hartmann Tyrell, "Potenz und Depotenzierung der Religion: Religion und Rationalisierung bei Max Weber," *Saeculum* 44 (1993): 300–347, here 306n20.

16. Ibid., 323.

17. Ibid., 311.

18. See Hans Joas, *Was ist die Achsenzeit?* (Basel: Schwabe, 2014), 26–35.

19. Max Weber, "Some Categories of Interpretive Sociology," *Sociological Quarterly* 22, no. 2 (Spring 1981): 151–80, here 155. The English translation uses "ethical" for Weber's *gesinnungshaft*, which does not really convey the meaning of Weber's statement. See Max Weber, "Über einige Kategorien der verstehenden Soziologie," in *Gesammelte Aufsätze zur Wissenschaftslehre*, by Max Weber (Tübingen: Mohr Siebeck, 1973), 427–74, here 433.

20. Of the vast and, of course, also controversial literature, here I will mention just an excellent overview: Rivka Feldhay, "Religion," in *The Cambridge History of Science*, vol. 3, *Early Modern Science*, ed. Katharine Park and Lorraine Daston (Cambridge: Cambridge University Press, 2008), 727–55. It distinguishes three main narratives on the relationship between religion and science as it has developed over the course of history (eternal conflict; peaceful coexistence; affinities and interactions), affirms the relative validity of each narrative and, above all, emphasizes how the religious upheavals of the early modern period and the development of modern science led to changes whose complexity is not well conveyed by any of the three narratives.

21. The standard text by Keith Thomas, *Religion and the Decline of Magic* (New York: Scribner, 1971), is highly compatible with Weber's narrative of disenchantment. For the debate on this book, see the introduction by the editors in Jonathan Barry, Marianne Hester, and Gareth Roberts, eds., *Witchcraft in Early Modern Europe: Studies in Culture and Belief* (Cambridge: Cambridge University Press, 1996), 1–45. On the history of the "miracle," see Lorraine Daston and Katharine Park, *Wonders and the Order of Nature 1150–1750* (New York: Zone, 2001). For a critique, see Michael Saler, "Modernity and Enchantment: A Historiographic Review," *American Historical Review* 111 (2006): 692–716, esp. 703–5. Saler writes: "In this respect, enchantment waxed rather than waned by the time of the Enlightenment, countering more linear narratives of progressive disenchantment" (703).

22. Reinhart Koselleck, *Critique and Crisis: Enlightenment and the Pathogenesis of Modern Society* (1959; Cambridge, MA: MIT Press, 1988).

23. Hans Joas, "The Contingency of Secularization: Reflections on the Problem of Secularization in the Work of Reinhart Koselleck," in *The Benefit of Broad Horizons: Intellectual and Institutional Preconditions for a Global Social Science. Festschrift for Björn Wittrock on the Occasion of His 65th Birthday*, ed. Hans Joas and Barbro Klein (Leiden: Brill, 2010), 87–104; now also in Joas, *Under the Spell of Freedom*, 132–46. The expression "our post-theological age" appears in Koselleck's foreword to *Critique and Crisis*, 3.

CHAPTER 4

1. Bertolt Brecht, "Peinlicher Vorfall," in *Gesammelte Werke*, by Bertolt Brecht (Frankfurt am Main: Suhrkamp, 1967), 10:861–62. Thanks to David Dollenmayer (Worcester Polytechnic Institute) for his help in translating this poem.

2. See Werner Mittenzwei, *Das Leben des Bertolt Brecht* (Berlin [GDR]: Aufbau, 1986), 2:106–10.

3. Bertolt Brecht, *Arbeitsjournal*, entry of August 14, 1943 (Frankfurt am Main: Suhrkamp, 1973).

4. Alfred Döblin, letter to Wilhelm Hausenstein of January 31, 1947, in *Briefe* (Olten: Walter, 1970), 364.

5. Alfred Döblin, *Der unsterbliche Mensch: Ein Religionsgespräch* (1946; Frankfurt am Main: Fischer, 2016), 158.

6. William James, "The Will to Believe" (1897), in *The Will to Believe and Other Essays in Popular Philosophy*, by William James (New York: Longmans, Green, 1905), 1–31, esp. 6.

7. Hans Joas, *The Genesis of Values* (Chicago: University of Chicago Press, 2000), 41.

8. Knut Hamsun, *Mysteries*, trans. Gerry Bothmer (New York: Farrar, Straus and Giroux, 1971), 64–65.

9. Paul Tillich, *The Courage to Be* (New Haven, CT: Yale University Press, 1952), 35. On Tillich's thinking, see Hans Joas, "Indebted Freedom," in *Under the Spell of Freedom: Theory of Religion after Hegel and Nietzsche*, by Hans Joas (New York: Oxford University Press, 2024), 196–214.

10. Paul Tillich, *Systematic Theology*, 4th ed. (Chicago: University of Chicago Press, 1955), 1:61–62.

11. See André Dubus, *Adultery and Other Choices* (Boston: David R. Godine, 1977), 168–70.

12. Richard Schröder, "Wie beim Handy, so beim Glauben: 'Wechseln Sie einfach den Anbieter!' Funktioniert das?" *Chrismon* 5 (2003): 46.

13. Paul Tillich, *Gesammelte Werke* (Stuttgart: Evangelisches Verlagswerk, 1970), 8:93.

14. Paul Ricœur and Andre LaCocque, *Penser la Bible* (Paris: Seuil, 1998), 279–304. On Ricœur's philosophy, see Joas, *Under the Spell of Freedom*, 213–25.

CHAPTER 5

1. Hans Joas, *Faith as an Option: Possible Futures for Christianity* (Stanford, CA: Stanford University Press, 2014).

2. Charles Taylor, *A Secular Age* (Cambridge, MA: Harvard University Press, 2007). On this, see Hans Joas, "The Secular Option, Its Rise and Consequences: Charles Taylor," in *Under the Spell of Freedom: Theory of Religion after Hegel and Nietzsche*, by Hans Joas (New York: Oxford University Press, 2024), 147–60.

3. Joas, *Faith as an Option*, 46–49.

4. William James, "The Will to Believe" (1897), in *The Will to Believe and Other Essays in Popular Philosophy*, by William James (New York: Longmans, Green, 1905), 1–31, here 3.

5. First described by Robert Wuthnow, *The Restructuring of American Religion* (Princeton, NJ: Princeton University Press, 1988).

6. Robert Putnam and David Campbell, *American Grace: How Religion Divides and Unites Us* (New York: Simon & Schuster, 2010).

7. Here I draw on passages from a number of my own earlier works.

8. Ernest Burgess and Harvey Locke, *The Family: From Institution to Companionship* (New York: American Book Company, 1945).

9. Philip Jenkins, *The Next Christendom: The Coming of Global Christianity* (Oxford: Oxford University Press, 2002).

10. Karl Rahner, "Theologische Grundinterpretation des II. Vatikanischen Konzils," in *Schriften zur Theologie*, by Karl Rahner (Cologne: Belziger, 1980), 14:287–302. See also Chapter 2 in this book in connection with how to organizationally guarantee the universalism of Christianity.

11. Rahner, "Theologische Grundinterpretation," 14:297.

12. David M. Thompson, "Introduction: Mapping Asian Christianity in the Context of World Christianity," in *Christian Theology in Asia*, ed. Sebastian C. H. Kim (Cambridge: Cambridge University Press, 2008), 3–21, here 13–14.

13. See Chapter 6 in this book for more discussion.

14. Charles Taylor, in particular, has examined this rise in depth. See his *Sources of the Self: The Making of the Modern Identity* (Cambridge, MA: Harvard University Press, 1989). Building on these ideas and developing them further is Magnus Schlette, *Die Idee der Selbstverwirklichung: Zur Grammatik des modernen Individualismus* (Frankfurt am Main: Campus, 2013).

15. Of his extensive oeuvre, I will mention just his lecture delivered in 1925 at the Lessing-Hochschule in Berlin: Max Scheler, "Die Formen des Wissens und die Bildung," in *Philosophische Weltanschauung*, by Max Scheler (Munich: Lehnen, 1954), 16–48. On Scheler's philosophy of value, see Hans Joas, *The Genesis of Values* (Chicago: University of Chicago Press, 2000), 84–102; on his philosophy of religion, see Joas, *Under the Spell of Freedom*, 69–84.

16. The literature on the subject of self-optimization has grown exponentially in recent years. Of the scholarly literature, I will mention just Jürgen Straub, *Das optimierte Selbst: Kompetenzimperative und Steigerungstechnologien in der Optimierungsgesellschaft* (Gießen: Psychosozial-Verlag, 2019); Anja Röcke, *Soziologie der Selbstoptimierung* (Berlin: Suhrkamp, 2021). For a brilliant journalistic discussion, see Alexandra Schwartz, "Improving Ourselves to Death," *New Yorker*, January 15, 2018, https://www.newyorker.com/magazine/2018/01/15/improving-ourselves-to-death.

17. Martin Buber, *I and Thou* (1923; New York: Scribner, 1958).

18. For example, in Romano Guardini and Otto Friedrich Bollnow, *Begegnung und Bildung* (Würzburg: Werkbund-Verlag, 1956), 9–24.

19. Martin Heidegger, *Gelassenheit* (Pfullingen: Neske, 1956). English translation: *Discourse on Thinking* (New York: Harper & Row, 1966).

20. Joas, *Faith as an Option*, 126–37.

21. Victor Turner, *The Ritual Process: Structure and Anti-structure* (1969; New York: Routledge, 2017).

22. Hans Joas, *The Power of the Sacred: An Alternative to the Narrative of Disenchantment* (New York: Oxford University Press, 2021), 87.

CHAPTER 6

1. Émile Durkheim, *Suicide: A Study in Sociology* (1897; New York: Free Press, 1951).

2. Jack D. Douglas, *The Social Meanings of Suicide* (Princeton, NJ: Princeton University Press, 1967).

3. Quotations from the novel are referenced in the text through the volume and page number (German/English). See Alfred Döblin, *November 1918*, 4 vols. (Munich: dtv, 1978). An abbreviated English translation of vols. II and III has been published in one volume: Alfred Döblin, *A People Betrayed: November 1918: A German Revolution*, trans. John E. Woods (New York: Fromm International Publishing, 1983); translation of vol. IV: Alfred Döblin, *Karl and Rosa: November 1918: A German Revolution*, trans. John E. Woods (New York: Fromm International Publishing, 1983). Vol. I remains untranslated, so citations from it are rendered into English by the translator of this book, Alex Skinner.

4. For a discussion, see Chapter 4 in this book.

5. This is the tendency, for example, in Theodore Ziolkowski, *Modes of Faith: Secular Surrogates for Lost Religious Belief* (Chicago: University of Chicago Press, 2007), 132–39.

6. Of the—often excellent—secondary literature, I would like to mention the following as particularly important to me: Helmuth Kiesel, *Literarische Trauerarbeit: Das Exil- und Spätwerk Alfred Döblins* (Tübingen: Niemeyer, 1986), 271–486; Manfred Auer, *Das Exil vor der Vertreibung: Motivkontinuität und Quellenproblematik im späten Werk Alfred Döblins* (Bonn: Bouvier, 1977), 56–102; David B. Dollenmayer, *The Berlin Novels of Alfred Döblin* (Berkeley: University of California Press, 1988), 124–78. For a useful overview of the research, see Wulf Koepke, *The Critical Reception of Alfred Döblin's Major Novels* (New York: Camden House, 2003), 178–203.

7. Alfred Döblin, "Epilog," in *Autobiographische Schriften und letzte Aufzeichnungen*, by Alfred Döblin (Olten: Walter, 1980), 439–51, here 448.

8. The similarity to Döblin's last novel (*Hamlet oder Die lange Nacht nimmt ein Ende*; English translation: *Tales of a Long Night* [New York: Fromm 1984]) is unmistakable. See my interpretation in Hans Joas, *Die lange Nacht der Trauer: Erzählen als Weg aus der Gewalt?* (Gießen: Psychosozial-Verlag, 2014).

9. This sounds like a prescient attempt to get to grips with tendencies toward "self-optimization" (see Chapter 5 in this book).

10. Werner Stauffacher, "Einführung," in Döblin, *November 1918*, 1:9–64, here 58.

11. Apart from Kiesel, this also applies to Günter Niggl, "Antwort auf das Inferno der Zeit: Das Spätwerk Alfred Döblins," in *Zeitbilder: Studien und Vorträge zur deutschen Literatur des 19. und 20. Jahrhunderts*, by Günter Niggl (Würzburg: Königshausen & Neumann, 2005), 115–24, here 121; Roland Dollinger, *Totalität*

und Totalitarismus im Exilwerk Döblins (Würzburg: Königshausen & Neumann, 1994), 190; Dollinger, however, presents salvation history and the critical description of history as alternatives (on 164, for example), which is why his study ends with an accusation of "historical repression" (209); original reflections on Döblin's understanding of history can be found in Meike Mattick, *Komik und Geschichtserfahrung: Alfred Döblins komisierendes Erzählen in "November 1918: Eine deutsche Revolution"* (Bielefeld: Aisthesis Verlag, 2003).

12. See Chapter 2 in this book. At the end of his second "religious dialogue" ("The Struggle with the Angel"), Döblin points out that the prayer Jesus himself taught his disciples does not refer to "My Father" but to "Our Father," to "our bread" and "our debts." "You are meant to be with the others. The tribulations of these others, whom you must help, call out to you, liberating you from your ego" (Alfred Döblin, *Der unsterbliche Mensch / Der Kampf mit dem Engel* [1950–52; Frankfurt am Main: Fischer, 2016], 595).

13. See Karl Griewank, *Der neuzeitliche Revolutionsbegriff: Entstehung und Entwicklung* (Weimar: Böhlau, 1955); James H. Billington, *Fire in the Minds of Men: Origins of the Revolutionary Faith* (New York: Basic Books, 1980).

14. Ernst Troeltsch, "Rück- und Umblick (Februar 1919)," in *Spectator-Briefe und Berliner Briefe (1919–1922)*, by Ernst Troeltsch, ed. Gangolf Hübinger, KGA (Berlin: De Gruyter, 2015), 14:53.

15. Christina Althen, *Machtkonstellationen einer deutschen Revolution: Alfred Döblins Geschichtsroman "November 1918"* (Frankfurt am Main: Peter Lang, 1993), 153.

16. On both, with details of the research literature, see Hans Joas, *War and Modernity* (Cambridge: Polity, 2003).

17. This is recognized by Oliver Jahraus, "Subjekte der Geschichte—Geschichten des Subjekts: Döblins Erzählwerk 'November 1918,'" in *Der Erste Weltkrieg als Katastrophe: Deutungsmuster im literarischen Diskurs*, ed. Claude D. Conter, Oliver Jahraus and Christian Kirchmeier (Würzburg: Königshausen & Neumann, 2014), 175–92.

18. Very precise evidence is provided for this view by Anthony W. Riley, "The Aftermath of the First World War: Christianity and Revolution in Alfred Döblin's 'November 1918,'" in *The First World War in German Narrative Prose*, ed. Charles N. Genno and Heinz Wetzel (Toronto: University of Toronto Press, 1980), 93–117, esp. note 33 (114–15).

19. Wolfgang Frühwald, "Rosa und der Satan: Thesen zum Verhältnis von Christentum und Sozialismus im Schlussband von Alfred Döblins Erzählwerk 'November 1918,'" in *Internationale Alfred-Döblin-Kolloquien Basel 1980 / New York 1981 / Freiburg 1983*, ed. Werner Stauffacher (Bern: Peter Lang, 1986), 239–56, here 248.

20. Kiesel, *Literarische Trauerarbeit*, 334.

21. Alfred Döblin, "Christentum und Revolution," in *Schriften zur Literatur*, by Alfred Döblin (Olten: Walter, 1963), 379–83, here 382.
22. Ibid.

CHAPTER 7

1. Quoted in Steven Lukes, "Leszek Kołakowski 1927–2009," *Proceedings of the British Academy* 172 (2011): 201–11, here 202.
2. Leszek Kołakowski, *Chrétiens sans Église: La conscience religieuse et le lien confessionnel au XVIIe siècle* (Paris: Gallimard, 1969). The Polish title refers to "ties to the church" rather than "confessional ties."
3. A characteristic case is François Bondy, "Kołakowski: Grundmuster und Exempel. 'Christen ohne Kirche'—'Sozialisten ohne Partei'?," *Europäische Ideen* 33 (1977): 12–17.
4. Statements made during the various phases of his development can in retrospect be interpreted as anticipating his later ideas.
5. Since I cannot read Polish-language texts and much of Kołakowski's early work has never been translated, I base my remarks on this first phase primarily on the available secondary literature. Particularly important to me in this regard and to the entire chapter is the remarkable book by Christian Heidrich, *Leszek Kolakowski: Zwischen Skepsis und Mystik* (Frankfurt am Main: Neue Kritik, 1995). Also Gesine Schwan, *Leszek Kolakowski: Eine Philosophie der Freiheit nach Marx* (Stuttgart: Kohlhammer, 1971); Bogdan Piwowarczyk, *Lire Kolakowski: La question de l'homme, de la religion et de l'Église* (Paris: Cerf, 1986).
6. As he explained, for example, in conversation with Danny Postel: Danny Postel, "On Exile, Philosophy and Tottering Insecurely on the Edge of an Unknown Abyss," *Daedalus* 134 (2005): 82–88, here 86.
7. Quoted in Heidrich, *Zwischen Skepsis und Mystik*, 54.
8. Ibid., 65.
9. Ibid., 49.
10. Ibid., 66.
11. Schwan, *Leszek Kolakowski*, 46–49.
12. Heidrich, *Zwischen Skepsis und Mystik*, 86–87.
13. Józef Tischner, "Leszek Kolakowski—Anmerkungen zu seinem Denken," in *Der unmögliche Dialog: Christentum und Marxismus in Polen*, by Józef Tischner (Graz: Styria, 1982), 217–32, here 223. The de facto development of this "impossible" dialogue into a "possible" one is further explored in Hella Dietz, *Polnischer Protest: Zur pragmatistischen Fundierung von Theorien sozialen Wandels* (Frankfurt am Main: Campus, 2015).
14. This can be traced in his essays of the early 1960s.
15. Jürgen Habermas, *Theorie und Praxis: Sozialphilosophische Studien* (1957; Frankfurt am Main: Suhrkamp, 1971), 448–50.

16. Heidrich, *Zwischen Skepsis und Mystik*, 74, 76.
17. Ibid., 90.
18. Ibid., 100.
19. Ibid., note 66.
20. Leszek Kołakowski, "Religiöse Symbole und humanistische Kultur" (1967), in *Geist und Ungeist christlicher Traditionen*, by Leszek Kołakowski (Stuttgart: Kohlhammer, 1971), 90–112, here 111.
21. With reference to a 1962 Polish publication by Kołakowski, see Marcin Król, "Leszek Kołakowski: Le philosophe et la religion," *Esprit* 106, no. 10 (1985): 63–81, here 66. Kołakowski does not seem to have been referring to Max Weber's famous comments on his religious nonmusicality.
22. I endeavored to elaborate this perspective in my book *The Genesis of Values* (Chicago: University of Chicago Press, 2000).
23. This project is bound to be aporetic if one cleaves to the idea that philosophical teachings as such could fundamentally change people's practice and experience. The picture changes if the practical side, such as spiritual exercises, is also taken into account, which applied to the Stoics in particular. Pioneering in this respect is Pierre Hadot, *Qu'est-ce que la philosophie antique?* (Paris: Gallimard, 1995), esp. 265–352.
24. In doing so, I deviate somewhat from the accounts mentioned in note 5, because I ascribe to his book *Chrétiens sans Église* a more significant position within Kołakowski's intellectual journey.
25. Lucien Goldmann, *The Hidden God: A Study of Tragic Vision in the Pensées of Pascal and the Tragedies of Racine* (London: Routledge, 1964).
26. Kołakowski, *Chrétiens sans Église*, 352. All subsequent page numbers in this book are cited in the main text itself.
27. There is no room here for a more detailed account. For an excellent brief summary, see Henry Mottu, "'Chrétiens sans Église' de Kołakowski," *Revue de Théologie et de Philosophie* 23 (1973): 308–31.
28. Michel de Certeau, *The Mystic Fable. Vol. 1, Sixteenth and Seventeenth Centuries* (Chicago: University of Chicago Press, 1985), 307n36.
29. Pierre Chaunu, "Deuxième ou troisième Réforme? Le XVIIe siècle des hétérodoxes," *Annales* 25 (1970): 1574–90. Further information on reviews can be found in Heidrich, *Zwischen Skepsis und Mystik*, 249–50. In 2014, the journal *Archives de Sciences Sociales des Religions* devoted an entire special issue to Kołakowski's book (166/2014). It might also be worthwhile to compare Kołakowski's accounts with those of Ernst Troeltsch in his *Social Teachings*; the latter also deals in depth with Jean de Labadie and the emergence of Pietist cell groups as well as "separatist" approaches. One would then have to scrutinize how the typology of Christian forms of community set out in the title essay of this book relates to Kołakowski's findings.

30. Mottu, "'Chrétiens sans Église' de Kołakowski," 328.

31. Leszek Kołakowski, *The Presence of Myth* (Chicago: University of Chicago Press, 2001). The book was written in Polish in 1966.

32. Ibid., 148.

33. To borrow from the subtitle of my book *Under the Spell of Freedom: Theory of Religion after Hegel and Nietzsche* (New York: Oxford University Press, 2024).

34. Leszek Kołakowski, "The Priest and the Jester: Reflections on the Theological Heritage of Contemporary Thought" (1959), in *The Two Eyes of Spinoza—and Other Essays on Philosophers*, by Leszek Kołakowski (South Bend, IN: St. Augustine's Press, 2004), 239–62.

35. These questions cannot be dealt with adequately here. On this topic, see Hans Joas, *The Power of the Sacred: An Alternative to the Narrative of Disenchantment* (New York: Oxford University Press, 2021), 154–94. It would be necessary to make a comparison above all with the conception of myth in Robert N. Bellah, *Religion in Human Evolution: From the Paleolithic to the Axial Age* (Cambridge, MA: Harvard University Press, 2011). Incidentally, the preface of that volume ends with a reference to Kołakowski (xxiv).

36. Heidrich, *Zwischen Skepsis und Mystik*, 20.

37. Martin Jay, "A Missed Opportunity: Leszek Kolakowski in Berkeley," *Salmagundi* 166/167 (2010): 3–9.

38. Leszek Kołakowski, *Modernity on Endless Trial* (Chicago: University of Chicago Press, 1990), 9.

39. Heidrich, *Zwischen Skepsis und Mystik*, 351–57, in his account of the critique expounded by Polish philosopher Helena Eilstein.

40. Kołakowski, *Modernity on Endless Trial*, 63–74.

41. Ibid., 14–31.

42. Tadeusz Mazowiecki, "Un-Vollendetes: Leszek Kołakowski und die Religion," in *Partei nehmen für die Hoffnung: Über Moral in der Politik*, by Tadeusz Mazowiecki (Freiburg: Herder, 1990), 66–86, here 83–84. My book *The Sacredness of the Person: A New Genealogy of Human Rights* (Washington, DC: Georgetown University Press, 2013) attempted to elaborate this idea.

43. See my books *Sind die Menschenrechte westlich?* and *Friedensprojekt Europa?* (Munich: Kösel, 2015 and 2020, respectively).

44. For more details, see Joas, *The Genesis of Values*, esp. 161–86.

45. Kołakowski, "The Priest and the Jester," 253.

46. Leszek Kołakowski, *Metaphysical Horror* (Chicago: University of Chicago Press, 2001).

47. Heidrich, *Zwischen Skepsis und Mystik*, 352, with reference to an interview in *Tygodnik Powszechny* 7 (1989): 1–2, here 2.

48. My thanks go to Christian Heidrich and Michał Kaczmarczyk (Gdańsk) for comments on my text and on the Polish debate.

CHAPTER 8

1. Hannah Arendt, *The Origins of Totalitarianism* (1951; London: Deutsch, 1986), 79.
2. Steven Lukes, *Émile Durkheim: His Life and Work* (Harmondsworth, UK: Penguin, 1977), 347–49.
3. Charles Maurras, *Au signe de Flore* (Paris: Bernard Grasset, 1933), 81. See Ernst Nolte, *Der Faschismus in seiner Epoche* (Munich: Piper, 1984), 92.
4. Émile Durkheim, "Individualism and the Intellectuals" (1898), in *Emile Durkheim on Morality and Society*, ed. Robert N. Bellah (Chicago: University of Chicago Press, 1986), 43–57, esp. 43; subsequent page numbers in the text refer to this essay. I have elaborated on Durkheim's ideas in Hans Joas, *The Sacredness of the Person: A New Genealogy of Human Rights* (Washington, DC: Georgetown University Press, 2013).
5. See Hans Joas, *The Creativity of Action* (Chicago: University of Chicago Press, 1996).
6. Immanuel Kant, *Groundwork for the Metaphysics of Morals* (1785; Oxford: Oxford University Press, 2002), 235.
7. Ibid., 236.
8. Émile Durkheim, *The Division of Labor in Society* (1893; New York: Free Press, 1997), 201–2.
9. For a more detailed examination of this issue, see Chapter 4 in this book.
10. Émile Durkheim, *The Elementary Forms of Religious Life* (1912; Oxford: Oxford University Press, 2001), 242–75; Émile Durkheim, *The Evolution of Educational Thought* (1938; London: Routledge, 1977); Émile Durkheim, *Professional Ethics and Civic Morals* (London: Routledge, 1991).
11. Niklas Luhmann, *Law as a Social System* (Oxford: Oxford University Press, 2004), 417.
12. Durkheim, *Professional Ethics*, 88.
13. Émile Durkheim, "Deux lois de l'évolution pénale" (1901), in *Journal sociologique*, by Émile Durkheim (Paris: Presses Universitaires de France, 1969), 244–73.
14. Michel Foucault, *Discipline and Punish: The Birth of the Prison* (New York: Vintage, 1977).
15. Randall Collins in particular has persistently championed such an interpretation.
16. Émile Durkheim, "Débat sur l'éducation sexuelle" (1911), in *Textes*, by Émile Durkheim (Paris: Editions de Minuit, 1975), 2:241–51.
17. Ibid., 248.

CHAPTER 9

1. Immanuel Kant, *Groundwork for the Metaphysics of Morals* (1785; Oxford: Oxford University Press, 2002), 235–36.

2. For more on Kant and especially Durkheim, see Chapter 8 in this book.
3. See Hans Joas, *Sind die Menschenrechte westlich?* (Munich: Kösel, 2015).

CHAPTER 10

1. This chapter is based on ideas set out in more detail in my book *Kirche als Moralagentur?* (Munich: Kösel, 2016).
2. The terminology here has fluctuated over the course of intellectual history. While in William James morality appears only as restrictive and religion as attractive, Émile Durkheim distinguishes between different types of morality. What matters to me is not the terminology but the distinction between "restrictive" and "attractive." These trains of thought are broadly developed in Hans Joas, *The Genesis of Values* (Chicago: University of Chicago Press, 2000).
3. Wolfgang Huber, *Kirche in der Zeitenwende: Gesellschaftlicher Wandel und Erneuerung der Kirche* (Gütersloh: Verlag Bertelsmann Stiftung, 1998).
4. Friedrich Wilhelm Graf, *Kirchendämmerung: Wie die Kirchen unser Vertrauen verspielen* (Munich: Beck, 2011).
5. For my discussion of the ideas and ministry of the late Cardinal Francis George of Chicago, see Hans Joas, "Public Religion, Secularism, and the Ethos of Love," in *Secularism, Catholicism, and the Future of Public Life*, ed. Gary J. Adler Jr. (New York: Oxford University Press, 2015), 155–64. The expressions quoted in what follows come from Cardinal Francis George, specifically his book *God in Action: How Faith in God Can Address the Challenges of the World* (New York: Doubleday, 2011). One of the most important contributions to the critique of the excessive politicization of the Christian churches in the United States and an alternative vision of "faithful presence" has been presented by James Davison Hunter, *To Change the World: The Irony, Tragedy, and Possibility of Christianity in the Late Modern World* (New York: Oxford University Press, 2010).
6. Irmgard Schwaetzer, "Grußwort auf der Vollversammlung des Zentralkomitees der deutschen Katholiken" (May 25, 2016, Leipzig).
7. H. Richard Niebuhr, *Christ and Culture* (1951; New York: Harper, 2001), first quotation on 237. On this thinker, see also Chapter 2 in this book; and Hans Joas, *Under the Spell of Freedom: Theory of Religion after Hegel and Nietzsche* (New York: Oxford University Press, 2024), 256–76.
8. Niebuhr, *Christ and Culture*, 178.
9. Michael Walzer, *Spheres of Justice: A Defense of Pluralism and Equality* (New York: Basic Books, 1983), 31–63.
10. William A. Barbieri Jr., *Constitutive Justice* (New York: Palgrave Macmillan, 2015), 100.
11. I have endeavored to clarify these issues in earlier writings, my engagement with Max Scheler and Paul Ricœur being particularly instructive in that context. See Joas, *The Genesis of Values*, chaps. 6 and 10; Hans Joas, "Liebe, Gabe, Gerechtigkeit," in *Die Zehn Gebote: Ein widersprüchliches Erbe?*, ed. Hans Joas (Cologne: Böhlau,

2006), 175–83; Hans Joas, *The Sacredness of the Person: A New Genealogy of Human Rights* (Washington, DC: Georgetown University Press, 2013), 97–139.

12. Max Weber, *Gesammelte Aufsätze zur Religionssoziologie*, vol. 1 (1920; Tübingen: Mohr Siebeck, 1988), for example, 546.

13. Cardinal Karl Lehmann, "Catholic Christianity," in *Secularization and the World Religions*, ed. Hans Joas and Klaus Wiegandt (Liverpool: Liverpool University Press, 2009), 23–45.

14. For an excellent account of this, see Michael Borgolte, *Christen, Juden, Muselmanen: Die Erben der Antike und der Aufstieg des Abendlandes 300 bis 1400 n. Chr.* (Berlin: Siedler, 2006).

CHAPTER 11

1. Hans Joas, *Kirche als Moralagentur?* (Munich: Kösel, 2016). See also Chapter 10 in this book. The present chapter refers to the discussion volume: Jochen Sautermeister, ed., *Kirche—nur eine Moralagentur? Eine Selbstverortung* (Freiburg: Herder, 2019). Unless otherwise stated, the contributions to this volume are the subject of my response here. All the page numbers in the main text refer to it.

2. "Konsens und Konflikt: Politik braucht Auseinandersetzung. Zehn Impulse der Kammer für Öffentliche Verantwortung der EKD zu aktuellen Herausforderungen der Demokratie in Deutschland (Französische Friedrichstadtkirche, Berlin, 21. August 2017)." *epd-Dokumentation* 44 (November 1, 2017). See also my commentary in the same publication: Hans Joas, "Um die 'konstitutive Gerechtigkeit' streiten," 16–17.

3. Ulrich H. J. Körtner, *Für die Vernunft: Wider Moralisierung und Emotionalisierung in Politik und Kirche* (Leipzig: Evangelische Verlagsanstalt, 2017).

4. Annette Schavan, "Gewissen bilden, nicht Gewissen ersetzen wollen," 81–96.

5. See Chapter 1 in this book.

6. Now available without my contribution (which was published separately) as Claas Cordemann and Gundolf Holfert, eds., *Moral ohne Bekenntnis? Zur Debatte um Kirche als zivilreligiöse Moralagentur* (Leipzig: Evangelische Verlagsanstalt, 2017).

7. Hans Joas, *The Sacredness of the Person: A New Genealogy of Human Rights* (Washington, DC: Georgetown University Press, 2013); Hans Joas, *Sind die Menschenrechte westlich?* (Munich: Kösel, 2015).

8. See Chapter 10 in this book.

9. Jan Brezger, *Internationale Freizügigkeit als Menschenrecht* (Frankfurt am Main: Campus, 2018).

10. See the essay by Günther Roth, "Max Weber's Ethics and the Peace Movement Today," *Theory and Society* 13 (1984): 491–511. I built on these ideas in the chapter "Ideologies of War" in Hans Joas, *War and Modernity* (Cambridge: Polity, 2003), 55–81, here 206n20.

11. Ulrich H. J. Körtner, "Moralisierung und Entmoralisierung des christlichen Glaubens," 97–116.

12. Peter Dabrock, "'Nicht Politik machen, Politik möglich machen': Zur begrenzten Legitimität religiöser Moral," 35–56.

13. With this term I allude to the essay by Sighard Neckel and Jürgen Wolf, "Die Faszination der Amoralität: Zur Systemtheorie der Moral," *Prokla* 18 (1988): 57–77. For my critique of Luhmann, see Hans Joas, *The Creativity of Action* (Chicago: University of Chicago Press, 1996), 209–23; Hans Joas and Wolfgang Knöbl, *Social Theory: Twenty Introductory Lectures* (Cambridge: Cambridge University Press, 2009), 249–80. Peter Dabrock is aware of the difference between Luhmann and myself but sees it as more superficial than it is (38–41).

14. Eberhard Schockenhoff, "Für eine Kirche, die sich einmischt: Die Problematik kirchlicher Stellungnahmen zu politischen Streitfragen," 57–80.

15. I am grateful to the editor of the discussion volume for making this clear in his own discussion of my book when he writes: "In his social scientific-theological critique, Hans Joas in no way advocates an innocuous, apolitical Christianity. Instead his core concern is to expose observable moralizing tendencies with respect to political issues on the part of the church and to problematize them insofar as they are inappropriate on theological/religious, political and ethical grounds" (see Jochen Sautermeister, "'Kirche als Moralagentur?' Theologisch-ethische Überlegungen zur moralischen und politischen Relevanz von Kirche in der Gesellschaft," *Münchener Theologische Zeitschrift* 68 [2017]: 292–305, here 298). He also recognizes the centrality in my argument of moral universalists' particular moral obligations (297).

16. Magnus Striet, "Jenseits von Heteronomie—oder: Kirche als Glaubensagentur," 117–35, here 135n6.

17. Hans Joas, *The Genesis of Values* (Chicago: University of Chicago Press, 2000); Hans Joas, ed., *Was sind religiöse Überzeugungen?* (Göttingen: Wallstein, 2003).

18. For more on this, see Part III, "The Search for a Different Kind of Freedom," in Hans Joas, *Under the Spell of Freedom: Theory of Religion after Hegel and Nietzsche* (New York: Oxford University Press, 2024), 163–72, especially my remarks on theonomy and autonomy in the introduction, 167–70.

19. See also Hans Joas, *The Power of the Sacred: An Alternative to the Narrative of Disenchantment* (New York: Oxford University Press, 2021), 99–106; and the title essay in this book (Chapter 2). Notable in this vein is Ulrich Schmiedel, *Elasticized Ecclesiology: The Concept of Community after Ernst Troeltsch* (New York: Palgrave Macmillan, 2017).

20. Günter de Bruyn, *Der neunzigste Geburtstag* (Frankfurt am Main: S. Fischer, 2018), 140.

21. Ibid., 143.

22. Ibid., 144.

Bibliography

Althen, Christina. *Machtkonstellationen einer deutschen Revolution: Alfred Döblins Geschichtsroman "November 1918."* Frankfurt am Main: Peter Lang, 1993.
Arendt, Hannah. *The Origins of Totalitarianism.* 1951. London: Deutsch, 1986.
Auer, Manfred. *Das Exil vor der Vertreibung: Motivkontinuität und Quellenproblematik im späten Werk Alfred Döblins.* Bonn: Bouvier, 1977.
Barbato, Mariano. "Double Bind: Der Synodale Weg und die Entmachtung des katholischen Klerus." *Herder Korrespondenz* 75, no. 10 (2021): 24–26.
Barbieri, William A., Jr. *Constitutive Justice.* New York: Palgrave Macmillan, 2015.
Barry, Jonathan, Marianne Hester, and Gareth Roberts, eds. *Witchcraft in Early Modern Europe: Studies in Culture and Belief.* Cambridge: Cambridge University Press, 1996.
Bellah, Robert N. *Religion in Human Evolution: From the Paleolithic to the Axial Age.* Cambridge, MA: Harvard University Press, 2011.
Berger, Peter L. "A Bleak Outlook Is Seen for Religion." *New York Times,* April 25, 1968, 3.
Billington, James H. *Fire in the Minds of Men: Origins of the Revolutionary Faith.* New York: Basic Books, 1980.
Bogner, Daniel. *Ihr macht uns die Kirche kaputt . . . , . . . doch wir lassen das nicht zu.* Freiburg: Herder, 2019.
Bondy, François. "Kołakowski: Grundmuster und Exempel. 'Christen ohne Kirche'—'Sozialisten ohne Partei'?" *Europäische Ideen* 33 (1977): 12–17.
Borgolte, Michael. *Christen, Juden, Muselmanen: Die Erben der Antike und der Aufstieg des Abendlandes 300 bis 1400 n. Chr.* Berlin: Siedler, 2006.
Brecht, Bertolt. *Arbeitsjournal.* Frankfurt am Main: Suhrkamp, 1973.
Brecht, Bertolt. "Peinlicher Vorfall." In *Gesammelte Werke,* by Bertolt Brecht, 10:861–62. Frankfurt am Main: Suhrkamp, 1967.
Brezger, Jan. *Internationale Freizügigkeit als Menschenrecht.* Frankfurt am Main: Campus, 2018.
Bruyn, Günter de. *Der neunzigste Geburtstag.* Frankfurt am Main: S. Fischer, 2018.
Buber, Martin. *I and Thou.* 1923. New York: Scribner, 1958.

Burge, Ryan P. *The Nones: Where They Come From, Who They Are, and Where They Are Going*. Minneapolis: Fortress Press, 2021.
Burgess, Ernest, and Harvey Locke. *The Family: From Institution to Companionship*. New York: American Book Company, 1945.
Casanova, José. "Religion, the Axial Age, and Secular Modernity in Bellah's Theory of Religious Evolution." In *The Axial Age and Its Consequences*, edited by Robert N. Bellah and Hans Joas, 191–221. Cambridge, MA: Harvard University Press, 2012.
Certeau, Michel de. *The Mystic Fable. Vol. 1, Sixteenth and Seventeenth Centuries*. Chicago: University of Chicago Press, 1985.
Chaunu, Pierre. "Deuxième ou troisième Réforme? Le XVIIe siècle des hétérodoxes." *Annales* 25 (1970): 1574–90.
Cordemann, Claas, and Gundolf Holfert, eds. *Moral ohne Bekenntnis? Zur Debatte um Kirche als zivilreligiöse Moralagentur*. Leipzig: Evangelische Verlagsanstalt, 2017.
Daniélou, Jean. *Why the Church?* Chicago: Franciscan Herald Press, 1975.
Daston, Lorraine, and Katharine Park. *Wonders and the Order of Nature 1150–1750*. New York: Zone, 2001.
Davie, Grace. *Religion in Modern Europe: A Memory Mutates*. Oxford: Oxford University Press, 2000.
Dewey, John. *A Common Faith*. New Haven, CT: Yale University Press, 1934.
Dietz, Hella. *Polnischer Protest: Zur pragmatistischen Fundierung von Theorien sozialen Wandels*. Frankfurt am Main: Campus, 2015.
Dilcher, Gerhard. "Der Staat als herrschaftlich-genossenschaftlich verfasstes Gemeinwesen." In *Staat und Historie: Leitbilder und Fragestellungen deutscher Geschichtsschreibung vom Ende des 19. bis zur Mitte des 20. Jahrhunderts*, edited by Walter Pauly and Klaus Ries, 113–42. Baden-Baden: Nomos, 2021.
Döblin, Alfred. *Briefe*. Olten: Walter, 1970.
Döblin, Alfred. "Christentum und Revolution." In *Schriften zur Literatur*, by Alfred Döblin, 379–83. Olten: Walter, 1963.
Döblin, Alfred. "Epilog." In *Autobiographische Schriften und letzte Aufzeichnungen*, by Alfred Döblin, 439–51. Olten: Walter, 1980.
Döblin, Alfred. *Hamlet oder Die lange Nacht nimmt ein Ende*. 1956. Munich: dtv, 1987. English translation: *Tales of a Long Night*. New York: Fromm, 1984.
Döblin, Alfred. *November 1918*. 4 vols. Munich: dtv, 1978. An abbreviated English translation of vols. II and III has been published in one volume: *A People Betrayed: November 1918: A German Revolution*, translated by John E. Woods. New York: Fromm International Publishing, 1983. Translation of vol. IV: *Karl and Rosa: November 1918: A German Revolution*, translated by John E. Woods. New York: Fromm International Publishing, 1983.

Döblin, Alfred. *Der unsterbliche Mensch / Der Kampf mit dem Engel*. 1950–52. Frankfurt am Main: Fischer, 2016.
Döblin, Alfred. *Der unsterbliche Mensch / Ein Religionsgespräch*. 1946. Frankfurt am Main: Fischer, 2016.
Dollenmayer, David B. *The Berlin Novels of Alfred Döblin*. Berkeley: University of California Press, 1988.
Dollinger, Roland. *Totalität und Totalitarismus im Exilwerk Döblins*. Würzburg: Königshausen & Neumann, 1994.
Douglas, Jack D. *The Social Meanings of Suicide*. Princeton, NJ: Princeton University Press, 1967.
Dubus, André. *Adultery and Other Choices*. Boston: David R. Godine, 1977.
Durkheim, Émile. "Débat sur l'éducation sexuelle." 1911. In *Textes*, by Émile Durkheim, 2:241–51. Paris: Editions de Minuit, 1975.
Durkheim, Émile. "Deux lois de l'évolution pénale." 1901. In *Journal sociologique*, by Émile Durkheim, 244–73. Paris: Presses Universitaires de France, 1969.
Durkheim, Émile. *The Division of Labor in Society*. 1893. New York: Free Press, 1997.
Durkheim, Émile. *The Elementary Forms of Religious Life*. 1912. Oxford: Oxford University Press, 2001.
Durkheim, Émile. *The Evolution of Educational Thought*. 1938. London: Routledge, 1977.
Durkheim, Émile. "Individualism and the Intellectuals." 1898. In *Emile Durkheim on Morality and Society*, edited by Robert N. Bellah, 43–57. Chicago: University of Chicago Press, 1986.
Durkheim, Émile. *Professional Ethics and Civic Morals*. London: Routledge, 1991.
Durkheim, Émile. *Suicide: A Study in Sociology*. 1897. New York: Free Press, 1951.
Etzioni, Amitai. *Modern Organizations*. Englewood Cliffs, NJ: Prentice Hall, 1964.
Feldhay, Rivka. "Religion." In *The Cambridge History of Science*, vol. 3, *Early Modern Science*, edited by Katharine Park and Lorraine Daston, 727–55. Cambridge: Cambridge University Press, 2008.
Foucault, Michel. *Discipline and Punish: The Birth of the Prison*. New York: Vintage, 1977.
Francis, E. K. "Toward a Typology of Religious Orders." *American Journal of Sociology* 55, no. 5 (1950): 437–49.
Frühwald, Wolfgang. "Rosa und der Satan: Thesen zum Verhältnis von Christentum und Sozialismus im Schlussband von Alfred Döblins Erzählwerk 'November 1918.'" In *Internationale Alfred-Döblin-Kolloquien Basel 1980 / New York 1981 / Freiburg 1983*, edited by Werner Stauffacher, 239–56. Bern: Peter Lang, 1986.
George, Francis. *God in Action: How Faith in God Can Address the Challenges of the World*. New York: Doubleday, 2011.

Gierke, Otto von. *Das deutsche Genossenschaftsrecht*. 4 vols. 1868–1913. Darmstadt: WBG, 1954.

Goldmann, Lucien. *The Hidden God: A Study of Tragic Vision in the Pensées of Pascal and the Tragedies of Racine*. London: Routledge, 1964.

Gorski, Philip. *American Babylon: Christianity and Democracy before and after Trump*. New York: Routledge, 2020.

Graf, Friedrich Wilhelm. *Kirchendämmerung: Wie die Kirchen unser Vertrauen verspielen*. Munich: Beck, 2011.

Griewank, Karl. *Der neuzeitliche Revolutionsbegriff: Entstehung und Entwicklung*. Weimar: Böhlau, 1955.

Guardini, Romano. "Zwischen zwei Büchern." 1965. In *Vom Sinn der Kirche / Die Kirche des Herrn*, by Romano Guardini, 105–13. Mainz: Grünewald, 1990.

Guardini, Romano, and Otto Friedrich Bollnow. *Begegnung und Bildung*. Würzburg: Werkbund-Verlag, 1956.

Gustafson, James M. *Treasure in Earthen Vessels: The Church as a Human Community*. 1961. Louisville, KY: Westminster John Knox Press, 2009.

Habermas, Jürgen. *Theorie und Praxis: Sozialphilosophische Studien*. Frankfurt am Main: Suhrkamp, 1971.

Hadot, Pierre. *Qu'est-ce que la philosophie antique?* Paris: Gallimard, 1995.

Hamsun, Knut. *Mysteries*. Translated by Gerry Bothmer. New York: Farrar, Straus and Giroux, 1971.

Heidegger, Martin. *Gelassenheit*. Pfullingen: Neske, 1956. English translation: *Discourse on Thinking*. New York: Harper & Row, 1966.

Heidrich, Christian. *Leszek Kolakowski: Zwischen Skepsis und Mystik*. Frankfurt am Main: Neue Kritik, 1995.

Honigsheim, Paul. "Religionssoziologie." In *Die Lehre von der Gesellschaft: Ein Lehrbuch der Soziologie*, edited by Gottfried Eisermann, 119–81. Stuttgart: Enke, 1958.

Honneth, Axel. *The Critique of Power: Reflective Stages in a Critical Social Theory*. Cambridge, MA: MIT Press, 1991.

Huber, Wolfgang. *Kirche in der Zeitenwende: Gesellschaftlicher Wandel und Erneuerung der Kirche*. Gütersloh: Verlag Bertelsmann Stiftung, 1998.

Hunter, James Davison. *To Change the World: The Irony, Tragedy, and Possibility of Christianity in the Late Modern World*. New York: Oxford University Press, 2010.

Inglehart, Ronald F. "Giving Up on God: The Global Decline of Religion." *Foreign Affairs* 99 (2020): 110–18.

Jahraus, Oliver. "Subjekte der Geschichte—Geschichten des Subjekts: Döblins Erzählwerk 'November 1918.'" In *Der Erste Weltkrieg als Katastrophe: Deutungsmuster im literarischen Diskurs*, edited by Claude D. Conter, Oliver Jahraus and Christian Kirchmeier, 175–92. Würzburg: Königshausen & Neumann, 2014.

James, William. "The Will to Believe." 1897. In *The Will to Believe and Other Essays in Popular Philosophy*, by William James, 1–31. New York: Longmans, Green, 1905.

Jaspers, Karl. *The Origin and Goal of History*. 1949. New York: Routledge, 2010.

Jay, Martin. "A Missed Opportunity: Leszek Kolakowski in Berkeley." *Salmagundi* 166/167 (2010): 3–9.

Jenkins, Philip. *The Next Christendom: The Coming of Global Christianity*. Oxford: Oxford University Press, 2002.

Ji Zhe. *Religion, modernité et temporalité: Une sociologie du bouddhisme chan contemporain*. Paris: CNRS Éditions, 2016.

Joas, Hans. "The Contingency of Secularization: Reflections on the Problem of Secularization in the Work of Reinhart Koselleck." In *The Benefit of Broad Horizons: Intellectual and Institutional Preconditions for a Global Social Science. Festschrift for Björn Wittrock on the Occasion of His 65th Birthday*, edited by Hans Joas and Barbro Klein, 87–104. Leiden: Brill, 2010.

Joas, Hans. *The Creativity of Action*. Chicago: University of Chicago Press, 1996.

Joas, Hans, ed. *David Martin and the Sociology of Religion*. London: Routledge, 2018.

Joas, Hans. *Do We Need Religion? On the Experience of Self-Transcendence*. Boulder, CO: Paradigm, 2008.

Joas, Hans. *Faith as an Option: Possible Futures for Christianity*. Stanford, CA: Stanford University Press, 2014.

Joas, Hans. *Friedensprojekt Europa?* Munich: Kösel, 2020.

Joas, Hans. *The Genesis of Values*. Chicago: University of Chicago Press, 2000.

Joas, Hans. *Kirche als Moralagentur?* Munich: Kösel, 2016.

Joas, Hans. *Die lange Nacht der Trauer: Erzählen als Weg aus der Gewalt?* Gießen: Psychosozial-Verlag, 2014.

Joas, Hans. "Liebe, Gabe, Gerechtigkeit." In *Die Zehn Gebote: Ein widersprüchliches Erbe?*, edited by Hans Joas, 175–83. Cologne: Böhlau, 2006.

Joas, Hans. "Mutter Kirche." *Herder Korrespondenz* 75, no. 12 (2021): 15–16.

Joas, Hans. *The Power of the Sacred: An Alternative to the Narrative of Disenchantment*. New York: Oxford University Press, 2021.

Joas, Hans. "Public Religion, Secularism, and the Ethos of Love." In *Secularism, Catholicism, and the Future of Public Life*, edited by Gary J. Adler Jr., 155–64. New York: Oxford University Press, 2015.

Joas, Hans. *The Sacredness of the Person: A New Genealogy of Human Rights*. Washington, DC: Georgetown University Press, 2013.

Joas, Hans. "Die säkulare Option: Ihr Aufstieg und ihre Folgen." *Deutsche Zeitschrift für Philosophie* 57 (2009): 293–300.

Joas, Hans. *Sind die Menschenrechte westlich?* Munich: Kösel, 2015.

Joas, Hans. "Um die 'konstitutive Gerechtigkeit' streiten." In "Konsens und Konflikt: Politik braucht Auseinandersetzung. Zehn Impulse der Kammer für Öffentliche Verantwortung der EKD zu aktuellen Herausforderungen der Demokratie in Deutschland (Französische Friedrichstadtkirche, Berlin, 21. August 2017)." *epd-Dokumentation* 44 (November 1, 2017): 16–17.

Joas, Hans. *Under the Spell of Freedom: Theory of Religion after Hegel and Nietzsche.* New York: Oxford University Press, 2024.

Joas, Hans. "Wann glauben Religionen an sich selbst?" *Frankfurter Allgemeine Zeitung*, August 3, 2015, 9.

Joas, Hans. *War and Modernity.* Cambridge: Polity, 2003.

Joas, Hans. *Was ist die Achsenzeit?* Basel: Schwabe, 2014.

Joas, Hans, ed. *Was sind religiöse Überzeugungen?* Göttingen: Wallstein, 2003.

Joas, Hans, and Wolfgang Knöbl. *Social Theory: Twenty Introductory Lectures.* Cambridge: Cambridge University Press, 2009.

Joas, Hans, and Robert Spaemann. *Beten bei Nebel: Hat der Glaube eine Zukunft?* Freiburg: Herder, 2018.

Johnson, Ian. *The Souls of China: The Return of Religion after Mao.* New York: Pantheon, 2017.

Kant, Immanuel. *Groundwork for the Metaphysics of Morals.* 1785. Oxford: Oxford University Press, 2002.

Kaufmann, Franz-Xaver. *Kirchenkrise: Wie überlebt das Christentum?* Freiburg: Herder, 2011.

Kiesel, Helmuth. *Literarische Trauerarbeit: Das Exil- und Spätwerk Alfred Döblins.* Tübingen: Niemeyer, 1986.

Koepke, Wulf. *The Critical Reception of Alfred Döblin's Major Novels.* New York: Camden House, 2003.

Kołakowski, Leszek. *Chrétiens sans Église: La conscience religieuse et le lien confessionnel au XVIIe siècle.* Paris: Gallimard, 1969.

Kołakowski, Leszek. *Metaphysical Horror.* Chicago: University of Chicago Press, 2001.

Kołakowski, Leszek. *Modernity on Endless Trial.* Chicago: University of Chicago Press, 1990.

Kołakowski, Leszek. *The Presence of Myth.* Chicago: University of Chicago Press, 2001.

Kołakowski, Leszek. "The Priest and the Jester: Reflections on the Theological Heritage of Contemporary Thought." 1959. In *The Two Eyes of Spinoza—and*

Other Essays on Philosophers, by Leszek Kołakowski, 239–62. South Bend, IN: St. Augustine's Press, 2004.

Kołakowski, Leszek. "Religiöse Symbole und humanistische Kultur (1967)." In *Geist und Ungeist christlicher Traditionen*, by Leszek Kołakowski, 90–112. Stuttgart: Kohlhammer, 1971.

Körtner, Ulrich H. J. *Für die Vernunft: Wider Moralisierung und Emotionalisierung in Politik und Kirche*. Leipzig: Evangelische Verlagsanstalt, 2017.

Koselleck, Reinhart. *Critique and Crisis: Enlightenment and the Pathogenesis of Modern Society*. 1959. Cambridge, MA: MIT Press, 1988.

Król, Marcin. "Leszek Kołakowski: Le philosophe et la religion." *Esprit* 106, no. 10 (1985): 63–81.

Lauster, Jörg. *Die Verzauberung der Welt: Eine Kulturgeschichte des Christentums*. Munich: Beck, 2014.

Lehmann, Karl. "Catholic Christianity." In *Secularization and the World Religions*, edited by Hans Joas and Klaus Wiegandt, 23–45. Liverpool: Liverpool University Press, 2009.

Locke, John. *A Letter concerning Toleration: Latin and English Texts Revised and Edited with Variants and an Introduction by Mario Montuori*. The Hague: Nijhoff, 1963.

Luhmann, Niklas. *Law as a Social System*. Oxford: Oxford University Press, 2004.

Lukes, Steven. *Émile Durkheim: His Life and Work*. Harmondsworth, UK: Penguin, 1977.

Lukes, Steven. "Leszek Kołakowski 1927–2009." *Proceedings of the British Academy* 172 (2011): 201–11.

Martin, David. "The Denomination." *British Journal of Sociology* 33, no. 1 (1962): 1–14.

Martin, David. *A General Theory of Secularization*. Oxford: Blackwell, 1978.

Marx, Reinhard. *Ist Kirche anders? Möglichkeiten und Grenzen einer soziologischen Betrachtungsweise*. Paderborn: Schöningh, 1990.

Marx, Reinhard. *Kirche überlebt*. Munich: Kösel, 2015.

Mattick, Meike. *Komik und Geschichtserfahrung: Alfred Döblins komisierendes Erzählen in "November 1918. Eine deutsche Revolution."* Bielefeld: Aisthesis Verlag, 2003.

Maurras, Charles. *Au signe de Flore*. Paris: Bernard Grasset, 1933.

Mazowiecki, Tadeusz. "Un-Vollendetes: Leszek Kołakowski und die Religion." In *Partei nehmen für die Hoffnung: Über Moral in der Politik*, by Tadeusz Mazowiecki, 66–86. Freiburg: Herder, 1990.

Mittenzwei, Werner. *Das Leben des Bertolt Brecht*. Vol. 2. Berlin (GDR): Aufbau, 1986.

Mottu, Henry. "'Chrétiens sans Église' de Kołakowski." *Revue de Théologie et de Philosophie* 23 (1973): 308–31.

Neckel, Sighard, and Jürgen Wolf. "Die Faszination der Amoralität: Zur Systemtheorie der Moral." *Prokla* 18 (1988): 57–77.

Niebuhr, H. Richard. *Christ and Culture*. 1951. New York: Harper, 2001.

Niebuhr, H. Richard. *The Purpose of the Church and Its Ministry: Reflections on the Aims of Theological Education*. New York: Harper, 1956.

Niebuhr, H. Richard. *The Social Sources of Denominationalism*. New York: Holt, 1929.

Niggl, Günter. "Antwort auf das Inferno der Zeit: Das Spätwerk Alfred Döblins." In *Zeitbilder: Studien und Vorträge zur deutschen Literatur des 19. und 20. Jahrhunderts*, by Günter Niggl, 115–24. Würzburg: Königshausen & Neumann, 2005.

Nolte, Ernst. *Der Faschismus in seiner Epoche*. Munich: Piper, 1984.

Norris, Pippa, and Ronald F. Inglehart. *Sacred and Secular: Religion and Politics Worldwide*. Cambridge: Cambridge University Press, 2004.

Oexle, Otto Gerhard. "Max Weber und das Mönchtum." In *Max Webers Religionssoziologie in interkultureller Perspektive*, edited by Hartmut Lehmann and Jean Martin Ouédraogo, 311–34. Göttingen: Vandenhoeck & Ruprecht, 2003.

Piwowarczyk, Bogdan. *Lire Kolakowski: La question de l'homme, de la religion et de l'Église*. Paris: Cerf, 1986.

Pollack, Detlef, and Gerhard Wegner, eds. *Die soziale Reichweite von Religion und Kirche*. Würzburg: Ergon, 2017.

Postel, Danny. "On Exile, Philosophy and Tottering Insecurely on the Edge of an Unknown Abyss." *Daedalus* 134 (2005): 82–88.

Putnam, Robert, and David Campbell. *American Grace: How Religion Divides and Unites Us*. New York: Simon & Schuster, 2010.

Rahner, Karl. *Grundkurs des Glaubens: Einführung in den Begriff des Christentums*. Freiburg: Herder, 1984.

Rahner, Karl. "Theologische Grundinterpretation des II. Vatikanischen Konzils." In *Schriften zur Theologie*, by Karl Rahner, 14:287–302. Cologne: Belziger, 1980.

Ricœur, Paul, and Andre LaCocque. *Penser la Bible*. Paris: Seuil, 1998.

Riley, Anthony W. "The Aftermath of the First World War: Christianity and Revolution in Alfred Döblin's 'November 1918.'" In *The First World War in German Narrative Prose*, edited by Charles N. Genno and Heinz Wetzel, 93–117. Toronto: University of Toronto Press, 1980.

Röcke, Anja. *Soziologie der Selbstoptimierung*. Berlin: Suhrkamp, 2021.

Roth, Günther. "Max Weber's Ethics and the Peace Movement Today." *Theory and Society* 13 (1984): 491–511.

Sahoo, Sarbeswar. *Pentecostalism and Politics of Conversion in India*. Preface by Hans Joas. Delhi: Cambridge University Press, 2018.

Saler, Michael. "Modernity and Enchantment: A Historiographic Review." *American Historical Review* 111 (2006): 692–716.

Sautermeister, Jochen. "'Kirche als Moralagentur?' Theologisch-ethische Überlegungen zur moralischen und politischen Relevanz von Kirche in der Gesellschaft." *Münchener Theologische Zeitschrift* 68 (2017): 292–305.

Sautermeister, Jochen, ed. *Kirche—nur eine Moralagentur? Eine Selbstverortung*. Freiburg: Herder, 2019.

Scheler, Max. "Die Formen des Wissens und die Bildung." In *Philosophische Weltanschauung*, by Max Scheler, 16–48. Munich: Lehnen, 1954.

Schlette, Magnus. *Die Idee der Selbstverwirklichung: Zur Grammatik des modernen Individualismus*. Frankfurt am Main: Campus, 2013.

Schmiedel, Ulrich. *Elasticized Ecclesiology: The Concept of Community after Ernst Troeltsch*. New York: Palgrave Macmillan, 2017.

Schröder, Richard. "Wie beim Handy, so beim Glauben: 'Wechseln Sie einfach den Anbieter!' Funktioniert das?" *Chrismon* 5 (2003): 46.

Schulze, Reinhard. *Der Koran und die Genealogie des Islam*. Basel: Schwabe, 2015.

Schwaetzer, Irmgard. "Grußwort auf der Vollversammlung des Zentralkomitees der deutschen Katholiken." Leipzig, May 25, 2016. https://www.domradio.de/artikel/ekd-praeses-wuerdigt-katholikentag-leipzig.

Schwan, Gesine. *Leszek Kolakowski: Eine Philosophie der Freiheit nach Marx*. Stuttgart: Kohlhammer, 1971.

Schwartz, Alexandra. "Improving Ourselves to Death." *New Yorker*, January 15, 2018. https://www.newyorker.com/magazine/2018/01/15/improving-ourselves-to-death.

Silber, Ilana Friedrich. *Virtuosity, Charisma, and Social Order: A Comparative Sociological Study of Monasticism in Theravada Buddhism and Medieval Catholicism*. Cambridge: Cambridge University Press, 1995.

Silver, Daniel. "Religion without Instrumentalization." *Archives Européennes de Sociologie* 47 (2006): 421–34.

Stark, Werner. "The Place of Catholicism in Max Weber's Sociology of Religion." *Sociological Analysis* 29 (1968): 202–10.

Stark, Werner. "The Routinization of Charisma: A Consideration of Catholicism." *Sociological Analysis* 26 (1965): 203–11.

Stark, Werner. *The Sociology of Religion: A Study of Christendom*. Vols. 2 and 3. New York: Fordham University Press, 1967.

Stauffacher, Werner. "Einführung." In *November 1918*, by Alfred Döblin, 1:9–64. Olten: Walter, 1991.

Straub, Jürgen. *Das optimierte Selbst: Kompetenzimperative und Steigerungstechnologien in der Optimierungsgesellschaft*. Gießen: Psychosozial-Verlag, 2019.

Taylor, Charles. *A Secular Age*. Cambridge, MA: Harvard University Press, 2007.

Taylor, Charles. *Sources of the Self: The Making of the Modern Identity*. Cambridge, MA: Harvard University Press, 1989.

Thomas, Keith. *Religion and the Decline of Magic*. New York: Scribner, 1971.

Thompson, David M. "Introduction: Mapping Asian Christianity in the Context of World Christianity." In *Christian Theology in Asia*, edited by Sebastian C. H. Kim, 3–21. Cambridge: Cambridge University Press, 2008.

Tillich, Paul. *The Courage to Be*. New Haven, CT: Yale University Press, 1952.

Tillich, Paul. *Gesammelte Werke*. Vol. 8. Stuttgart: Evangelisches Verlagswerk, 1970.

Tillich, Paul. *Systematic Theology*. 4th ed. Vol. 1. Chicago: University of Chicago Press, 1955.

Tipton, Steven M. *Public Pulpits: Methodists and Mainline Churches in the Moral Argument of Public Life*. Chicago: University of Chicago Press, 2007.

Tischner, Józef. "Leszek Kolakowski—Anmerkungen zu seinem Denken." In *Der unmögliche Dialog: Christentum und Marxismus in Polen*, by Józef Tischner, 217–32. Graz: Styria, 1982.

Troeltsch, Ernst. *Augustin, die christliche Antike und das Mittelalter*. Munich: Oldenbourg, 1915.

Troeltsch, Ernst. "Die Kirche im Leben der Gegenwart." 1911. In *Gesammelte Schriften*, by Ernst Troeltsch, 2:91–108. Tübingen: Mohr Siebeck, 1913.

Troeltsch, Ernst. "Review of Peter A. Clasen, 'Der Salutismus." *Historische Zeitschrift* 115 (1915): 327–30; also in Ernst Troeltsch, *Rezensionen und Kritiken (1915–1923)*, KGA, 13:84–87. Berlin: De Gruyter, 2010.

Troeltsch, Ernst. "Rück- und Umblick (Februar 1919)." In *Spectator-Briefe und Berliner Briefe (1919–1922)*, by Ernst Troeltsch, edited by Gangolf Hübinger, KGA, 14:53. Berlin: De Gruyter, 2015.

Troeltsch, Ernst. *Die Soziallehren der christlichen Kirchen und Gruppen*. 1912. Edited by Friedrich Wilhelm Graf, KGA, vol. 9. Berlin: De Gruyter, 2021. English translation: *The Social Teaching of the Christian Churches*. London: Allen & Unwin, 1931.

Turner, Victor. *The Ritual Process: Structure and Anti-structure*. 1969. New York: Routledge, 2017.

Tyrell, Hartmann. "Potenz und Depotenzierung der Religion: Religion und Rationalisierung bei Max Weber." *Saeculum* 44 (1993): 300–347.

Vesper, Stefan. "Schlicht privat: Von den freien Vereinigungen in der Kirche." *Salzkörner* 24, no. 1 (2018): 8–9.

Walzer, Michael. *Spheres of Justice: A Defense of Pluralism and Equality.* New York: Basic Books, 1983.
Weber, Max. *Economy and Society.* 1922. Berkeley: University of California Press, 1978.
Weber, Max. *Gesammelte Aufsätze zur Religionssoziologie.* Vol. 1. 1920. Tübingen: Mohr Siebeck, 1988.
Weber, Max. *The Religion of China.* New York: Free Press, 1951.
Weber, Max. "Über einige Kategorien der verstehenden Soziologie." In *Gesammelte Aufsätze zur Wissenschaftslehre*, by Max Weber, 427–74. Tübingen: Mohr Siebeck, 1973. English translation: "Some Categories of Interpretive Sociology." *Sociological Quarterly* 22, no. 2 (Spring 1981): 151–80.
Wegner, Gerhard. *Wirksame Kirche: Sozio-theologische Studien.* Leipzig: Evangelische Verlagsanstalt, 2019.
Wichelhaus, Manfred. *Kirchengeschichtsschreibung und Soziologie im neunzehnten Jahrhundert und bei Ernst Troeltsch.* Heidelberg: Winter, 1965.
Wuthnow, Robert. *The Restructuring of American Religion.* Princeton, NJ: Princeton University Press, 1988.
Ziolkowski, Theodore. *Modes of Faith: Secular Surrogates for Lost Religious Belief.* Chicago: University of Chicago Press, 2007.

Name Index

Adorno, Theodor W., 102
Alaric I (King of the Visigoths), 33
Angelus Silesius (Johann Scheffler), 99–100
Arendt, Hannah, 107
Arnold, Matthew, 142
Augustine of Hippo, 20, 33

Barbieri, William, 130
Barrès, Maurice, 47
Bedford-Strohm, Heinrich, 124
Benedict XVI (Pope), 125
Berger, Peter, 13
Bergson, Henri, 91
Bérulle, Pierre de, 99–100
Bismarck, Otto von, 35, 125
Bloch, Ernst, 101
Bonhoeffer, Dietrich, 143–44
Bourignon, Antoinette, 99
Brecht, Bertolt, 43–45, 75
Buber, Martin, 67
Burgess, Ernest, 62

Calvin, John, 38
Camphuysen, Dirk, 99
Casanova, José, 10, 137
Comte, Auguste, 110

Dabrock, Peter, 7, 136, 139, 141, 143–44, 164n13

Daniélou, Jean, xi–xiv
de Bruyn, Günter, 145–46
Dewey, John, 3
Dickens, Charles, 129
Diefenbach, Hans, 86
Döblin, Alfred, 6, 43–45, 51, 74–90
Dreyfus, Alfred, 106–7
Dubček, Alexander, 87
Dubus, André, 54
Durkheim, Émile, 63, 73, 107–18, 121, 143, 162n2

Ebert, Friedrich, 85, 88
Eckhart von Hochheim (Meister Eckhart), 55
Eisler, Hanns, 43
Eliade, Mircea, 101
Elias, Norbert, 115

Feldhay, Rivka, 153n20
Feuchtwanger, Lion, 43
Foucault, Michel, 25–26, 114
Francis (Pope), 69, 124, 133, 144
Francis of Assisi, 55
Frederick the Great (King of Prussia), 33

Gerhardt, Paul, 56–57
Gierke, Otto von, 26
Gilson, Etienne, 93

Name Index

Goffman, Erving, 115
Goldmann, Lucien, 98
Graf, Friedrich Wilhelm, 124, 127
Granach, Alexander, 43
Grass, Günter, 75
Guardini, Romano, 16, 67

Habermas, Jürgen, 4, 6, 67–68, 95, 102, 105
Halík, Tomáš, 137
Hamsun, Knut, 47–48
Hegel, Georg Wilhelm Friedrich, xiii, 4, 19, 40, 101
Heidegger, Martin, 67
Hemmerle, Klaus, 141
Herder, Johann Gottfried, 40, 109
Honigsheim, Paul, 22–23
Huber, Wolfgang, 104, 124, 126–27
Humboldt, Wilhelm von, 40, 66
Husserl, Edmund, 67, 91

Inglehart, Ronald, 2, 8

James, William, 46, 53, 60–61, 98, 126, 142, 162n2
Jaspers, Karl, 15, 101–2
Jenkins, Philip, 63
John Paul II (Pope), 141
John XXIII (Pope), 103
Joyce, James, 74

Kant, Immanuel, 39, 68, 108–9, 121, 130, 142–43
Käßmann, Margot, 124
Kaufmann, Franz-Xaver, 148n1
Kierkegaard, Søren, 78
Klinsmann, Jürgen, 59–60
Kołakowski, Leszek, 6, 91–105, 159n21, 159n29

Kortner, Fritz, 43
Körtner, Ulrich, 136, 139–40, 143–44
Koselleck, Reinhart, 42

Labadie, Jean de, 99, 159n29
Lassalle, Ferdinand, 122
Lenin, Vladimir Ilyich, 82, 86–88
Liebknecht, Karl, 75, 82, 87–89
Locke, John, 17
Lorre, Peter, 43
Louis XIV (King of France), 98
Luckmann, Thomas, 13
Ludendorff, Erich, 34
Ludendorff, Mathilde, 34
Luhmann, Niklas, 113, 139
Luther, Martin, 129
Luxemburg, Rosa, 75–76, 86–89

Mann, Heinrich, 43
Mann, Thomas, 43
Mao Zedong, 11, 14
Maritain, Jacques, 93
Martin du Gard, Roger, 107
Martin, David, 34, 149n13
Marx, Reinhard, 148n1
Maurras, Charles, 107
Mazowiecki, Tadeusz, 104
Merkel, Angela, 135, 139–40, 145
Merleau-Ponty, Maurice, 95
Michnik, Adam, 91
Montesquieu, 28
Mounier, Emmanuel, 93

Niebuhr, H. Richard, xiii, 20–22, 129, 138
Niebuhr, Reinhold, 20
Nietzsche, Friedrich, 25, 37, 101
Norris, Pippa, 2
Noske, Gustav, 88

Obama, Barack, 128
Otto, Rudolf, 98

Parsons, Talcott, 113
Pascal, Blaise, 46, 91, 98
Paul of Tarsus, 63, 134
Paul VI (Pope), xi, 69
Proust, Marcel, 107

Racine, Jean, 98
Rahner, Karl, 22–23, 63
Reinhard, Wolfgang, 104
Resing, Volker, 1
Ribéry, Franck, 60
Ricœur, Paul, 58, 144
Rousseau, Jean-Jacques, 108

Saler, Michael, 153n21
Sartre, Jean-Paul, 95
Sautermeister, Jochen, 164n15
Schavan, Annette, 7, 136, 138–41, 144
Scheler, Max, 65–68, 98
Schleiermacher, Friedrich, xiii, 33–34, 40, 51, 66
Schnitzler, Arthur, 50
Schockenhoff, Eberhard, 136, 140–44
Schröder, Richard, 140
Schulze, Gerhard, 54
Schwaetzer, Irmgard, 128
Spaemann, Robert, xii, 1
Spinoza, Baruch, 91

Stark, Werner, 21–22
Striet, Magnus, 136, 142–44

Taylor, Charles, 36, 60–61, 137
Tebartz-van Elst, Franz-Peter, 125
Thomas, Keith, 153n21
Thompson, David, 63
Tillich, Paul, 32, 50–51, 55–56, 101, 144
Tischner, Józef, 94–95
Troeltsch, Ernst, xiii, 16–22, 24–25, 84, 159n29
Turner, Victor, 70

Voltaire, 33

Walzer, Michael, 129–30, 138
Wanke, Joachim, 64
Weber, Max, xiii, 4, 16–19, 21–22, 33, 37–39, 56, 90, 98, 131, 138, 143, 153n21, 159n21
Wegner, Gerhard, 150n27
Weigel, Helene, 43
Weizsäcker, Richard von, 139
Wilson, Woodrow, 89
Wuerl, Donald, 41

Xi Jinping, 11

Zé Roberto (José Roberto da Silva Júnior), 60
Zola, Émile, 106

Subject Index

Anglicanism, 20
anti-Semitism, 34, 93, 106, 145
areligiosity, 9, 96–97, 103
atheism, xi, xiv, 9, 47, 55–56, 96, 110
Axial Age, 15, 38–39, 102

Baptists, 68
Buddhism, 11, 14–15, 31, 37, 54, 59–60, 64, 67, 71, 81, 133

Catholicism, xi–xiv, 1–4, 7–8, 10–11, 14, 16–18, 20–24, 27–28, 31, 34–35, 43, 47, 59–60, 63–64, 67–73, 75, 78, 93–96, 99–100, 103–4, 118, 124–25, 128, 130, 133–34, 141, 143, 145. *See also* religion in Germany
Christianization, 31, 63, 74
church (as a form of social organization in Christianity), xi, xiii–xiv, 2–4, 8, 11–20, 24–25, 132, 137, 145
church
    as cooperative, 26–27
    as mission, 8, 29, 126, 134, 144
    as moral agency, 4, 35, 125–28, 131–37, 139, 141, 144
    pluralism within, 19, 23, 133, 138, 141

    self-sacralization of, 126
    universality of, xi, 21–25, 28–29
church reform, xii, 7–8, 22–25, 28, 99, 103, 137
church sociology, 13–14
church–state, relation between, 3, 17, 26–27, 30, 35, 126–27, 131, 133
colonialism, 21–22, 32, 63, 104–5, 121–22
communism, 11, 14, 25, 31, 35, 41, 45, 70–71, 83, 86, 91–95, 102–4, 122, 125, 141
Confucianism, 11–12, 14, 133
Congregationalism, 21
conversion, 43–44, 56, 63, 73–74, 76, 78–79, 81–83, 85–86, 88, 90, 92
Council, Second Vatican, xi–xii, xiv, 22–23, 63, 103, 144
Counter-Reformation, 69, 99

Daoism, 11, 14, 31
"democratization" of the church / synodal structures/power within the church, 8, 25–29, 93, 99, 134
denomination (as a form of social organization in Christianity), 20–21, 23–24

Subject Index

differentiation, (functional), 111–13, 118, 139, 148n1
disenchantment, xiii, 4, 33, 37–41, 90
Dreyfus affair, 106–8, 111, 118

ecstasy, (collective), 47–50, 54, 63, 83, 116
Enlightenment, 3, 28, 37, 40, 42, 92, 100
esotericism, 30, 35, 54
ethics of conviction vs. ethics of responsibility, 127, 136, 138–40
experience, (interpretation/articulation of), 4, 47–56, 65, 70, 72–74, 97–98, 101, 115, 126, 132, 142
experience, sacramental, 53–55

fascism, 25, 74, 88, 93, 106–7, 118–19, 122
freedom, religious, 21, 23, 60, 118

globalization (of religion), 8, 22, 24, 60, 62–63, 113, 126, 132

Hinduism, 14, 64, 133
human rights/dignity, xiii, 8, 34, 69, 74, 93, 104, 106–14, 116–23, 127, 129, 133, 137–38, 143
humanism, 74, 77, 96, 121

idealism, xiii, 4, 19, 40–41
imperialism, 11, 21, 104, 122
individualism, 35, 55, 66, 108–14, 117–18, 129
individualization, 3, 18, 24, 66, 118, 126
Islam, 14, 55, 60–61, 74, 118, 133, 145

Jansenism, 98
Judaism, 14, 21, 34, 36–37, 40, 43, 55, 63, 67, 73, 75, 83, 106, 110, 129, 133, 145

Kulturkampf (Germany), 35, 125

liberalism, 27, 34, 74, 90
Lutheranism, 68, 99, 137

magification, 37–40
Marxism, 11, 36, 42, 45, 68, 74, 91–98, 102–3
materialism, 19, 36, 98
Methodism, 21
migration policy, 7, 35, 124, 127, 131, 135, 137–41, 146
modernization, 1–2, 9–11, 31–34, 37, 45
Mormonism, 32
mysticism / spiritual community (as a form of social organization in Christianity), xi–xii, 3, 13, 18–20, 24–25, 97, 99–103, 105, 132

nationalism, xiv, 21, 34, 66, 80, 93, 106, 117, 145
Nazism, 34–35, 83, 118–20, 122, 125–27

optionality of faith/religion, 11, 61–64, 126, 132
Orthodox Christianity, 20, 22–23

patchwork, religious, 54–55, 60, 64–65
Pentecostalism, 32, 41
Pietism, 18, 159n29

pluralism, (genuine) religious, xiii, 3, 5, 20–21, 34, 45, 61–63, 127, 132–33
privatization of religion, 13, 32
Protestantism, xiii, 3, 10–11, 16–17, 20–21, 25, 31–34, 39, 45, 59, 62, 68–69, 73–74, 99, 118, 128–29, 133–34, 140, 143, 145. *See also individual entries*; religion in Germany

Quakerism, 21

Reformation, 14, 20, 26, 37–38, 40, 92, 99–100, 125
Reformed Christianity, 3, 38, 99–100
religion in
    Africa, 31–32, 63–64
    Asia, 30, 32, 63–64, 67, 132–33
    China, 8, 10–12, 14–15, 31, 63, 74
    Europe, xii, 8, 11, 17, 20, 22, 29, 31–36, 38, 45–46, 60–64, 67, 74, 76, 89, 103–4, 118, 127, 132
    Germany, xii, 1–2, 8, 16–17, 24–25, 30–31, 33–35, 59–60, 70–71, 145; Catholic/Protestant Church in Germany 1, 35, 59–60, 70, 124–28, 131, 133–37, 139, 141, 144–45
    India, 32, 67
    Latin America, 31–32, 74
    South Korea, 31, 63, 74
    the United Kingdom, 31, 36, 100
    the United States, xii, 2, 8–10, 19–21, 32, 41, 45–46, 62–63, 68, 74, 100, 117, 127–30
    the West, 22, 24, 30–31, 41–42, 74

religion, utility/(anthropological) necessity of, 4, 38, 44, 46–47, 56–57, 98, 101, 103, 111
religion/morality–politics, relation between, 10, 14, 18, 30, 34–36, 127–28, 136–41, 144
religion–morality, relation between, 25, 39, 46, 57–58, 69–70, 105, 136, 141–44
religion–science, relation between, 25, 37, 39–40, 56, 68, 153n20
religious orders / monasticism (as a form of social organization in Christianity), 21–22, 24
restrictive vs. attractive, 4, 105, 126, 130–31, 141–43, 162n2
revitalization, religious, 8, 11, 21, 24, 31–32, 36, 38
Revolution, French, 33, 107–8, 117–18, 125
Revolution of 1848–49 (Germany), 34, 75
Revolution of 1918–19 (Germany), 76, 79–90

sacralization, 37–40, 95–96
sacralization/sacredness of the person, xiii, 104–5, 108–11, 114–16, 121–22, 143
sacredness / the sacred, xi, xiii, 25, 38, 56, 67, 70–71, 98, 103, 108–10, 114, 116, 121, 132, 143
sect (as a form of social organization in Christianity), 3, 16–24, 132
"secular option" (Taylor), 36, 38, 60–62
secularity/secularism, 4, 11, 36, 38, 64, 71, 74, 100, 104, 118, 122, 126, 128, 137, 144

secularization, xiv, 2, 8–10, 14, 31–42, 45–46, 60–61, 63, 68–69, 71, 105, 125, 145
secularization thesis/theory, 1–2, 4, 10, 32–33, 37, 41–42, 45
self-optimization/self-realization, 3–4, 24, 60, 64–70, 72, 109, 118, 125
self-transcendence, 4, 38, 47–49, 53–57, 65, 67, 70, 79, 97, 110, 116
   in relation to morality, 47, 49, 51
   in relation to religion/faith, 51–56
   positive or negative versions of, 50–51
socialism, 41–42, 76, 87–90, 94
spirituality, 2, 13, 30, 35, 67, 69
state church, 17, 22, 26, 34
supranaturalism (of the church), 16–17

transcendence, 15, 24–25, 37–38, 40, 69, 108, 114, 145
transcendentalization, 37–40

universalism, moral, xiii–xiv, 4–5, 8, 14–16, 19–21, 23–27, 29, 34, 40, 69, 90, 93, 105, 107–8, 117–18, 122, 126, 128, 130–33, 138–39
   vs. particular obligation, 129–31, 133, 138

values, (articulation of), 25, 36, 50–51, 57–58, 64–65, 69–70, 96, 101–2, 104–5, 109–10, 113, 115–20, 122–23, 129–30, 142–43
violence, 15, 50, 76, 81–83, 85–89, 107, 127, 129

World War, First, 24–25, 34, 37, 76–77, 79–83, 85–86, 89–90, 139

Cultural Memory in the Present

Jean-Luc Marion, *Revelation Comes from Elsewhere*
Peter Sloterdijk, *Out of the World*
Christopher J. Wild, *Descartes' Meditative Turn: Cartesian Thought as Spiritual Practice*
Eli Friedlander, *Walter Benjamin and the Idea of Natural History*
Helmut Puff, *The Antechamber: Toward a History of Waiting*
Raúl E. Zegarra, *A Revolutionary Faith: Liberation Theology Between Public Religion and Public Reason*
David Simpson, *Engaging Violence: Civility and the Reach of Literature*
Michael Steinberg, *The Afterlife of Moses: Exile, Democracy, Renewal*
Alain Badiou, *Badiou by Badiou*, translated by Bruno Bosteels
Eric Song, *Love against Substitution: Seventeenth-Century English Literature and the Meaning of Marriage*
Niklaus Largier, *Figures of Possibility: Aesthetic Experience, Mysticism, and the Play of the Senses*
Mihaela Mihai, *Political Memory and the Aesthetics of Care: The Art of Complicity and Resistance*
Ethan Kleinberg, *Emmanuel Levinas's Talmudic Turn: Philosophy and Jewish Thought*
Willemien Otten, *Thinking Nature and the Nature of Thinking: From Eriugena to Emerson*
Michael Rothberg, *The Implicated Subject: Beyond Victims and Perpetrators*
Hans Ruin, *Being with the Dead: Burial, Ancestral Politics, and the Roots of Historical Consciousness*
Eric Oberle, *Theodor Adorno and the Century of Negative Identity*
David Marriott, *Whither Fanon? Studies in the Blackness of Being*
Reinhart Koselleck, *Sediments of Time: On Possible Histories*, translated and edited by Sean Franzel and Stefan-Ludwig Hoffmann
Devin Singh, *Divine Currency: The Theological Power of Money in the West*
Stefanos Geroulanos, *Transparency in Postwar France: A Critical History of the Present*
Sari Nusseibeh, *The Story of Reason in Islam*
Olivia C. Harrison, *Transcolonial Maghreb: Imagining Palestine in the Era of Decolonialization*
Barbara Vinken, *Flaubert Postsecular: Modernity Crossed Out*
Aishwary Kumar, *Radical Equality: Ambedkar, Gandhi, and the Problem of Democracy*
Simona Forti, *New Demons: Rethinking Power and Evil Today*
Joseph Vogl, *The Specter of Capital*
Hans Joas, *Faith as an Option*

Michael Gubser, *The Far Reaches: Ethics, Phenomenology, and the Call
    for Social Renewal in Twentieth-Century Central Europe*
Françoise Davoine, *Mother Folly: A Tale*
Knox Peden, *Spinoza Contra Phenomenology: French Rationalism from Cavaillès to Deleuze*
Elizabeth A. Pritchard, *Locke's Political Theology: Public Religion and Sacred Rights*
Ankhi Mukherjee, *What Is a Classic? Postcolonial Rewriting and Invention of the Canon*
Jean-Pierre Dupuy, *The Mark of the Sacred*
Henri Atlan, *Fraud: The World of Ona'ah*
Niklas Luhmann, *Theory of Society, Volume 2*
Ilit Ferber, *Philosophy and Melancholy: Benjamin's Early
    Reflections on Theater and Language*
Alexandre Lefebvre, *Human Rights as a Way of Life: On Bergson's Political Philosophy*
Theodore W. Jennings, Jr., *Outlaw Justice: The Messianic Politics of Paul*
Alexander Etkind, *Warped Mourning: Stories of the Undead in the Land of the Unburied*
Denis Guénoun, *About Europe: Philosophical Hypotheses*
Maria Boletsi, *Barbarism and Its Discontents*
Sigrid Weigel, *Walter Benjamin: Images, the Creaturely, and the Holy*
Roberto Esposito, *Living Thought: The Origins and Actuality of Italian Philosophy*
Henri Atlan, *The Sparks of Randomness, Volume 2: The Atheism of Scripture*
Rüdiger Campe, *The Game of Probability: Literature and Calculation from Pascal to Kleist*
Niklas Luhmann, *A Systems Theory of Religion*
Jean-Luc Marion, *In the Self's Place: The Approach of Saint Augustine*
Rodolphe Gasché, *Georges Bataille: Phenomenology and Phantasmatology*
Niklas Luhmann, *Theory of Society, Volume 1*
Alessia Ricciardi, *After La Dolce Vita: A Cultural Prehistory of Berlusconi's Italy*
Daniel Innerarity, *The Future and Its Enemies: In Defense of Political Hope*
Patricia Pisters, *The Neuro-Image: A Deleuzian Film-Philosophy of Digital Screen Culture*
François-David Sebbah, *Testing the Limit: Derrida, Henry,
    Levinas, and the Phenomenological Tradition*
Erik Peterson, *Theological Tractates*, edited by Michael J. Hollerich
Feisal G. Mohamed, *Milton and the Post-Secular Present: Ethics, Politics, Terrorism*
Pierre Hadot, *The Present Alone Is Our Happiness, Second Edition:
    Conversations with Jeannie Carlier and Arnold I. Davidson*
Yasco Horsman, *Theaters of Justice: Judging, Staging, and
    Working Through in Arendt, Brecht, and Delbo*
Jacques Derrida, *Parages*, edited by John P. Leavey
Henri Atlan, *The Sparks of Randomness, Volume 1: Spermatic Knowledge*
Rebecca Comay, *Mourning Sickness: Hegel and the French Revolution*

*For a complete listing of titles in this series, visit the
Stanford University Press website, www.sup.org.*

The authorized representative in the EU for product safety and compliance is:
Mare Nostrum Group
B.V Doelen 72
4831 GR Breda
The Netherlands

www.ingramcontent.com/pod-product-compliance
Lightning Source LLC
Chambersburg PA
CBHW032059230426